ON THE FIELD OF GLORY

ON THE FIELD OF GLORY

BY
HENRYK SIENKIEWICZ

TRANSLATED AND EDITED BY
MIROSLAW LIPINSKI

HIPPOCRENE BOOKS, INC.
New York

For information, address:
HIPPOCRENE BOOKS, INC.
171 Madison Avenue
New York, NY 10016

Library of Congress Cataloging-in-Publication Data

Sienkiewicz, Henryk, 1846-1916.
   [Na polu chwaly. English]
   On the field of glory / by Henryk Sienkiewicz; translated and
edited by Miroslaw Lipinski.
       p. cm.
   ISBN 0-7818-0762-X
       1. Poland--History--John III Sobieski, 1674-1696--Fiction.
   I. Lipinski, Miroslaw. II. Title
   PG7158.S4 N3513   1999
   891.8'536--dc21   99-055811

Printed in the United States of America.

INTRODUCTION

ON *the Field of Glory* takes place against the backdrop of one of the most heroic phases in Polish history, when Poland still occupied a position of great importance and influence in Europe. The battle that it leads up to, at the siege of Vienna by the Turks in 1683, has been considered for over three centuries as one of the most decisive contests in European history. The fate of Western Europe lay in the balance, as the Ottoman forces under Kara Mustapha waited at the capital of the Holy Roman Empire for entry not only into the city but the symbolic heart of European and Christian power. Over two months before this important battle, the Holy Roman Emperor, Leopold, fled Vienna with his family, leaving Count Starhemberg and the Duke of Lorraine the task of its protection. As a terrible siege of the capital ensued, a request for assistance was sent to Jan Sobieski III, King of Poland, who had signed a treaty of alliance with Leopold. Polish might and blood, it seemed, were needed for the salvation of Europe.

The last great ruler of Poland, Jan Sobieski III, and his renowned army of nobles were perfect material for a supremely patriotic novelist like Sienkiewicz. As the book began to take form in 1903, Sienkiewicz, impelled by publishers and populace and his own romantic imagination, envisioned a new trilogy that would follow his bestselling first one (*With Fire and Sword, The Deluge, Pan Wolodyjowski*), already a national bible to the Polish people and known in a multitude of translations worldwide. But Sienkiewicz found the task too demanding of his energies at the time, so a new trilogy never materialized. As it happens, such a circumstance makes this novel a delightful addition to the earlier series of books, a fond revisit to the beloved milieu of seventeenth century Poland. After all, *On the Field of Glory* takes place less than ten years after the last event depicted in the final book of the *Trilogy, Pan Wolodyjowski,* and the titular hero of that book is remembered affectionately by a character, a comrade and pupil of the little knight, in the current novel.

Readers familiar with the *Trilogy* will find much here to admire. As usual Sienkiewicz plots well, and presents characters who live and breathe in the time period being described. The poetry of his imagery is unmatched; the strength of his vision undaunted. The story brims with robust humor, rousing adventure and touching romance. *On the Field of Glory* is a fitting farewell from a master storyteller to a century of Polish history that he conquered so remarkably with his pen.

A note on the current translation: Not only has this translation used the authoritative Polish text edited by Julian Krzyzanowski, it also has been referenced to an earlier English translation by Jeremiah Curtin, Sienkiewicz's foremost English translator during his lifetime. In cases where the earlier translation was most accurate, passages from it have been retained, with modification. Primary among all concerns has been the desire to render a translation that is as true in style, spirit and content to the original as possible.

With this in mind, the translation employs the unique Polish form of addressing a man as "Pan," a married lady as "Pani," and an unmarried woman as "Panna," as well as the endings of Polish last names for women.

As for the epilogue, necessary for readers unfamiliar with what actually happened at Vienna in 1683, it is not written by Sienkiewicz, who stopped his novel before Sobieski reaches Vienna. Using seasoned texts written by Count John Sobieski (a distant relative of the king) and Count A.J. Orchowski, this constructed epilogue hopefully maintains, at least in small part, the special antique flavor and historical passion found in the novel itself.

I dedicate this translation to my mother, Milada.

Miroslaw Lipinski

Cast of Characters

JACEK TACZEWSKI — young noble, last of the famed Taczewskis

ANULKA SIENINSKA — beautiful young ward of Gideon Pagowski

STANISLAW CYPRIANOWICZ — rival of Jacek Taczewski

SERAFIN CYPRIANOWICZ — Stanislaw's father, wealthy landowner of Jedlinka

FATHER WOYNOWSKI — earthy priest, ex-soldier, Jacek's substitute father

GIDEON PAGOWSKI — stern old noble; owner of Belczaczka

THE BUKOJEMSKIS (Jan, Mateusz, Lukasz, Marek) — good-hearted brothers, always ready for a fight or a drink

MARCIAN KRZEPECKI — grotesque-figured young man who lusts after Anulka Sieninska

CHAPTER 1

THE winter of 1682-83 was so severe that even the oldest people could not remember one like it. Rain fell continually during the autumn, and in the middle of November the first frost arrived, confining waters and coating trees with a glass-like shell. In the forests, icicles formed on pines, and branches began to break. During the first days of December, after frequent biting frosts, birds flew into towns and villages, and even wild beasts came out of dense forests and drew near human habitation. Around the time of Saint Damasius' Day the heavens became clouded, and then snow fell without pause for ten days. It covered the country to a height of two ells, hid forest roads and fences, and even covered cottage windows. Men had to make pathways through the drifts with shovels to get to their granaries and stables, and when the snow finally stopped, a ringing frost arrived once again and trees gave out noises that sounded like gunshots.

During those days, for safety's sake, peasants, who had to go to the wilderness for wood, did not travel other than in groups, and even then they were careful that night should not find them too far from their homes. After the setting of the sun, no man dared step outside his door without a pitchfork or a hatchet, and dogs gave out, until morning, short frightened yelps, as they usually do when barking at wolves.

It was on such a night and in such a fierce frost that a great equipage on runners pushed along a forest road, drawn by four horses and surrounded by attendants. At the front, on a strong beast, rode a man with a pole and a small iron pot hanging on its end. Pitch was burning in this pot, not to light up the road, for the moon lit the way, but to frighten wolves away from the party. A driver sat on the box of the equipage, and a postilion rode on a saddled horse, while at each side of the sleigh rode two men armed with muskets and slingshots.

The party moved forward very slowly, since the road was little beaten and in places the snowdrifts, especially at the turnings, rose like waves.

This slowness both irritated and disturbed Pan Gideon Pagowski, who, relying on his numerous attendants and their weapons, had decided on making the journey, though in Radom he was warned of the possible danger, particularly since one had to pass the Kozienicki Wilderness to reach Belczaczka, his home.

In those times this immense forest began a good distance before Jedlinka, and continued far beyond Kozienice to the Vistula River, and toward the other side of the Stezyca and northward to Ryczywol.

It had seemed to Pan Gideon that if he left Radom before midday, he would quite easily reach Belczaczka at sunset. Meanwhile he had been forced in a number of places to open the road bordered by hurdles; some hours were lost at this labor, so that he arrived at Jedlinka about twilight. There, his party was warned again to remain in the village for the night; but since a pitch light had been found at the blacksmith's to burn before the coach, Pan Gideon commanded the journey to continue.

And now night had found him in the wilderness.

It was difficult to go faster because the snowdrifts were getting higher, so Pan Gideon became more and more troubled and at last fell to swearing, but in Latin, lest he frighten the two ladies who were with him, Pani Winnicka, his relative, and Panna Sieninska, his adopted daughter.

Because she was young and carefree, Panna Sieninska was not too afraid. On the contrary, she drew aside the leather curtain at the window and, commanding the horseman on her side not to block the view, looked with joy at the drifts and the pine trunks covered with long strips of snow, over which reddish gleams from the pitch pot played and made, with the greenish moonlight, moving figures quite pleasing to her eye. Then she pursed her lips and began to blow out air, and was amused to see that her breath was visible and rosy from the fire.

But Pani Winnicka, who was old and fainthearted, began to complain:

"Why did we leave Radom, or why did we not at least pass the night in Jedlinka, since we were warned of the danger? All this because of someone's stubbornness. There is still a long stretch of road to Belczaczka, and all of it runs through a forest where wolves can doubtlessly meet us, unless Raphael, the Archangel and patron of travelers, takes pity on our wanderings—pity we are not worthy of, unfortunately."

When he heard this, Pan Gideon lost all patience. That was all that was needed! Talk of being lost in the wilderness!

The road was, after all, evident, and as for wolves, well, they would or would not come. He had good attendants, and besides, a wolf is not anxious to meet with a soldier—not only because he fears him far more than a common man, but also because of a certain liking the sharp-witted beast has for soldiers.

The wolf understands well that no town dweller or peasant will give him food *gratis*; only a soldier will feed wolves and, at times, in abundance; hence, it is not without reason that men have called war "the wolf's harvest."

But in speaking thus and praising the wolves in some small degree, Pan Gideon was still not quite convinced of their affection; so he was considering whether to command an attendant to slip down from his horse and sit next to the young lady. In such a case, he himself would defend one door of the coach and the attendant the other, while the freed horse would either rush off ahead or escape in the rear, thus drawing the wolves after it.

But the time to do this had not arrived, according to Pan Gideon. Meanwhile, he placed a knife and two pistols on the front seat, near his ward; these he wished to have near him since he only had the use of his right hand.

The party advanced about a furlong farther in quiet, and the road grew wider. Pan Gideon, who knew the way perfectly, drew breath as if somewhat relieved.

"The Malikow field is not far," he said.

Whatever the situation, he expected more safety in that open space than in the forest.

But just then the attendant in front turned his horse suddenly and, rushing to the coach, spoke hurriedly to the driver and to others, who answered abruptly, as men do when there is no time for loitering.

"What is it?" asked Pan Gideon.

"A noise in the field."

"Is it wolves?"

"Some outcry. God knows what!"

Pan Gideon was on the point of commanding the horseman with the torch to spring forward and see what was happening, when he remembered that in cases like this it was better not to be without fire and important to have all his people together; furthermore, defense in the open is easier than in a forest, so he commanded the equipage to move on.

After a while, however, the servant showed up again at the coach window.

"Wild boars, master," he said.

"Wild boars?"

"I heard a horrible grunting to the right of the road."

"Praise God for that!"

"Perhaps wolves have attacked them."

"Praise God for that also! We shall pass by unharmed. Move on!"

The attendant's supposition proved accurate.

Coming out onto the field, they saw to the right of the road, at a distance of two or three bow-shots, a dense crowd of wild boars surrounded by a circle of lively wolves. A terrible grunting, in which there was not fear but rage, reverberated ever more loudly. As the coach advanced toward the middle of the field, the attendants saw from their riding positions that the wolves had not yet dared to jump the herd, but instead were pressing it tighter and tighter.

The boars had arranged themselves in a round mass, the young in the middle, the strong heads on the outside, forming, as it were, a dangerous, moving fortress, impenetrable and fearless, that glittered with white tusks.

Between the circle of wolves and that wall of tusks and snouts could be seen a white, snowy ring, lit up, just as the entire field was, by the bright light of the moon.

Only a few of the wolves sprang up to the boars, but they withdrew quickly, as if frightened by the clatter of the tusks and the more terrible outbursts of grunting.

If the wolves would have come into close contact with the herd, the battle would have absorbed them completely, and the coach might have passed by unmolested; but, since this had not happened, there was concern that they might abandon their dangerous attack to seek another.

Indeed, after a while, a few started to separate themselves from the pack and run toward the coach. Others followed. But the sight of armed men disconcerted them.

Some began to gather behind the procession, others placed themselves a dozen or so steps from it or ran around in maddened dashes, as if urging themselves on.

The attendants wished to fire, but Pagowski forbade them for fear that gunshots might draw the entire pack.

Meanwhile, the horses, though accustomed to wolves, began to lean to their side and turn their heads, snorting loudly. Then something much worse happened, something that increased the danger a hundredfold.

The young horse carrying the torchbearer reared all of a sudden, once, then twice, and rushed to the side.

The horseman, knowing that if he were to fall he would be immediately torn to pieces, seized the pommel but at the same time let go of the pole with the torch, which sank deeply into the snow.

The resinous chips sparkled, then went out, leaving only the light of moon on that glade.

The coachman, a Russian by birth from the neighborhood of the castle in Pomerania, began to pray; the Mazovian attendants fell to cursing.

Emboldened by the darkness, the wolves pressed on with greater audaciousness, and other wolves ran up from the direction of the battle with the wild boars. A few came up quite close, snapping their teeth, their hair bristling at the nape of their necks. Their eyes glittered with green and blood-red hues.

A truly terrible moment had arrived.

"Shall we shoot, master?" asked one of the attendants.

"Frighten them with shouts," replied Pagowski.

Sharp cries of "ahu, ahu!" reverberated. The horses gained courage, and the wolves, upon whom the voices of men make an impression, withdrew a dozen or so steps.

But an even stranger thing happened.

Suddenly, behind the coach, forest echoes repeated the shouts of the attendants but with greater force. At the same time there were heard what seemed like outbursts of wild laughter, and a moment later a group of horsemen darkened both sides of the coach and rushed with the full speed of their horses toward the herd of wild boars and the wolves that encircled them.

In the twinkling of an eye, both boars and wolves, abandoning their places, scattered about the field, as if a whirlwind had dispersed them. Gunshots were heard, shouts, and again those strange bursts of laughter. Pan Pagowski's attendants also rushed after the horsemen, so that only the coachman and the attendant sitting on the lead horse remained by the coach.

Inside the coach such a great amazement prevailed that for a while no one dared to speak.

"And the word became flesh!" cried out Pani Winnicka finally. "Help must have come from heaven above."

"Let it be blessed wherever it came from," replied Pan Pagowski. "It was almost over for us."

Panna Sieninska, wanting to add her own word, said:

"God sent those young knights!"

How Panna Sieninska could have known that these were knights— and young ones at that—was difficult to guess, as the riders had passed the sleigh like a whirlwind; but no one questioned her about this, for both of the old folks were too taken up with what had occurred.

Meanwhile, the sounds of pursuit were still heard on the glade for the space of a few Hail Marys, and not too far from the coach a wolf, apparently its back broken from a sling-shot, sat on its haunches and howled from pain with such a horrible voice that it made the flesh creep.

The attendant in the front jumped to the ground and went to finish off the wolf, for the horses were beginning to struggle and kick, so that the sleigh pole cracked.

But, after a while, the party of horsemen blackened the field of snow again.

They came in a disorderly crowd in a mist, for though the night was bright and clear, the exhausted horses were smoking in the frost like chimneys.

The horsemen approached with laughter and singing, and when they were close, one of them shot up to the sleigh, and asked in a resonant, merry voice:

"Who is traveling?"

"Pagowski of Belczaczka. Whom should I thank for our rescue?"

"Cyprianowicz of Jedlinka!"

"The Bukojemskis!"

"Thanks to your lordships! God sent you in time. Thanks!"

"Thanks!" repeated a young feminine voice.

"Glory to God that it was in time!" replied Cyprianowicz, raising his fur cap.

"How did you find out about us?"

"No one told us, but as the wolves are running in packs, we rode out to save people; and since a distinguished person has been found, the greater is our joy and service to God," said Cyprianowicz politely.

"And our supply of wolves' skins," added one of the Bukojemskis.

"Real knightly work," replied Pan Gideon, "and a wonderful deed for which, God grant, I will show my gratitude as soon as possible. I think that the wolves have lost their desire for human flesh now and that we shall reach home in safety."

"That is not so certain. The wolves might be encouraged to try again soon."

"There's no help for that. We will not give in!"

"There is help, namely, if we escort your lordship right to your doorstep. We may also be able to save someone else along the road."

"I dared not ask for that, but since such is the generosity of your lordships, then let it be so, for my ladies will be less fearful."

"I am not afraid, but deeply indebted," replied Panna Sieninska.

Pan Pagowski gave the order and the train moved forward. But they had barely gone a dozen or so steps, when the cracked sleigh pole broke completely and the coach came to a standstill.

A new delay ensued.

The attendants did indeed have ropes, and they immediately began to fix the broken parts, but it was not known if such improvised work would not come apart after several stajes.

So the young Cyprianowicz thought for a moment, after which, raising his fur cap again, he said:

"It is closer to Jedlinka through the fields than to Belczaczka. Honor our house, your lordship, and spend the night there. I do not know what could meet us in the depth of the forest—and it may turn out that our number is too small against all those wolves who will undoubtedly run to the road from the entire wilderness. Somehow I will manage to have the coach pulled, and the closer, the better. Truthfully speaking, the honor will be greater than the service, but it is almost *dura necessitas*, so I should not let pride stand in the way."

Pan Pagowski did not respond right away, for he felt a rebuke in those words.

He called to mind that when the elder Cyprianowicz had paid him a visit at Belczaczka two years ago, he received him politely, to be sure, but with a certain haughtiness—and he did not repay the visit at all, the reason being that the elder Cyprianowicz was *homo novus*—only noble for two generations—and an Armenian in origin, whose grandfather still traded in mercers in Kamieniec.

Jacob, the son of that merchant, had served in the artillery under the great Chodkiewicz, and had distinguished himself at the battle of Chocim so splendidly that through the influence of Stanislaw Lubomirski he received his nobility and the domain of Jedlinka for life. That life estate was given to his heir, Serafin, in return for a loan given the Commonwealth after the Swedish invasion.

The young man who had come to the travelers with such effective assistance was Serafin's son.

Pagowski felt this rebuke all the more, since the words "I should not let pride stand in the way" had been uttered by the young Cyprianowicz rather impudently and with special emphasis.

But it was precisely that chivalrous fancy that pleased the old noble, and besides, it was difficult to refuse the man who had saved him, and the road to Belczaczka was indeed long and dangerous, so not hesitating any longer, he said:

"Without your lordship's help the wolves might be gnawing our bones now—let me at least pay you back with goodwill. . . . Let us go!"

Cyprianowicz had the coach bound.

The pole was broken as if an axe had gone through it, so they tied one end of each rope to a runner, the other to a saddle, and everyone moved forward briskly in a large but merry group, amid shouts from the attendants and songs from the Bukojemskis.

It was not too far to Jedlinka, which was more of a forest settlement than a village. Soon, therefore, there opened up before the travelers a wide field some several dozen stajes in length, or rather a spacious clearing enclosed on four sides by woods, and on it a dozen or so homesteads, whose roofs, covered with snow, were shining and glittering in the moonlight.

A little farther on, beyond the peasant cottages, one could see the farm buildings standing in a circle about a courtyard, and in the interior a mansion, very misshapen, for it had been altered by the Cyprianowiczes from a residence in which once lived the king's foresters into something that was too big for such a small clearing.

A bright light glowed from its windows, giving a rosy hue to the snow lying on the mound at the front of the mansion, the bushes growing before the building and the well sweeps sticking out to the right of the farmyard.

It was evident that Cyprianowicz was expecting his son, and perhaps guests from the road who might come with him, for barely had the coach reached the gate when several servants ran out with torches, and after them the master of the house himself, dressed in a marten coat and a weasel-fur cap on his head, which he immediately took off at sight of the coach.

"What welcome guests has the Lord sent to our wilderness?" he asked, descending the steps of the porch.

The young Cyprianowicz kissed his father's hand and informed him whom he had brought, while Pan Pagowski, getting out of the coach, said:

"I have long wanted to do as grievous necessity has forced me today, and so I bless all the more the compulsion which has agreed so exquisitely with my desires."

"Various adventures befall men, but for this adventure I am happy, so that I joyously ask you to my chambers."

Saying this, Pan Serafin bowed again, and gave his arm to Pani Winnicka, after whom the rest of the company entered the house.

Immediately upon entering, the guests were seized by that feeling of satisfaction which is always felt by travelers when they come out of darkness and cold into warm and lighted rooms. In the hallway and in the other rooms fires were blazing away in spacious tiled chimneys, and besides this, the servants began to light candles here and there, which began to glow about the rooms.

Pan Pagowski looked around with a certain astonishment, for the typical noble house was far from the wealth that struck one's eyes at the manor of the Cyprianowiczes.

By the light of the fires and candles, one could see in each room furnishings such as might not even be found in many a castle: chests and Italian chairs of carved wood, here and there clocks and Venetian glass, chandeliers cast in worthy brass, Oriental weapons inlaid with turquoise and hanging from tapestries knitted with silver threads. On the floors were soft Crimean kilims, and on the two long walls two arras, which could have constituted the decoration of any magnate's chamber.

"These came to them from trade," thought Pan Gideon with a certain amount of anger, "and now they can lord over the nobility and swagger of wealth not won by the sword."

But the kindness and sincere hospitality of the Cyprianowiczes disarmed the old noble, and when a moment later he heard the clatter of utensils in the neighboring dining room, he became completely appeased.

In the meantime, hot spiced wine was served to warm the guests who had come out of the cold. A conversation began concerning the recent danger the party had experienced. Pan Pagowski praised highly the young Cyprianowicz for going out to save people on the roads, without regard to the biting frost, the difficulty, and the danger.

"Indeed, thus acted famous knights in the old days," he said. "Riding around the world, they defended people from dragons, evil spirits, and various other beasts."

"And if any one of them happened to rescue some beautiful princess," said the young Cyprianowicz, "then he would be as happy as we are at the moment."

"True!" the four Bukojemski brothers cried out with enthusiasm. "No knight saved a more beautiful maiden! As God is dear to me, he speaks the truth!"

Panna Sieninska smiled pleasantly, so that two charming dimples appeared on her cheeks, and she lowered her eyes.

But the compliment seemed a little too familiar to Pan Pagowski, for Panna Sieninska, though an orphan without property, was descended from magnates, so he changed the conversation, and asked:

"Have your lordships been riding about the roads long in this fashion?"

"Since the great snows fell, and we shall keep on riding until the frosts let up," replied the young Stanislaw Cyprianowicz.

"And how many wolves did you manage to kill?"

"Enough so that everyone has wolf skins."

Here the Bukojemskis started to laugh loudly, sounding like four horses neighing, and when they calmed down a bit, the oldest, Jan, said:

"His Majesty will be proud of his foresters."

"True," replied Pan Pagowski. "And I have heard that your lordships are the chief foresters in this, the king's wilderness. But do not the Bukojemskis originate in the Ukraine?"

"We are of the same stock."

"Indeed . . . indeed . . . a good stock, the Jelo-Bukojemskis. . . . There are members connected by marriage to some renowned families. . . ."

"And to St. Peter!" cried out Lukasz Bukojemski.

"Eh?" asked Pan Pagowski.

And he started to look around sternly and suspiciously at the brothers, as if trying to determine if they were making fun of him. But their faces were sincere, and with deep conviction they nodded their heads, confirming in this way the words of their brother. So Pan Pagowski was quite astonished, and repeated:

"Relatives of St. Peter? And *quo modo?*"

"Through the Przegonowskis!"

"Indeed! And the Przegonowskis?"

"Through the Uswiatows!"

"And the Uswiatows through someone else," said the old noble with a smile now. "And so on, to the birth of Christ. . . . Yes! It is a good thing to have relatives in the senate here on earth—how much better then to have them in the senate in the heavens. Promotion is certain in that case. . . . But how did your lordships make your way from the Ukraine to our Kozienicki Wilderness, for, as I heard, you have been here for several years?"

"For three years. The rebellion has long since leveled everything in the Ukraine, and later even the boundaries were altered. We did not want to serve the Tartar pagans, so first we served in the army, and then became tenants here and there until a relative of ours, Pan Malczynski, made us chief foresters here."

"Yes," said the old Cyprianowicz. "It seems strange to me that we have found ourselves side by side in this wilderness, for though we are not from these parts, the changing fortunes of men have brought us here. The heritage of your lordship," here he turned to Pagowski, "is likewise, as far as I know, in Russia near the Pomeranian castle."

Pan Pagowski quivered at this, as if someone had touched an open wound on his body.

"I had and still have property there," he said, "but those parts are loathsome to me, for only misfortunes struck me there like so many thunderbolts."

"God's will," replied Cyprianowicz.

"Of course it is vain to complain against it in a stronghold, but life is difficult. . . ."

"Your lordship, as is known, served long in the army."

"Until I lost my hand. I avenged both my country's wrongs and my own. And if the Lord Jesus will pardon one sin of mine for every pagan head I took, then there is hope that I will never see hell."

"To be sure, to be sure! Service is a merit, and suffering is a merit. It's best to drive out sad thoughts."

"I would gladly get rid of them, but they do not want to get rid of me. But enough of this. I will remain a cripple, and at the same time the guardian of this lady. For my old age I've moved to a calmer part of the country where Tartars do not venture, and I sit in Belczaczka, as you know."

"Quite so, and I have done a similar thing," said the old Cyprianowicz. "Though there is quiet now in those parts, the young men of our nation are eager for adventures on those trails, but those are terrible and sorrowful regions, after all, where everyone is mourning someone."

Pan Pagowski placed his hand to his forehead and kept it there for a while, after which he said in a sad voice:

"Indeed, only a peasant or a magnate can survive in those parts: a peasant because when a pagan onslaught comes he can escape to the woods and live there like a wild animal for months at a time; and a magnate because he has fortified castles and his own company which protects him. . . . But even then! The Zolkiewskis perished, the Danilowiczes perished. Of the Sobieskis, the brother of our gracious King Jan perished. . . . And how many more! One of the Wisniowieckis writhed on a rope in Stambul. Korecki was beaten to death with iron rods. The Kalinowskis were killed, and before that the Herburts and Jazlowieckis paid with blood tribute. At various times fell several Sieninskis, and they once ruled almost the entire land there. . . . What a graveyard! If I wanted to name everyone, I would not be done by the break of day. And if I were to name the nobles and not just the magnates, then a month would not be enough time."

"True, true! It is a wonder how the Lord God has multiplied this Turkish and Tartar rabble. For, after all, so many of them have been killed that when a peasant tills the land in the spring, his plough grinds against the skull of a pagan at every step. . . . Dear God, how many of them have been squashed just by our present king! . . . Their blood could fill a large river, and they still keep coming and coming!"

This was true.

The Commonwealth, consumed by anarchy and licence, could not afford strong armies that would be able to end, once and for all, the Turkish-Tartar onslaughts in one great war.

For that matter, all of Europe could not acquire such an army.

Nevertheless, in this Commonwealth lived a daring people who would in no way freely give their throats to the knife of the eastern invaders. On the contrary, on that terrible frontier, bristling with graves and steeped in blood—that is, in Podolia, in the Ukraine, and Red Russia—newer and newer waves of Polish settlers arrived, not only tempted by the fertile land, but by precisely a craving for continual wars, battles and adventures.

"The Poles," wrote the chronicler, Kromer, "go to Russia for skirmishes with the Tartars."

So streamed peasants from Mazovia, warlike nobles who were ashamed of "dying a common death in bed," and then mighty magnates appeared on these Red Lands, who, not content with defense at home, went frequently much farther—to Crimea or to Wallachia—seeking power, victory, death, salvation and glory.

It was even said that the Poles did not want one great war that would end everything so that they could continually indulge in battle. Though this was not true, it did not lessen the satisfaction of constant clouds of war to this proud tribe—and, once in a while, the invader paid for his audaciousness with blood.

Neither the Dobruda lands, nor those in Bialogrod, and certainly not those barren thickets in Crimea could sustain their wild inhabitants, so hunger drove them to the fertile frontier where abundant booty awaited, but also frequent death.

Fires lit up scenes of slaughter yet unknown to history. Single regiments routed and wiped out with sword and hoof Tartar armies ten times their number. Only boundless swiftness saved the invaders, for, in general, every Tartar army overtaken by the regular army of the Commonwealth was hopelessly lost.

There were expeditions, especially the smaller ones, from which no one came back to Crimea. Terrible in their time both to Tartars and Turks were the names of Pretficz and Chmielecki. Of knights of lesser importance, the following names were written in blood in their memories: Wolodyjowski, Pelka and the elder Ruszczyc—men who had been resting in their graves and in glory for several years or more. But even of the great ones, no one had shed as much blood of the followers of Islam as the present king, Jan Sobieski III.

At Podhajce, Kalusz, Chocim and Lwow were lying still unburied piles of pagan bones, whitening the broad fields like snow.

Until finally terror seized all the hordes.

Then the frontier breathed freely, and when the insatiable Turkish force started to seek easier conquests, the entire battered Commonwealth breathed freer.

Only painful memories remained.

Far away from the present abode of the Cyprianowiczes, in the vicinity of the Pomeranian castle, stood a tall cross on a hill with two lances which Pan Pagowski had raised some twenty years ago on the site of his burned manor—so that whenever he thought of that cross and all those people dear to him whom he had lost there, his old heart still pained him.

But since he was hard on himself and on others, and was embarrassed to let anyone see his tears and detested ready pity, he did not want to speak of his misfortunes any longer, and started to ask his host how he liked living in this wooded region.

And the elder Cyprianowicz said:

"Oh, what quiet, what quiet! When the trees are not rustling and soughing, and the wolves are not howling, one can almost hear the snow falling. There is peace, a fire in the chimney, and a jug of heated wine in the evening—one doesn't need more in old age."

"True. But what of your son?"

"A young bird flies away from the nest sooner or later. And the trees here whisper of a great war against the pagans!"

"Even gray falcons will fly off to that war. I would go myself, if not for this!"

Here Pan Pagowski shook his empty sleeve, in which only a stub of an arm remained near the shoulder.

Cyprianowicz poured him some wine:

"To the success of the Christian sword!"

"God grant it! Bottoms up!"

Meanwhile, the young Cyprianowicz treated Pani Winnicka, Panna Sieninska and the four Bukojemski brothers from a similar steaming jug. The ladies barely touched the tips of the glasses with their lips, but the Bukojemskis showed no such reluctance, and so the world seemed more joyous to them with every minute and Panna Sieninska more beautiful.

Unable to find the appropriate words to express their admiration, they started to look at her with amazement, while breathing heavily and nudging each other with an elbow.

Finally, Jan, the oldest of the four, said:

"It's no wonder that the wolves wanted to taste the bones and meat of your ladyship, for even a wild beast knows a real delicacy!"

The other three—Mateusz, Marek and Lukasz—slapped their thighs:

"Right on the mark!"

"A delicacy! Nothing less!"

"A marzipan!"

Hearing this, Panna Sieninska crossed her arms and, feigning terror, said to the young Cyprianowicz:

"Save me, sir, for I see that these gentlemen rescued me from the wolves only to eat me themselves."

"My dear lady," replied Cyprianowicz merrily, "Pan Jan Bukojemski said one shouldn't wonder about the behavior of the wolves, and I say do not wonder about the behavior of the Bukojemskis."

"Then I shall have to say: "Into whose hands—""

"Don't joke about holy things!" cried out Pani Winnicka.

"Ah, but these gentlemen are ready to eat auntie as well as me—is that not true?"

But this question went unanswered for a moment. In truth, it was easy to see by the expressions on their faces that the Bukojemskis had considerably less desire for this. But Lukasz, who had a sharper wit than his brothers, said:

"Let Jan speak; he is the eldest."

But Jan became disconcerted somewhat and answered:

"Who knows what will happen tomorrow!"

"A wise comment," noted Cyprianowicz, "but how does it apply here?"

"What are you saying?"

"I'm saying nothing, only asking why you are referring to tomorrow."

"Don't you know that love is worse than a wolf? A wolf you can kill, but love can never be killed."

"Yes, I know that, but that is another subject."

"If wit favors one, the subject matter is of less concern. . . ."

"Ha! If that is the case, then God grant us wit."

Panna Sieninska began to laugh behind her hand, and Cyprianowicz followed, and finally even the Bukojemskis joined in. But further conversation was interrupted by a female servant announcing that supper was ready.

The elder Cyprianowicz gave his arm to Pani Winnicka; Pan Pagowski followed them, while the young Cyprianowicz conducted Panna Sieninska.

"A debate with Pan Bukojemski is difficult," said the cheered up young lady.

"That's because his reasons are like restive horses, each trying to go his own way. But he told two truths that are difficult to deny."

"What is the first one?"

"That no person knows what will meet him tomorrow. I, for example, did not know that I would see your ladyship today."

"And the second truth?"

"That is it easier to kill a wolf than love. . . . That is a great truth."

Saying this, the young Cyprianowicz sighed, and the young lady lowered her dark eyelids and became silent.

Only after they had sat down to table did she say:

"You gentlemen must visit Belczaczka soon, so that my guardian can repay you for saving us and for your hospitality."

Pan Pagowski's sullen mood improved considerably during supper, and when the host toasted with florid words first the health of the ladies and then the respectable guest, the old noble answered quite courteously, giving thanks for the rescue from difficult straits and proclaiming his everlasting gratitude.

After that, they talked *de publicis*, of matters concerning the king, his victories, the Diet, which was supposed to meet in April, the war threatening the German Empire from the Turkish Sultan, for which Pan Hieronim Lubomirski, a knight of Malta, had already recruited Polish volunteers.

The Bukojemskis listened with no little interest to how every Pole was greeted with open arms in Germany, for the Turks did not think highly of the German cavalry, but were properly terrified of the Polish one.

Pan Pagowski criticized Lubomirski's pride somewhat, for he was wont to say of the German counts: "Ten of them could fit into one glove of mine." But he praised his knightly superiority, boundless courage and great skill in the art of war.

Hearing this, Lukasz Bukojemski declared for himself and his brothers that as soon as spring would come nothing could hold them back from joining Lubomirski, but as long as the frosts were strong, they would still kill wolves to avenge Panna Sieninska, a suitable thing to do. For, as Jan stated, while one cannot wonder at the actions of the wolves, the very thought that such an innocent little dove could have been their prey made the heart rage with anger, even as it made it difficult to withhold one's tears.

"It is a pity," he said, "that the skin of a wolf is so cheap, for Jews barely give you one thaler for three skins. But it is difficult to hold back one's tears, and even better to simply indulge them, for whoever does not lament oppressed innocence and virtue shows himself a barbarian unworthy of being called a knight or a noble."

Saying this, he did indeed shed his tears freely, while his brothers immediately followed his example, and though in the worst case wolves could only threaten the life and not the virtue of Panna Sieninska, the three brothers were so moved by what their brother had said that their hearts melted like heated wax.

After supper, they wanted to fire their pistols into the air in honor of the young lady, but their host opposed this, saying that he had a forester in the house, a man of great merit, who was sick and needed quiet.

Pan Pagowski, thinking that the sick man might be an impoverished relative, or in the worst case, a local noble, began through politeness to inquire about him; but finding out that the person was a domestic, he shrugged his shoulders and, looking with an unfavorable and surprised eye at the old Cyprianowicz, said:

"Ah, yes, I forgot what people say of your too kind heart!"

"God grant," replied Pan Serafin, "that this is the worst they say about me. I have much to thank him for, and everyone should be so fortunate, for he knows all about herbs and can find a remedy for every illness."

"It is surprising that he can cure others but not himself. Send him one day to my relative Pani Winnicka, who draws various *extracta* from herbs and applies them to people. Meanwhile, permit us to think of retiring, for the journey has fatigued me terribly and the wine has effected me a bit, just as it has the Bukojemskis."

The Bukojemskis were indeed tipsy, and their eyes were glazed over and tender, so when the young Cyprianowicz conducted them to the annex, where he would spend the night with them, they followed him with great uncertain steps along the snow, squeaking from the frost, surprised that the moon was smiling at them and sitting on the roof of the barn, instead of shining in the heavens.

But Panna Sieninska had made such a deep impression on them that they wanted to speak more of her.

The young Cyprianowicz did not feel inclined to go to sleep either, so he had a demijohn of mead brought, after which they sat by a great chimney, and by the bright light, they drank in silence at first, listening to the chirping of the crickets in the room.

Finally, the oldest brother, Jan, took in a deep breath and blew it out into the chimney with such force that the flame bent, and he said:

"Oh, Jesus! Weep for me, my dear brothers, for a sad fate has met me!"

"What fate? Speak, don't hide anything!"

"I am so in love that my legs are failing me."

"And I? Don't you think that I'm in love?" cried out Lukasz.

"And I?" shouted Mateusz.

"And I?" finished Marek.

Jan wanted to give them an answer, but could not do so right away for he got a case of the hiccups. He merely stared with great astonishment and started to look at them as if he were seeing them for the first time in his life.

Finally, his anger was reflected in his face.

"How's that, you sons of bitches?" he cried out. "You want to stand in my way and deprive me of happiness?"

"Oh, what's this?" replied Lukasz. "Is Panna Sieninska some inheritance that only the oldest brother can get? We are from the same father and mother, so if you call us sons of bitches, you're offending our parents in their graves. Each man is free to love whomever he chooses."

"Each man, except for the three of you since you should be *oboedientiam* to me."

"Should we listen to a nitwit the rest of our lives? Well?"

"You're blaspheming like a pagan dog!"

"You're blaspheming yourself. For Jacob was younger than Esau, and Joseph was the youngest of his brothers, so you are reprimanding the Holy Scriptures and barking against faith."

Driven into a corner, Jan could not find a ready answer, and when Mateusz made a comment about Cain, as being the oldest brother, he lost his head completely.

He swelled with anger, until finally he began to search with his right hand for his saber, which he did not have by his side anyway.

It is unknown where this could have led to if Marek, who had been holding his finger against his forehead, as if wrestling with some thought, had not suddenly cried out in a booming voice:

"I am the youngest brother, I am Joseph, so Panna Sieninska should be mine!"

The others immediately turned to him with turmoil written in their faces and fire in their eyes.

"What? For you? For you, you goose egg, you man of straw, you horse's scrofula, you empty mug, you drunkard! . . . For you?"

"Shut your mouths, for it is written in the Scriptures!"

"Where in the Scriptures, you idiot?"

"It doesn't matter, it is there. You are all drunk, not I!"

But here Stanislaw Cyprianowicz intervened.

"Are you not ashamed," he said, "being nobles and brothers, to start a quarrel? Is this the way you observe brotherly love? And what is the argument about? Is Panna Sieninska a mushroom in the forest that the first one who catches it can put it into his pottle? Pelicans have a custom—and they are not nobles or even people—that through family affection they give way to each other, and if they fail to catch any fish they feed each other with their own blood. You make mention of your dead parents, but they are turning over in their graves at the quarreling amongst their sons, whom they surely enjoined to do otherwise. To them even heavenly food is now tasteless, and they do not dare raise their eyes to the four evangelists whose names they gave you in holy baptism."

Thus spoke Cyprianowicz, and though at first he wanted to laugh a little, the more he spoke, the more he was stirred by his own words, for, indulging the company he was in, he was also somewhat drunk. However, the Bukojemskis were greatly moved by his speech and finally all ended in tears, while the eldest, Jan, cried out:

"Oh, for God's sake, kill me but don't call me Cain!"

At this, Mateusz, who had mentioned Cain, threw himself into his brother's arms.

"Brother, hand me over to the hangman for saying that!"

"Forgive me, for I will burst from sorrow!" called out Lukasz.

And Marek: "I was barking against the commandment like a dog!"

And they began to embrace each other; but at last Jan, freeing himself from his brothers, suddenly sat on a bench, unbuttoned his zupon, parted his shirt and baring his chest, began to speak in a broken voice:

"Here I am! Like a pelican! . . . Here I am!"

The others burst out crying even more loudly:

"A pelican! A real pelican! . . . As God is dear to me! A pelican!"

"Take Panna Sieninska!"

"She is yours! Take her."

"The youngest should take her. . . ."

"Never! That's not possible!"

"Damn her!"

"Damn her!"

"We don't want her!"

At that, Lukasz struck his thighs with his palms until the sound reverberated in the room.

"I know!" he cried out.

"What do you know? Speak, don't hide anything!"

"Let Cyprianowicz take her!"

When they heard this, the other brothers sprang up from their benches, so had the brotherly idea affected them, and all four surrounded Cyprianowicz.

"Take her, Stanislaw."

"You'll do us a great favor."

"If you love us!"

"Do this for us!"

"May God bless you!" cried out Jan, raising his eyes to heaven and stretching his arms over him.

Cyprianowicz, however, became red and stood dumbfounded, repeating:

"Good heavens! . . ."

But his heart throbbed in his breast at the very thought, for having been with his father amidst the dense forest for two years and having seen few people, he had not met such a beautiful girl in a long time.

He had seen such girls once in Brzezany, when his father sent him to that manor to acquire refinement and knowledge of public affairs. But he was still but a boy then, and time had erased those distant memories.

And now, when he saw unexpectedly amid the woods such a beautiful flower, he was told at once: "Take it!"

So he became terribly confused and repeated:

"Fear God! How can she be for you or me!"

But they urged him on, for like all tipsy people, they saw no obstacle to anything.

"None of us will be jealous of the other," said Lukasz, "and you take her! We are supposed to go to war anyway, for we've had enough of this caretaking in the forest. Thirty thalers for the entire, whole year. That's not enough for drink, let alone clothing! We sold our horses and use yours for chasing wolves, and work also. . . . Everyone knows it is a hard life for orphans. It's better to perish in war—but, if you love us, take her!"

"Take her!" cried out Jan, "and we will go to Rakusz, to Lubirski. We're going to help those Germans skin pagans."

"Take her now. . . ."

"Tomorrow! Straight to church! . . ."

But Cyprianowicz recovered from his astonishment and returned to a state of sobriety, as if he had not touched a drop all day.

"People, think about what you are saying! Do you think it is just a matter of your will or mine? What about her? What about Pan Pagowski, who is proud and unaccommodating? Even if in time she became my friend, he might prefer to see her sow seeds than be the wife of such an impoverished fellow like me, or anyone of you."

"Oh, pshaw!" exclaimed Jan. "Is Pan Pagowski the Castellan of Cracow or the grand hetman? If you are good enough for us, then he shouldn't be so particular. Are the Bukojemskis small fry for match-making? Woe to him! He's old, he doesn't have a long time to live, let him beware lest Saint Peter slam heaven's gate on his fingers. Saint Peter, say to him: 'You did not know, you son of a bitch, how to respect my blood relatives, so go to hell!' Say that to him after he dies! But we will not be slighted even while living. Why should we be slighted? Because we have no fortune, should we be held in contempt and treated like peasants? Is this the way we are paid for our service to our country, for our blood, for our wounds? Oh, brothers of mine, orphans of God, many an injustice has met us in life, but not one has been as grievous as this one."

"True, true!" exclaimed Lukasz, Marek and Mateusz plaintively.

And once again tears of grief flowed down their cheeks in abundance, but when they had cried themselves out, they started to seethe, for it seemed to them that such an offence to men of birth should not be for-gotten.

Marek, who was the most impulsive of the four brothers, was the first to address this matter.

"It is difficult to challenge him to a duel," he said, "for he is old and has no left arm, but if he were to show us any contempt, we must have satisfaction. What should we do? Think!"

"My legs froze in the cold," replied Lukasz, "and now are really burning. If not for this, I could find an answer straightaway."

"My head is burning, not my legs."

"You can't get something out of nothing."

"The pot calls the kettle black!" said Jan.

"You are starting a quarrel instead of thinking of an answer!" exclaimed Marek in anger.

But here Cyprianowicz came between them.

"An answer?" he asked. "To whom?"

"To Pagowski."

"What do you want an answer to?"

"What to? What do you mean: what to?"

And they began to look at one another, with no small astonishment, and then turned to Marek.

"What do you want of us?"

"What do *you* want? . . ."

"Let's adjourn this session!" exclaimed Cyprianowicz. "See, the fire is even dying down, and midnight has passed some time ago. The beds against the wall are waiting for us, and we deserve to rest, for we tired ourselves out in the frost."

Indeed, the fire did go out, and the room became plunged in darkness, so the advice of the host carried conviction to the Bukojemskis.

For a little time the conversation continued, but with ever decreasing intensity, and then a whispered prayer was heard, recited in low tones, then louder tones, and interrupted now and then with deep sighing.

The firebrands in the chimney began to be covered with ash and to blacken; once in a while, something squeaked in the dying fire, and crickets chirped sadly in the corners, as if in mourning for the light.

Then came the clatter of boots thrown from feet to the floor, after that a short interval of silence, and then a loud snoring from the four sleeping brothers.

But the young Cyprianowicz could not fall asleep, for all his thoughts circled around Panna Sieninska like lively bees about a flower.

How could he sleep with such a buzzing in his head!

In truth, he closed his eyes once and then twice, but seeing that it was useless, he thought:

"I will see if there is still a light in her room."

And he went out.

There was no light in her window, but the moonlight quivered on the uneven panes as on flowing water.

The world was silent and sleeping so soundly that even the snow seemed to slumber in the whirlpool of greenish moonlight.

"Do you know that you are paradise to me?" whispered the young Cyprianowicz, gazing at the silver window of the girl's room.

CHAPTER 2

IN keeping with his inborn hospitality and habit, the elder Cyprianowicz spared neither requests nor entreaties in trying to persuade his guests to stay longer in Jedlinka. He even knelt before Pani Winnicka, an act that did not come easily because of his gout, which, though moderate so far, was somewhat annoying. But nothing helped. Pan Pagowski insisted on setting out before midday, and one finally had to agree to this, for he declared that he was expecting guests at his home and had to be present. So, with the day bright and frosty, they started before noon in beautiful weather. The snow formations on the trees and the snow lying on the fields seemed covered with a thousand sparkles, which glittered so strongly in the sun that the eye could barely stand the gleams shooting from the heavens and the earth. The horses moved at a vigorous trot till their flanks panted; the sleigh runners whistled along the hard snow; the coach curtains were pushed back on both sides, and now at one window and then at the other appeared Panna Sieninska's rosy face, her eyes merry and her nose red from the frost—a bewitching picture, indeed.

And she rode as if she were a queen, for the coach was encircled by an "honorary guard" comprised of the Bukojemskis and the young Cyprianowicz. Riding on stalwart beasts from the Jedlinka stables (the Bukojemski brothers had sold or pledged not only their horses but the best of their sabers), they rushed forward on both sides, spurring and urging their horses with such impetus that chips of snow, sliced out from the frozen road by the horses' hoofs, whirred through the air like stone projectiles.

Perhaps Pan Pagowski was not that pleased with these bodyguards—at the moment of the coach's departure he had even begged the cavaliers not to trouble themselves, for the road was safe in the daytime and there had been no reports of any robbers in the wilderness—but when they insisted on conducting the ladies, there was nothing left for him to do but repay their politeness with an invitation to Belczaczka. He also obtained a promise from the elder Cyprianowicz to visit him, but only after several days, since it was difficult for an old man to tear himself free of his household so abruptly.

The journey passed quickly with the knights displaying their horsemanship and Panna Sieninska appearing at alternate sides of the coach. Only at the midway point did they stop at a forest inn, bearing the ominous name of "Robbery," to let their horses catch some breath. Next to the inn was a forge and a shed. A blacksmith was shoeing a horse before the forge, and near the inn stood several peasant sleighs attached to gaunt, hoar-frosted nags, who had their tails between their hind legs and bags of oats tied under their noses.

People came out of the inn to look at the coach surrounded by riders, and stood nearby. These were not peasants but potters from Kozienice who made their pots in the summer and transported them in sleighs during winter to sell in villages and especially at church fairs in the surrounding region. They thought that some great dignitary must be traveling in that coach escorted by such fine-looking nobles, so despite the frost, they removed their caps and looked on with curiosity.

The warmly dressed travelers did not leave the equipage, and the attendants remained mounted, but Pan Pagowski's page took a demijohn of wine and a pot into the inn to heat by the fire inside. Meanwhile Pan Pagowski beckoned the potters to come to him and inquired where they came from, where they were going, and if "danger from wild beasts" threatened anywhere.

"There's danger everywhere, your lordship," replied an old townsman, "but we travel in a single group and only during the day. We're waiting for our people from Przytyk and from other places. Perhaps some peasants will arrive, and if fifteen or twenty sleighs should gather, we will move out at night—and if not, then not, though we ride with clubs."

"Nothing has happened around here?"

"It appears wolves tore a Jew to bits in broad daylight. He was riding with geese, for goose feathers were scattered on the road, and of the man and the horse, only bones were found. Only by his skull-cap could people tell he was a Jew. And this morning a man came here on foot, a noble who passed the entire night in a pine tree. He says that his horse fell and that right before his eyes the wolves devoured the beast. He became so stiff in the tree that he could barely talk, and is sleeping now."

"What is his name? Did he say where he came from?"

"No. He only drank some heated beer and immediately afterward fell onto a bench as if he were dead."

Pan Pagowski turned to the cavaliers:

"Did you hear that, gentlemen?"

"Yes."

"We will probably have to wake him up and ask him a few questions. He has no horse now, so how can we leave him here? My page could give up his own horse and sit on one of the front coach animals. They say that the man is a noble. Perhaps he is from afar?"

"He must have been in a hurry," said Stanislaw Cyprianowicz, "since he was traveling at night—and alone. I will go and wake him up, and ask him a few questions."

But this proved unnecessary, for at that moment the page came out of the inn carrying a board with steaming mugs of wine, and upon reaching the coach, he said:

"I beg to tell you that Pan Taczewski is here."

"Pan Taczewski? What the devil is he doing here?"

"Pan Taczewski?" repeated Panna Sieninska.

"He is making himself presentable and will come out as soon as possible," said the page. "He almost knocked the board with the wine from my hand when he heard of your arrival—"

"No one asked you about the board."

The page shut his mouth immediately, as if the power of speech had been taken away from him, while Pan Pagowski grabbed a mug of wine, took one draught and then another, after which he said to Cyprianowicz with a certain distaste:

"That man is an acquaintance of ours, and, in a sense, our neighbor . . . from Czarnia. Humph! A rather giddy and carefree fellow. Of the line of Taczewski, apparently of note in these parts at one time."

Further explanations were interrupted by the appearance of Pan Taczewski, who, coming out hurriedly, walked with a firm stride toward the coach, but with a certain reservation depicted on his face. He was a young noble of medium stature, with wonderfully dark eyes, but lean as a flag pole. His head was covered with a Magyar cap, recalling, one might say, the time of King Bathory; he wore a gray coat lined with sheepskin and yellow Swedish boots that reached up to his hips. No one wore such boots in Poland nowadays, so it was apparent that they were spoils of war from the time of Jan Kazimierz and taken out of the storehouse when needed. While approaching, he looked now at Pan Pagowski, now at Panna Sieninska, and smiled, showing white, perfect teeth, but his smile was rather cheerless, and his face showed unease and even a trace of embarrassment.

When he reached the coach, he bowed, his Magyar cap in hand, and said:

"I am delighted to see Pani Winnicka, Panna Sieninska, and your grace in good health, for the road is dangerous; this I know from experience."

"Cover your head, sir, or your ears will freeze," said Pan Gideon curtly. "I thank you for your thoughtfulness. But why are you wandering through the wilderness?"

Taczewski shot a glance at the young lady, as if to ask, "Perhaps you know?" But seeing that she had her eyes downcast and was playing around with biting a ribbon on her hood, he answered in a rather cold voice:

"Well, the fancy struck me to gaze at the moon above the trees."

"A nice fancy. Did the wolves tear your horse to bits?"

"They only had the pleasure of devouring him, for I took his life myself."

"We know. And you spent the entire night in a pine tree, just like a crow."

At this the Bukojemskis burst into such vigorous laughter that their horses were put on their haunches, and Taczewski turned and measured them one after another with glances that were ice cold and as sharp as a sword blade.

After which, he said to Pagowski:

"Not like a crow, but like a horseless nobleman, at whom your grace is allowed to laugh, but not another, for it may prove unhealthy."

"Oho! Well, well!" repeated the Bukojemskis, advancing toward him on their horses. Their faces grew dark in a moment, and their mustaches quivered ominously, while Taczewski once again began to measure them, perking his head high.

But Pan Gideon spoke in a voice as severe and commanding as if he had power over all of them.

"No quarrels here, please! . . . This is Pan Taczewski," he said more mildly, turning to the knights, "and this is Pan Cyprianowicz and the Bukojemskis to whom, I can say, we owe our lives, for wolves attacked us yesterday. They came to our aid *insperate*, but with good result and in the nick of time."

"In the nick of time," repeated Panna Sieninska with emphasis, pouting a little and glancing at Cyprianowicz with gratitude. Taczewski's cheeks flushed, humiliation seemed to cross his face, his eyes misted, and he said, with boundless sorrow in his voice:

"In the nick of time, for they were in a group and fortunate to be on good horses, while my noble steed was devoured by wolves and I've lost my last friend. But," here he looked with greater friendliness at the Bukojemskis, "may your hands be blessed, gentlemen, for you have done that which with my whole being I would have wanted to do, but which God did not allow me. . . ."

Panna Sieninska was apparently fickle, like all women, but perhaps she was also sorry for Pan Taczewski, because suddenly her eyes became sweet and twinkling, her eyelids fluttered, and in an entirely different voice, she asked:

"Your old steed?. . . My God, I liked him so much and he knew me. My God!"

Taczewski immediately looked at her with immense gratitude.

"He knew you, gracious lady, he knew you. . . ."

"Don't worry so much, Pan Jacek."

"I worried before, but then it was on horseback. Now I will worry on foot. God will reward you, however, for your kind words."

"Meanwhile mount that mouse-colored horse," said Pan Pagowski. "The page will ride next to the leader, or else get on top of the rear of the coach. There is an extra cloak there. Put it on, for you have been freezing all night, and now the cold is increasing."

"No, thank you," replied Taczewski. "I deliberately left my fur mantle behind and am warm!"

"Very well, let's be on our way!"

And after a moment they started. Jacek Taczewski took his place beside the left window of the coach, Stanislaw Cyprianowicz at the right, so that the young lady sitting in front could, without turning her head around, freely glance at one and the other.

CHAPTER 3

BUT the Bukojemskis were displeased at Taczewski's presence and angry that he had taken a place at the side of the coach, so they brought their horses together until the animals' heads almost touched, and began to converse and consult with one another.

"He looked at us with insolence," said Mateusz. "As God is in heaven, he wanted to slight us."

"Now he has turned his horse's backside to us. What do you say to that?"

"He cannot turn his horse's head around, for horses do not travel backwards like a crab. But he has a thing for that young lady, that is certain," observed Marek.

"You have sized things up well. See how he strains his ears and bends forward. If his stirrup leather breaks, he will fall."

"That son of a bitch will not fall, for he sits well and the straps are strong."

"Bend, bend, or we will bend you!"

"See that! Once again he smiles at her!"

"Well, my dear brothers? Are we to allow this?"

"Never, as long as we live! That girl is not for us—fine! But do you remember what we said the other day?"

"Of course! He must have guessed that, for one can see he is a sly fox, and now he is courting her to spite us."

"And in contempt of our orphanhood and poverty."

"Oh, take a look! A great magnate—on another man's horse!"

"Hey, we are not riding our own horses either!"

"At least we have one horse, so if three of us sit at home, the fourth can ride, even to war. But that fellow doesn't even have a saddle, for wolves tore it to bits."

"Yet he still has the nerve to be stuck up. What has he against us? Tell me!"

"We should ask him."

"Now?"

"Now, but diplomatically, so as not to offend old Pagowski. Only after we have heard what he has to say can we challenge him."

"And then he will be ours."

"Which of us shall do this?"

"I should because I am the eldest. First I will rub off the icicle from my mustache, and then go over to him!"

"Just remember what he tells you."

"I will repeat it word for word like a prayer."

Saying this, the eldest of the Bukojemskis began to rub off a lump of ice resting on his mustache, and then he urged his horse to Taczewski's, and spoke:

"Sir?"

"What?" asked Taczewski, turning his head from the coach reluctantly.

"What do you have against us?"

Taczewski glanced at him for a brief moment in surprise, and answered: "Nothing."

And shrugging his shoulders, he turned back to the coach.

Bukojemski rode on for some time in silence, thinking over whether to return to his brothers and report what Taczewski had said or to speak further. The latter course seemed preferable, so he spoke again:

"Because if you think you will get something out of this, then I will tell you what you will achieve, exactly what you said to me—nothing!"

On Taczewski's face was reflected boredom and annoyance. He understood that they were trying to pick a quarrel with him, but at the moment he had little desire to get into a fight. He knew, however, that he had to give some answer, and one that could end the conversation.

So he asked:

"Are those fellows brothers also?"

"Of course! But what do you mean by 'also'?"

"Think about it, sir, and now please don't interrupt my pleasant conversation."

Bukojemski rode beside Taczewski for ten or fifteen steps more, then drew reign.

"What did he say? Speak!" said his brothers.

He repeated what Taczewski had said. They were not happy.

"You did not know how to deal with him," said Lukasz. "You should have tickled his horse's stomach with your stirrup, or, since you know that his name is Taczewski, you should have said, 'Up a tree, Taczewski!'"

"Or you should have said: 'Since wolves ate your horse, you should go and buy a goat at Przytyk."

"We can still say those things to him, but what did it mean when he said: 'Are those fellows brothers also?'"

"Maybe he wanted to ask if we were dolts also!"

"Of course! As God is dear to me!" cried Marek. "What else could he think! Now what?"

"Either his death or ours. As God lives, what he says is open heresy. Stas needs to hear about this."

"Don't tell him anything, for since we've given the young lady to Stas, Stas would have to challenge him, and we must do that first."

"When?"

"It wouldn't be proper at Pagowski's. And we're almost at Belczaczka."

In fact, Belczaczka was not far distant. At the edge of the forest stood the cross marking Pagowski's land, a tin Savior hanging between two spears; on the right, where the road went around the woods, one could see vast meadows and a river lined by alders, and beyond the alders, on the opposite higher bank, the leafless tops of tall trees and smoke rising from cottages.

Soon the retinue was moving past these cottages, and when it had gone beyond the fences and farm buildings, Pan Pagowski's manor house appeared before the eyes of the riders.

The broad courtyard was surrounded by an old, decayed palisade that was overturned in places. No enemy had appeared in that region since the most ancient times, so no one gave much thought to the defense of the dwelling. There were two dovecotes in that spacious yard. On one side stood an annex, and on the other a granary, a storehouse and a large cheese house constructed in a checkered pattern of thin timber and planks. Before the manor and around the courtyard stood pillars with iron rings for the halters of horses; on each pillar sat a cap of frozen snow. The house was old and wide, with a low roof of straw. Hunting dogs were rushing around the yard, and in their midst a tame stork with a broken wing walked about in safety; apparently the bird had left its warm room a moment ago to get air and exercise in the cold weather.

At the manor, people were waiting for them, since Pagowski had sent a page ahead with news of their coming. The same page came out now to meet them and, bowing, said:

"Pan Grothus, the starost of Rajgrod, has arrived."

"Dear God!" cried Pan Pagowski. "Has he been waiting long?"

"Not even an hour. He wanted to go, but I told him that your lordship was on the way and would arrive soon."

"You spoke well."

Then he turned to his guests:

"Gentlemen. Pan Grothus is a relative on my wife's side. He must be returning to Warsaw from his brother's, for he is a deputy in the Diet. Please enter!"

In a moment they found themselves in a dining room in the presence of the starost of Rajgrod, whose head almost touched the ceiling, for in height he surpassed somewhat even the Bukojemskis and the rooms throughout the manor were exceedingly low. Pan Grothus was an ostentatious noble, with a look of wisdom in his eye, and the face and bald head of a supernumerary. A sword scar just above the nose and centered between his two eyebrows seemed like a furrow and gave his face a stern and angry expression. But he smiled pleasantly at Pagowski, and opened his arms to him, saying:

"Yes, it is I, a guest, greeting the host in his own house."

And Pagowski put a hand around his neck and said:

"A guest, a dear guest! God give you health for having dropped by, my fellow brother. What news?"

"Good news *de privatis*, and also *de publicis*, for war is coming."

"War! How's that? Already? Are we involved?"

"We are not involved yet, but an alliance with His Majesty the Emperor will be signed in March, and war is certain to follow."

Even though before the New Year there had been whispers of a war with the Turks, and there were even those who considered it inevitable, the confirmation of these rumors from the lips of such a notable person, and one so intimately acquainted with politics as Pan Grothus, made a great impression not only on Pan Pagowski but also his young guests. So right after the host presented them to the starost, a conversation ensued concerning the war, Tekeli and the bloody contests in Hungary, from which, as from a great conflagration, light reached the lands of Austria and Poland. This was to be a terrible war, before which the Roman Caesar and all the German lands trembled. The politically astute Pan Grothus declared that the Sublime Port would set in motion half of Asia and all Africa, and appear with such strength as the world had not yet seen. But these forecasts did not ruin the good mood of anyone; on the contrary, the valiant young men, bored with the long peace at home, listened with joy to the possibility of a war that opened the way to glory, service, and even profit.

And so when Mateusz Bukojemski heard the starost's words, he struck his knee so loudly that a reverberation was heard about the room, and exclaimed:

"Half of Asia, and what else? Ha! That's nothing new for us!"

"Nothing new—you speak the truth, sir!" replied the host, whose usually gloomy face lit up with fleeting joy. "If this war is a sure thing, then the call to arms will be issued soon, and recruitment will start. God grant it! God grant it as soon as possible. Remember old Dziewiatkiewicz at Chocim, blind in both eyes? His sons aimed his lance in the charge—and he struck the Janissaries like everyone else. But I have no son!"

"My lord brother, if anyone has the right to stay at home, it is you," said the starost. "It is a bad thing not to have a son in the war, worse not to have eyes, but not to have an arm is worst of all."

"I accustomed both hands to the saber," replied Pan Gideon, "and can hold reins in my teeth. And I would like to fall on the field against the pagans. Not because they have ruined my life. Not because of some private vengeance—no! But because of the following—and I speak openly: I am old now; I have seen much and have thought about many things. I have seen in this Commonwealth so much hatred among men, so much selfishness, so much disorder; I have seen our licence, the breaking of Diets, the disobedience, all manner of lawlessness, that I tell you, sirs, many times in desperation I have asked the Lord God: 'Why, Lord, did you create this Commonwealth of ours and our people?' It is only when the pagan sea swells, when that vile dragon opens its jaws to swallow the entire world and Christianity, when, as your graciousness says, the Roman Caesar and all the Germans lands tremble before that onslaught—it is only then that I shall finally know why God created us and what kind of responsibility He placed upon us. The Turks themselves speak of this. Let others tremble—we will not, just as we did not before. Let our blood flow even if it has to be to the last drop—and let my blood be joined with the blood of my brothers. Amen!"

Pagowski's eyes glittered, and he became very moved, but he did not allow himself to shed tears, perhaps because he had already cried them out a long time ago or, perhaps, because he was as hard on himself as he was on others. Nevertheless, Pan Grothus put an arm around his neck, kissed him on both cheeks, and said:

"True, true! There is much evil among us, and only with our blood can we settle our accounts with God. That service, that guard which God has charged us with, is our nation's destiny. And the time is coming when we shall render this service. This is so! There are tidings from the pagan that the onslaught will be directed on Vienna. We will go there, and in front of the whole world will show that we are nothing but soldiers of Christ, created for the defense of the faith and the Cross. All those nations who have till now lived safely behind our backs, will see in the clear light of day how we carry out our mission, and with God's will, the memory of our service and glory shall not be forgotten as long as the world exists."

At these words, enthusiasm seized the young men. The Bukojemskis sprang from their chairs, and began to call out in loud voices:

"God grant it! When are the enlistments taking place? God grant it!"

And Cyprianowicz said:

"Even the soul is eager to go! We are ready this very day!"

Only Taczewski was silent, and his expression did not brighten. The news which had filled all hearts with joy was for him only a source of pain and bitterness. His thoughts and his eyes were directed at Panna Sieninska, who was bustling merrily about the dishes on the table, and they spoke to her with reproach and boundless sorrow:

"Had it not been for you, I would have gone to some nobleman's manor and—even though I might not have found fortune—I would at least have some nice weapons and a horse, and would now join up with a company to find either death or glory. Your charming ways, your glances, your good words, which you threw at times to me like alms, have resulted in this, that I have stayed on these last field-patches almost dying of hunger. I have not seen the world because of you and have not gained any refinement. How have I wronged you, someone who has taken my soul and body into a Tartar-like captivity? . . . Why, I would rather die than not see you for one year. I lost my last horse in hurrying to save you, but you just laughed and looked upon another with gratitude. And now what am I to do? War is coming. Should I become a servant or be disgraced among foot soldiers? What have I done to you that you have never been compassionate to me?"

Thus did Jacek Taczewski complain, and he felt his misery the more because he was a noble of a great knightly family, albeit one terribly poor. And though it was not true that Panna Sieninska never had compassion toward him, it was true that because of her he had never gone out into the world, but rather remained at pasture, as it were, with two serfs, frequently unable to afford the basic necessities of life. He had been seventeen and she thirteen when he fell madly in love with her— and for these past five years he loved her, each year with greater depth and greater sorrow, for his love seemed without hope. At first Pan Pagowski received him gladly, as a descendent of a great family that had once owned much land in these parts, but later when Pagowski became aware of where things stood, he began to be curt with him and on occasion even cruel. He did not bar him from visiting his house, but kept him at a distance from his daughter, for, quite simply, he had other hopes and plans for her. And Panna Sieninska herself tested her powers over him and played with his love just like every girl plays with flowers in a meadow. Sometimes she bends over one of those flowers, at other times she plucks one; sometimes she puts one in her hair to later throw it away or forgets about flowers altogether to then return and look for new ones. Taczewski had never told her of his love, but she knew of it perfectly, though she pretended not to know, as she pretended that she did not want to know anything about what was happening within him. She did with him what she wanted. Once when bees were chasing her, she sought refuge under his cloak and cuddled up to his breast, but afterward she would not forgive him this for two days. At times she treated him almost with disdain, and when it seemed to him that everything was finally over, with one sweet look, with one warm word she would fill him with boundless joy and hope. But when he was not present at Belczaczka for several days, either because of a wedding, a name day, or a hunt in the neighborhood, she really missed him; yet when he returned she took revenge on him for her longing, and tormented him for a long time. His worst moments came when there were guests at the manor, and among them happened to be some young man who was good-looking as well as intelligent. At those times Jacek Taczewski thought that her heart did not possess even simple compassion. This is precisely what he was thinking now because of Cyprianowicz. And everything that Pan Grothus had told of the coming war added still more bitterness to the already overflowing cup of his thoughts.

Taczewski was quite accustomed to maintaining control over himself at Pan Pagowski's house; nevertheless, as he listened to the conversation between Panna Sieninska and Stanislaw Cyprianowicz, he could hardly sit in place during supper. The unhappy youth saw that Cyprianowicz pleased her very much, for he was, in fact, a valiant, likeable and not at all stupid fellow. The conversation at table continually revolved around the forthcoming levies. Cyprianowicz, learning from Pan Grothus that perhaps he himself would be recruiting in these parts, suddenly turned to the young lady, and asked:

"And what company do you prefer, lady?"

And the young lady glanced at his shoulders and replied:

"The hussars."

"Because of their wings?"

"Yes. I once saw hussars and thought that they were an army from heaven. Afterward I dreamed of them for two nights."

"I do not know whether you will dream of me should I become a hussar, but it is certain that I will frequently dream of you—and also with wings."

"How so?"

"As an angel."

Panna Sieninska lowered her eyes, so that a shadow fell on her rosy cheeks from her eyelids, and said after a moment:

"Become a hussar, sir."

Taczewski gritted his teeth and drew a hand over his sweaty brow, but during the supper he got neither a word nor a glance from Panna Sieninska. Only when everyone had risen from the table, and in the room there was noise of chairs moving, did a sweet, beloved voice murmur in his ear:

"Will you also go to war?"

"To die! To die!" replied Jacek.

And in this answer there was such genuine anguish that the beloved voice was heard again, as if moved:

"Why cause people to grieve?"

"No one will weep for me."

"How do you know?" murmured the feminine voice a third time.

After which she went to the other guests as quickly as a wonderful vision in a dream, to bloom like a rose at the other end of the room.

Meanwhile, after the meal, the older gentlemen sat over cups of mead and, after they had their fill of discussing public affairs, they began to chat about private ones. Pan Grothus followed Panna Sieninska for a while with tender eyes, after which he said:

"What a candle! Take a look, lord brother, at those youths who are flying like moths to a flame! But it is no wonder, for if not for our age, we would also be flying."

But Pan Pagowski waved a hand in displeasure.

"Moths they are, gray moths, nothing more."

"How so? Why, Taczewski is no yeoman."

"But he is an impoverished nobleman. The Bukojemskis are also not yeomen. They even declare that they are related to Saint Peter, which may help them get a promotion in heaven, but here on earth, in the king's wilderness, they are nothing but gamekeepers."

Pan Grothus was surprised at this relationship of the Bukojemskis, no less than Pan Pagowski when he had first heard of it, so he began to inquire about it in detail, until finally he laughed out loud and said the following:

"Saint Peter—he was a great apostle and I have no desire to detract from his honor, particularly as, feeling my age, I shall need his good graces soon, but speaking between you and me—as far as a relative is concerned . . . well, there is not much to boast of. That noble person was a fisherman, nothing more. Now if you talk to me about Saint Joseph, who is descended from King David, that is something else!"

"I only say this: that there is no one here suitable for the girl—and I'm not just speaking about these youths you see here under my roof, but about all the eligible men in the entire region."

"What about that young man sitting near Pani Winnicka? He seems like a nice gentleman."

"Cyprianowicz? Yes! He is nice, but of Armenian descent and of a family that has belonged to the nobility for only three or four generations."

"Then why invite these young men? Cupid is treacherous, and before you know it, you will find yourself in a mess."

Pan Pagowski, who had already stated how much he had owed the young men when he had introduced them, now explained in detail about the attack of the wolves and the assistance he had received, and how through simple gratitude he was compelled to invite his rescuers to his home.

"True, true," acknowledged Pan Grothus, "but Amor may work his wonders here, for the girl's blood is not water."

"Ah, she's a slippery weasel," replied Pan Pagowski. "She can and will bite, and will slip out from between a man's fingers—and no ordinary person can catch her. Great blood has this inborn virtue that it does not yield, but must prevail and rule. I am not a person who is easily led by the nose, but I give in to her and not just once. It is true that I owe the Sieninskis a lot, but even if that were not so, when she stands before me and proceeds to move her tresses from one shoulder to the other, tilting her head and glancing at me, then she frequently gets her way. More than once I have thought what an honor and blessing from God it is that this last child, this last heiress of such a renowned family, finds herself under my roof. . . . Of course you know about the Sieninskis— once all of Podolia was theirs. In truth, the Danilowiczes, the Zolkiewskis and the Sobieskis rose to prominence because of them. His Majesty the King should remember this, the more so since almost nothing remains of that vast fortune, and if the girl is to have anything, it will only be that which remains after me."

"But what will your relatives say?"

"I have only distant relatives who will not be able to prove their kinship. Nevertheless, I am bothered at times by the thought that after my death there could be some difficulties—legal proceedings, disputes—as is usually the case in our country. I am speaking chiefly of my wife's relatives, for I received a portion of my possessions from her as well as Belczaczka."

"I shall not bring a lawsuit," said Pan Grothus with a smile, "but I cannot vouch for anyone else."

"That's just it! That's just it! Recently I have been thinking of going to Warsaw and asking the king himself to be this orphan's guardian in the future, but his mind is occupied with other things now."

"If you had a son it would be a simple matter to give the girl to him."

Pan Pagowski glanced at the Rajgrod starost with such a pained look that the starost stopped speaking in midsentence. Both men were silent for a long time, after which Pan Gideon said in a voice broken by emotion:

"I could answer you, lord brother, with what Virgil said: '*Infadum iubes renovare dolorem.*' [You command me to bring up unspeakable sorrow.] Yes, it would be a simple matter. I will tell you that if it were not for this simple matter, then perhaps I would have died a long time ago. My son was seized by the horde as a child. It has happened, and not just once, that people have returned from pagan captivity when the memory of them has faded. . . . For years and years I have waited for a miracle and have lived in that hope. Even today, after a drink or two, I think: 'Perhaps now it will come to pass!' God is greater than man's hopes. But these moments of hope are brief, and my pain is long and constant. . . . No! Why should I delude myself? My blood will not be mingled with the blood of the Sieninskis, and if relatives will tear away at my fortune, then this last child in her family, to whom I owe everything, will be without a penny in the world!"

Both drank in silence again. Pan Grothus was thinking how to alleviate the pain he had unintentionally caused his host and how to cheer him up. Finally an idea came to him which he considered quite good.

"There's a way out for everything," he said. "And you will be able to make certain the girl is not left penniless, no matter what."

"How can I do that?" asked Pan Pagowski with a certain unease.

"Does it not happen that old men take as wives even girls not yet fully grown? An *exemplum* in history is the great hetman Koniecpolski, who, though older than you, married an unripe girl. It is true, of course, that he died the first night after the wedding because of all the rejuvenating elixirs he took, but neither Pan Makowski, pocillator of Radom, nor Pan Rudnicki, Master of the Royal Hunt, died, though both were over seventy years old. . . . Besides, you are hardy fellow. Should the Lord God bless you, so much the better; but if not, then you will leave the young widow in peace and wealth, and at that point she can choose whatever husband she likes."

Whether such an idea had ever entered Pan Pagowski's head, it was difficult to say; it was enough that, upon hearing the words of the Raj-grod starost, he became greatly confused, and with a somewhat trembling hand, poured the starost some mead, which overflowed his cup so that the worthy liquor began to drip from the table onto the floor. Then he said:

"Let us drink! To the success of Christian arms!"

"That's a different matter," replied Pan Grothus, following the course of his thoughts, "but as far as this one is concerned, think over what I have told you—for it seems to me that I've found the solution."

"What are you talking about! What does one thing have to do with the other! Drink some more."

Further conversation was interrupted by the movement of chairs at the larger table. Pani Winnicka and Panna Sieninska wanted to retire. The young lady's voice, resonant as a silver bell, began to repeat: "Goodnight, sir; goodnight, sir." Then she curtsied wonderfully to Pan Grothus, kissed Pan Pagowski's hand, rubbed her nose and forehead against his shoulder like a cat, and left. Cyprianowicz, the Bukojemskis and Taczewski also left right after the ladies. Only the two older men remained in the room, and they chatted a long time, for Pan Gideon commanded a new demijohn of even worthier mead be brought to them.

CHAPTER 4

WHETHER by pure chance or through a prank on the part of the young lady, the four Bukojemskis were given a large room in the annex, while Cyprianowicz and Taczewski had a smaller room to themselves. This perturbed the two men somewhat, and in order not to speak to each other, they began their prayers straightaway and recited them longer than usual. Nevertheless, when they had finished, an embarrassing silence ensued that weighed heavily on both, for though they did not have friendly feelings toward each other, they felt that it would not be proper to betray this and that they should be diplomatic for a while, particularly at the home of Pan Pagowski.

Taczewski ungirded his saber, drew it out of the scabbard, looked at the edge by the light of the hearth and began to polish it with a kerchief.

"After a frost," he said half to himself, half to Cyprianowicz, "it sweats in a warm room and rusts immediately."

"And last night your saber must have been truly ice cold," replied Cyprianowicz.

He said this without any evil intent, and only because it occurred to him that Taczewski had indeed spent the night in a ringing frost; but the other man immediately rested the point of his blade on the floor and looked keenly into his eyes.

"Are you referring to the fact that I sat in a pine tree?"

"Yes," answered Stanislaw straightforwardly. "There was no hearth there, of course."

"And what would you have done in my position?"

Cyprianowicz wished to reply: "the same as you," but the question was put to him so sharply that he said:

"Since I was not there, why should I concern myself with that?"

Anger flashed across Jacek's face, but to restrain himself, he began to blow on the saber and rub it with greater vigor. Finally he returned it to the scabbard, and said: "God sends both good and bad occurrences."

And his eyes, which a moment ago had been gleaming, exhibited once again their usual sadness, for just then he remembered his one friend, his horse, that wolves had torn to pieces.

Meanwhile the door opened, and the four Bukojemski brothers entered the room.

"The frost has let up, and the snow is steaming," said Mateusz.

"There will be a fog," added Jan.

And then they noticed Taczewski, whom they had not seen at first.

"Oh!" exclaimed Lukasz, turning to Cyprianowicz. "So this is the company you're keeping?"

All four brothers put their hands on their hips and cast challenging looks at Jacek.

He, meanwhile, seized a chair and, pushing it to the middle of the room, turned it suddenly toward the Bukojemskis and sat astride it like a horse, rested his elbows on the arms, raised his head, and answered them with an equally challenging look.

Thus they stayed facing each other: he, in his Swedish boots, his legs placed far apart; they, standing shoulder to shoulder, enormous, threatening, aggressive.

Cyprianowicz saw that it was coming to a quarrel, but he also wished to laugh. Thinking he could prevent an altercation at any moment, he let them stare at each other.

"Well, what a bold fellow!" he thought to himself about Taczewski. "Nothing confounds him."

Meanwhile the silence continued, unendurable and amusing at the same time. Jacek felt this himself, for he was the first to break it:

"Have a seat, my dear sirs," he said. "Not only do I request but beg you to do so."

The Bukojemskis looked at one another with astonishment, confused at this unexpected turn.

"What's that? What? What is he thinking of? . . ."

"Please! Please!" repeated Jacek, pointing to some stools.

"We will remain standing, for it pleases us to do so. Understand?"

"Too much ceremony."

"What ceremony?" cried out Lukasz. "Do you claim to be a bishop or a senator, you—you Pompeius?"

Taczewski did not move from his chair, but his back began to shake as if from sudden laughter.

"But, sir, why do you call me Pompeius?" he asked.

"Because it suits you."

"But perhaps you say that because you're a simpleton?"

"Strike, whosoever believes in God!" exclaimed Jan.

But Jacek apparently also had enough of talk, for he suddenly sprang from his chair toward the Bukojemskis like a cat.

"Listen, you loafers," he said with a voice as cold as steel. "What do you want of me?"

"Blood!" cried out Mateusz Bukojemski.

"You won't escape this time!" shouted Marek.

"Step outside immediately!" added Mateusz, grasping at the saber at his side.

But Cyprianowicz stepped in quickly between them.

"I will not allow this!" he cried out. "This is another man's house."

"True!" attested Taczewski. "This is another man's house, and I will not dishonor Pan Pagowski by paying you back under his roof, but tomorrow I will find you!"

"Then we will seek you out tomorrow!" roared Mateusz.

"You've been trying to pick a quarrel all day long. Why? I do not know because I've never met you before, nor have you met me. But you must answer for this. I will face not only four but ten men if insulted."

"Oh, well, well!" exclaimed Jan. "One man will be enough in this case. It is evident that you have not heard of the Bukojemskis."

But Taczewski turned suddenly to Cyprianowicz.

"I spoke of four," he said, "but perhaps you wish to join these cavaliers?"

Cyprianowicz bowed politely.

"As long as you are asking me. . . ."

"But we are first, and according to seniority. We will not back down from this. We have promised her to you and will cut up anyone who stands in your way."

Taczewski looked sharply at the Bukojemskis, understood in one moment what they were talking about, and paled.

"So that's it, my dear sir?" he said, turning again to Cyprianowicz. "These are your hirelings, and you are hiding behind their sabers? A sure and very safe method, indeed, but whether it is noble and knightly is another thing! Pish! In what company do I find myself?"

Upon hearing this shameful accusation, Cyprianowicz, though good-natured, felt the blood rush to his face; the veins on his forehead swelled, lightning flashed from his eyes, his teeth gritted terribly, and he seized the hilt of his saber.

"Step outside! Step outside this instant!" he cried out in a voice choked with anger.

Sabers flashed, and the room brightened from the blades of steel, upon which fell light from the resinous chips glowing in the fireplace. But three of the Bukojemskis, springing between the opponents, stood as a wall between them, while the fourth seized Cyprianowicz by the shoulders and started to shout:

"Stas, for the love of God, restrain yourself! We are first!"

"We are first!" repeated the others.

"Let go of me!" exclaimed Cyprianowicz hoarsely.

"We are first!"

"Let go of me!"

"Hold Stas, while I deal with this man," shouted Mateusz.

And grabbing Taczewski by the hand, he began to pull him to the side in order to start right away, but Taczewski, regaining his presence of mind, wrenched the hand away, sheathed his saber, and said:

"I will choose who will go first and when. So I tell you: tomorrow, and not here, but in Wyrabek."

"Oh, you will not slip away. Now! Now!"

But Taczewski folded his arms over his chest.

"Ha! If you want to murder me under another man's roof, go right ahead."

At this, rage seized the brothers. They started to stamp the floor with their heels, pull at their mustaches, and pant like bears.

But not one dared to spring at Taczewski, so as not to bring dishonor upon himself!

He stood for some time, as if waiting to see if someone would jump him; finally he grabbed his Magyar cap, nestled it on his head, and said:

"So, I'm telling you: tomorrow! You will tell Pan Pagowski that you are going to visit me—and ask for the road to Wyrabek. Beyond the brook is a roadside Passion of Christ from the time of the plague. I will be waiting for you there at midday. . . . May that be the end of you!"

And these last words he uttered almost with sorrow, after which he opened the door and walked out.

In the yard the little dogs surrounded him, and knowing him well, they began to fawn on him. Involuntarily he looked at the posts near the windows, as if seeking his horse. He remembered that his horse was no longer on this earth, so he sighed and, feeling a cold breath of air, said to himself:

"The wind blows in the eyes of the poor man. I will go on foot!"

Meanwhile, in the room, the young Cyprianowicz was wringing his hands in pain and anger, and saying to the Bukojemskis with great bitterness:

"Who asked you for this? My worst enemy could not have crushed me more than all of you have with your service."

They, on the other hand, were most sorry for him, and fell to embracing him, one after the other.

"Stas," said Mateusz. "They sent a demijohn to our room for the night. For God's sake, cheer up!"

CHAPTER 5

THE world was still gray when Father Woynowski, lantern in hand, shuffled through the deep snow to the hares, pigeons and partridges that he raised in a granary in a special enclosure. A tame fox with a little bell on its neck followed his footsteps, and beside the fox went a spotted spitz dog and a badger who was not overcome with winter sleep in the priest's warm room. After slowly crossing the yard, the quartet stopped under the straw eaves of the granary, from which hung long icicles. The lantern swayed, a key was heard in the lock, the staple whined, the door squeaked louder than the key, and the old man went in with his animals. Sitting down on a block, he placed the lantern on the second block and, taking a linen bag filled with grain and cabbage leaves smelling of the cellar, began to toss them into the trough, yawning loudly.

Even before he began, three hares hopped immediately toward him from the dark corners of the recess. Then, their eyes shining in the lantern light like glittering rosary beads, pigeons and rust-colored partridges advanced in a dense flock, bobbing their heads on supple necks. Before long, the more daring pigeons began to peck at the trough, while the partridges advanced with caution, glancing now at the falling grain, now at the priest, now at the she-fox, with whom they had long been acquainted, for having been caught the past summer as chicks and raised at home since they were little, they saw her daily.

The priest kept tossing the grain and muttering the morning prayer at the same time:

"*Pater noster, qui es in coelis, sanctificetur nomen . . .*"

He stopped his work for a moment and turned to the fox, who, resting against him, trembled as if a fever were shaking her.

"Ah, your skin quivers every time you see them. Everyday it is the same thing. Learn to hold your inborn appetites in check, for your food is worthy and you don't suffer from hunger. Now, where was I?"

He closed his eyes as if waiting for an answer, and since he did not get it, he started over:

"*Pater noster, qui es in coelis, sanctificetur nomen tuum, adveniat regnum tuum . . .*"

Once again he interrupted himself.

"I see your hair is curling," he said, placing his hand on the she-fox's back. "Such is that vile nature in you that you not only must eat but also murder. Catch her, Filus, by the tuft, and if she becomes impolite then bite her. . . . *Adveniat regnum tuum.* . . . Oh you little devil, I know what you'd like to say! That man is *libenter perdices manducat,* but know this, that at least man gives partridges peace during fast days, while in you lies the soul of that obscene Luther, for you would devour meat even on Good Friday. *Fiat voluntas tua.* . . . Bunny, bunny, bunny! . . . *sicut in coelo . . .* here you are; here's a cabbage stump for all of you! . . . *et in terra.*"

And thus speaking he threw the pieces of cabbage, and then the grain again, grumbling a bit at the pigeons because they were approaching each other from behind, cooing and strutting, even though spring was still far away. Finally, when the bag was completely empty, he got up, raised the lantern, and was preparing to go, when Taczewski turned up at the threshold of the granary.

"Ah! Jacek!" he cried out. "What are you doing here so early?"

Taczewski kissed the priest's hand, and replied:

"I arrived for confession, reverend father, and at early mass I would like to approach the Lord's Table."

"To confession? That is fine, but why the urgency? Tell me straightaway, for this is not without reason!"

"I will speak openly. I must fight a duel today, and since one has a greater chance of meeting with a mishap fighting five men than one, I would like to absolve my soul of sins."

"Five men? Good heavens! What did you do to them?"

"That's just it: I did nothing. They sought a quarrel and have challenged me."

"Who are these people?"

"The Bukojemskis, foresters, and Cyprianowicz from Jedlinka."

"I know them. Come to the presbytery, and tell me what happened."

They went out. But in the middle of the farmyard, Father Woynowski stopped suddenly, looked sharply into Taczewski's eyes, and said:

"Listen, Jacek, is there a *mulier,* a woman, involved in this?"

Taczewski smiled sadly.

"Yes, and no," he said, "for she is at issue, but is innocent."

"Aha! Innocent! They are all innocent. But do you know what Ecclesiastes says of women?"

"I do not remember, reverend father."

"Neither do I, but what I have forgotten I will read to you in the house. *'Inveni amariorem morte mulierem, quae laqueus venatorum est et sagena cor eius.'* [I have found woman more bitter than death; her heart is a trap and a snare.] And he says something more, but in the end says: *'Qui placet Deo, effugiet illam, qui autem peccator est, capietur ab illa.'* [Whosoever is pleasing to God will escape her, but whosoever is a sinner will be caught by her.] I have warned you more than once not to stay at that house—and now you see the result."

"Well, it is easier for you to warn me than for me not to go there," replied Taczewski with a sigh.

"Nothing good will meet you in that house."

"That is certain," said the young cavalier quietly.

And they proceeded in silence toward the presbytery, the priest with a look of worry on his face, for he loved Jacek with his entire soul. When Jacek's father had died from the plague, the young man was left in the world without any near relation, without property, in Wyrabek with a few serfs, so the old man had surrounded him with tender care. He could not give him wealth, for, having an angelic soul, he distributed to the poor everything that his poor parish received, but he nevertheless helped him in secret, and besides, watched over him, taught him—and not only what was found in books, but the art of being a knight. For in his day he was a famed soldier, a comrade and friend of the famed Wolodyjowski, as well as a soldier under Czarniecki; he had gone through the entire Swedish conflict, and only after its completion had put on a cleric's robe because of some terrible misfortune. He loved Jacek, and valued not only his famed knightly lineage, but his noble and sad soul, similar to his own. So he was grieved over the young man's immense poverty and the ill-fated love that caused the young man to waste himself away in a little hole leading a half-peasant life instead of seeking fame and bread in the great wide world. Because of this he felt a certain distaste for the entire house at Belczaczka, and also took it ill of Gideon Pagowski that the old master treated his serfs so severely.

For him, however, these "hewers of wood and drawers of water" were the apple of his eye, but besides them, he loved everything that lived in the world: those animals that he scolded, birds, fish, and even the frogs that croaked in the sun-warmed waters during summer.

However, in this priest's robe walked not only an angel, but an old soldier, so now when he learned that Jacek was scheduled to fight five men, he thought only of this: what account the young man would give of himself and whether he would come out of the affair without sustaining an injury.

He halted right before the door of the presbytery, and said:

"You will not yield, I suppose? I have taught you everything I know, and what Wolodyjowski showed me."

"I would not like them to chop me to death," answered Taczewski with modesty, "for a great war with the Turks is approaching."

Hearing this, the old man's eyes shone like stars, and in one moment he seized Jacek by the loop of his doublet, and began to ask him questions:

"Praise the name of the Lord! How do you know this? Who told you?"

"The starosta, Pan Grothus," replied the young man.

The conversation between Jacek and the priest lasted long, as well as the confession before Mass; and when they finally found themselves after Mass in the presbytery and were seated for caudle, the mind of the old man was haunted continually by thoughts of war with the pagan, and because of this, he began to complain of the moral corruption and decline of piety in the Commonwealth.

"My God," he said, "the fields of glory and salvation are open, but you men prefer private quarrels and cutting each other up. Having a chance of giving your blood in the defense of the cross and the faith, you are ready to spill the blood of a brother. For whom? Why? For private grudges, or women, or similar worldly vanities. I know that in the Commonwealth this habit is old—for, *mea culpa*, in time of sinful and frivolous youth, I myself submitted to it. In winter camps, when the armies are occupied only with idleness and drinking, a day does not go by without a duel, but the Church censures them and upholds the law. Dueling is sinful at all times, and before a war with the Turks, the sin is greater, for every sword is needed, and every sword serves the true faith and the true God. That is why our king, who is *defensor fidei*, detests duels, and in the field, in the face of the enemy, where martial law dictates, they are punished severely."

"The king also fought in his youth, and not just once," replied Taczewski. "But what am I to do, reverend father? It was not I who offered the challenge; I was challenged. How can I fail to meet them?!"

"True, you must meet them! That is why my soul is distressed. Well, God will be on the side of the innocent one!"

Taczewski began to take leave of him, for midday was not more than two hours away and he had a long road ahead of him.

"Wait," said Father Woynowski. "I will not let you go like this. I will have my servant rack up a sleigh and go to the place of combat. For if at Pagowski's they know nothing of the duel, they will send no assistance, and how will it be if one of them, or you, should be wounded severely? Have you thought about this?"

"I have not, and they certainly will not."

"See! I will also go, but I will not be on the field but at your place in Wyrabek. I will take the viaticum and a boy with a bell too, for who knows what may happen? It is not proper, not at all, for a man of the cloth to be a witness to such things, but if it were not for this, I would gladly be there, even if just to raise your spirits."

And Taczewski looked at him with eyes as sweet as a girl's.

"May God reward you!" he said. "But I shall not lose heart, for even if I had to lay down my life—"

"Better be silent," said the priest, interrupting him. "Wouldn't it be better to face the Turk and die a more glorious death in that case?"

"That is true, reverend father; I will try not to let those cannibals swallow me at once."

Father Woynowski thought a moment, then said:

"But if I were to go to the field and explain to them the reward that would meet them in heaven were they to die at the hands of the pagan, would they perhaps give up the duel?"

"God forbid!" exclaimed Jacek passionately. "They would think that I sent you. God forbid! It is better that I go right now than hear such things."

"Ha! Then nothing can be done! Let's go!" said the priest.

And calling his servant, he commanded him to attach the horse to the sleigh with all speed, after which both he and Taczewski went out of the presbytery to personally help with the harnessing.

But when the priest saw in the courtyard the horse on which Jacek had come, he retreated in amazement, and exclaimed:

"In the name of the Father and the Son, where did you find such a thing?"

At the fence stood a poor hoarfrost-covered jade, its head drooping low, long hair hanging down from its jaws, and not much bigger than a full-grown goat.

"I borrowed her from a peasant," replied Taczewski. "Well, if I were to go on it to the Turkish war . . ."

And he began to laugh in painful duress.

To this the priest answered:

"It matters little on what horse you will go, as long as you come back on a Turkish one, and may God give you this, Jacek; but in the meantime put your saddle on my mount, for you cannot show yourself like this to those nobles."

After this, they finished up what was necessary and set off: the priest, a church boy with a bell, a driver for the sleigh, and Taczewski on horseback. The day was cloudy and somewhat misty, for a thaw had set in over the earth. Snow covered the frozen ground, but its surface had softened considerably, so that the horse hoofs sank noiselessly in it and the sleigh runners moved quietly along the even road. Immediately beyond Jedlinka they met wagons loaded with wood, accompanied by peasants on foot, who knelt at the sound of the bell, thinking that the priest was going with the Lord God to a dying man. Then began mist-covered fields lying next to the forest, empty and white, over which passed flocks of crows. The closer they got to the forest, the thicker the mist became; it rolled down, filling the area and stretching upward, so that after a while when the travelers heard croaking above them, they did not see any birds. The bushes by the roadside looked like ghosts. The world lost its usual distinctness and was transformed into some kind of vague, delirious land where nearby objects took on a hallucinatory look and distance became completely unknown.

Jacek rode along the silent snow, thinking about the duel awaiting him, and even more about Panna Sieninska, and he soliloquized in his mind, half to himself and half to her: "My love for you has always been constant, but I have no joy in my heart from it. In truth, I had little joy even before! But now, if I could just embrace your dear feet for one instant or hear a good word from you, or just know that you would be sad if some mishap met me. But all of this is like this mist, and you seem beyond this mist, and I do not know what is true, nor do I know what will be or what will befall me, nor what will happen. I know nothing."

And feeling a great sadness settle over him just as the dampness was settling into his clothes, Jacek sighed deeply and said:

"But I want this to end, once and for all!"

Father Woynowski was also attacked by sad thoughts.

"The boy's gone through hard times," he thought. "He has missed his youth, worried to the utmost over this ill-fated love of his, and now what? These bullies, the Bukojemskis, will cut him to pieces. Not too long ago, they hacked up Korzybski after a church fair. Even if they do not cut up Jacek, nothing good can come out of this duel. Dear God! This boy is as pure as gold—the last of a great knightly tree, the last nourishing drop of blood. . . . If he could only take care of himself now. . . . I hope to God that he hasn't forgotten those two strokes—one a feint under the guard with a side spring, the other a whirl through the cheek. . . ."

Then he cried out: "Jacek!"

But Jacek did not hear, for he had ridden ahead, and the old man did not call out again. On the contrary, he was quite disconcerted at the thought that it was not proper for a man of the cloth, who was traveling with the Sacrament, to think of such things. He began to repent and asked the Lord God for forgiveness.

Yet he felt more and more aggrieved in his soul. He was overcome by a sudden ill foreboding, which became almost a certainty, that this strange duel without seconds would end in the worst possible manner for Jacek.

Meanwhile they reached the crossroad, which on the right led to Wyrabek and on the left to Belczaczka. The driver stopped as he was commanded. Taczewski approached the sleigh and dismounted.

"I will go on foot to the shrine," he said, "for I would not know what to do with this horse while the sleigh takes you to my house and returns. Perhaps they are already there."

"It is not noon yet, though soon," replied the priest with a somewhat altered voice. "What a fog! The lot of you will have to grope your way through the duel!"

"One can see well enough!"

The cawing of unseen crows or ravens was heard once again above their heads.

"Jacek!" said the priest.

"I am listening."

"As long as this duel is to happen, do not forget the knights of Taczewo."

"They will not be ashamed of me, father, indeed not!"

The old man noticed that the young man's features had hardened, and while the eyes had not lost their sadness, they did not have in them that usual girlish sweetness.

So he said:

"That is good. But kneel now, so that I can bless you, and do not forget to make the sign of the cross yourself right before the duel."

Afterward, he made the sign of the cross over Jacek, who had knelt down on the snow.

Then Taczewski tied the horse behind the sleigh at the side of the peasant's own nag, kissed the priest's hand, and went off toward Belczaczka.

"Come back to me in one piece!" cried the priest after him.

No one was present yet at the wayside cross. Taczewski went around the shrine several times, after which he sat down on a stone at the foot of the crucifix and waited.

An immense silence hung about the place. Only great tearlike drops, formed by the damp mist and falling from the arms of the crucifix, struck the soft snow with a barely audible sound. That quiet, permeated with a certain sadness, and that misty emptiness, filled Jacek's heart with a new wave of sorrow. He felt alone as never before: "In truth, I am like a lone eagle in the world," he said to himself, "and that is my fate till I die."

And he waved his hand.

"So let it end once and for all."

With growing bitterness he thought that his opponents were in no hurry, because they were sitting now joyous at Belczaczka conversing with *her* and looking at her as much as they wanted.

But he was mistaken, for they too were in a rush. After a while the sound of loud talking came to him, and in the white mist loomed the four immense figures of the Bukojemskis, and a fifth, smaller figure, Cyprianowicz.

They were talking so loudly because they were arguing about who should slash at Taczewski first. For that matter the Bukojemskis were always quarreling among themselves about something, but this time the argument was with Cyprianowicz, who claimed that he, as the person most offended, should go first. They fell silent only upon sighting the cross and Jacek standing underneath it, and they raised their caps, whether out of respect for the Passion of Christ, or in greeting to their enemy, it was unknown.

Taczewski bowed to them in silence and drew out his saber, but his heart began to beat uneasily in his breast, for after all, there were five of them against his one, and besides, the Bukojemskis looked simply awesome: big men, broad shouldered, with broomlike mustaches, on which the mist had settled in gray dewdrops, and knit brows. In their faces was a kind of gloomy, murderous joy, as if they were delighted at the chance of spilling blood.

"Why am I placing my sound head under the sword?" thought Jacek.

But after this moment of unease, indignation at these rogues seized him, men whom he hardly knew and had never wronged, and who, for God knows what reason, had latched onto him and now had come to do away with him.

So he addressed them in his heart thus:

"Just you wait, you loafers. You have brought your heads here also!"

His cheeks reddened, and his teeth gritted with anger. They, meanwhile, threw off their cloaks and rolled up the sleeves of their zupans, which they unnecessarily did all together, each thinking that he would be the one to begin the duel. Finally they stood in a row, sabers drawn, and Taczewski stepped up to them and halted in the same pose. They looked at each other in silence.

Cyprianowicz broke the quiet:

"I will serve you first, sir."

"No! I am first, I am first!" repeated all the Bukojemskis in a chorus.

And when Cyprianowicz moved forward, the others immediately seized him by the elbows. A quarrel began again, in which Cyprianowicz inveighed against them as ruffians, and they him as a dandy, and each other as bastards. Jacek was shocked at all this, and said:

"I have never seen such cavaliers in all my life."

And he sheathed his saber into the scabbard.

"Choose, or I will go!" he said in a loud, firm voice.

"You choose!" cried out Cyprianowicz, in the hope that he would be chosen.

Mateusz Bukojemski began to shout that he would not allow any whippersnapper to order them about, and he shouted so that his front teeth, which were long like a rabbit's, glittered beneath his mustache. But he became silent when Taczewski, drawing his saber again, indicated him with its curved edge, and said:

"I choose you, sir."

The remaining brothers and Cyprianowicz drew back immediately, seeing that otherwise they would never agree, but their faces grew gloomy, for knowing the strength of Mateusz, they were almost certain that no work would be left for them when he had finished.

"Begin!" called out Cyprianowicz.

Taczewski felt his opponent's strength immediately upon the first meeting, for the saber quavered in his hand; he warded off the blow, however, and the next one, and after the third, he said to himself:

"He is not as skillful as he is strong."

And crouching somewhat for a better spring, he pressed on with vigor.

The other three brothers, lowering the points of their sabers, followed with open mouths the course of the duel. They saw now that Taczewski also "knew a few things" and that it would not be easy with him. After a while, they realized he knew things quite well indeed, and concern was reflected on their faces, for, despite their endless bickering among each other, they loved one another immensely. A cry of "Ah!" was rent from the breast of one, then the other, as each blow fell with greater strength. And meanwhile the blows became quicker and quicker, like lightning bolts. Taczewski was apparently gaining more confidence. He was calm, but sprang around like a wildcat, and ominous flashes shot out from his eyes.

"This is bad," thought Cyprianowicz.

All of a sudden a cry was heard. Mateusz's saber went down, and he raised both hands to his face, which in one instant was covered entirely with blood—and he tumbled to the ground.

At the sight of this, the other brothers bellowed like bulls, and in a twinkling of an eye they threw themselves in a rage at Jacek, not with the clear intention of attacking him all at once, but because each wished to be the first in avenging their brother.

And perhaps they would have cut him up with their sabers, if Cyprianowicz, springing in to assist him, had not cried out with all the force within him:

"A disgrace! Away! Murderers, not nobles! A disgrace! Away! Or you must deal with me, murderers! Away!"

And he began to slash at them at close quarters, until they could be compelled to come to their senses. Meanwhile, Mateusz raised himself up on his hands and turned toward them a face covered with what looked like a mask of blood, so Jan grabbed him under the armpits and sat him down on the snow, while Lukasz likewise rushed over to help him.

But Taczewski moved up to Marek, who was gritting his teeth, and began to repeat in a quick voice, as if fearing that the united attack might repeat itself for a second time:

"If you please! If you please!"

And once again sabers clanged ominously. But with Marek, who was as much stronger than Mateusz as he was less skillful, Taczewski had short work. Marek swished his great saber like a flail, so that Jacek struck his right shoulder blade immediately after the third meeting, cutting through the bone and incapacitating him.

Lukasz and Jan realized now that a most unpleasant task was before them and that this slender young man was, in reality, a wasp it would have been better not to provoke. Because of this they fought him with greater passion, but the duels ended as badly for them as it had for their brothers. Lukasz, cut through the cheek to the gums, fell with great force and, moreover, struck a stone hidden under the snow, while Jan, thought the most skilled of the brothers, had his saber and one finger fall to the ground in a moment.

Taczewski, without a scratch on him, looked upon his work as if in amazement, and those sparks, which a moment ago had glittered in his eyes, began to slowly die down. With his left hand, he straightened his Magyar cap, which had slipped a little over his right ear during the struggle, then removed it completely, took a deep breath, another, and turned to the cross, saying, half to Cyprianowicz and half to himself:

"I swear to God that I am innocent."

Stanislaw Cyprianowicz replied:

"Now it is my turn. But you are out of breath, sir, so perhaps you would like to rest while I cover my comrades with their cloaks, lest the hoarfrost get them before help arrives."

"Help is nearby," answered Taczewski, "for there in the mist is a sleigh with runners sent by Father Woynowski, and he himself is at my house. Allow me to go for the sleigh; these gentlemen will feel better in that than on the snow."

And he went while Cyprianowicz proceeded to cover the Bukojemskis, who were sitting shoulder to shoulder on the snow, with the exception of Jan. The latter, the least wounded, was kneeling before Mateusz, and holding up his own right hand lest the blood flow too freely from the severed finger, he washed with snow the face of his brother with his left hand.

"How are you?" asked Cyprianowicz.

"Ah, that son of bitch has bitten us," replied Lukasz, spitting out an abundant amount of blood. "But we will have our revenge."

"I cannot use my entire arm, for he injured my bone," added Marek. "Oh, the dog! . . . Oh!"

"And Mateusz is cut over the brows," said Jan. "One has to apply bread and a spider's web to the wound, but meanwhile I'm holding back the flow of blood with snow."

"If I hadn't been blinded by the blood," said Mateusz, "I would have . . ."

But he could not finish, for loss of blood had weakened him, and he was interrupted by Lukasz, who was suddenly seized by anger:

"Ah, he's cunning, the scoundrel," he said, "for he looks at you like a maiden, but stabs like a reptile."

"It's precisely that cunning which I cannot forgive!" cried out Jan.

Further conversation was interrupted by the snorting of horses. The sleigh loomed in the mist, then it was at the side of the Bukojemskis. Taczewski jumped down from the sleigh and commanded the driver to step down.

The peasant looked at the Bukojemskis, cast a quick glance at Taczewski and Cyprianowicz, and did not say a word, but his face seemed to reflect shock, and turning for a moment toward the horses, he crossed himself.

After this, the three of them began to raise the wounded and move them in their cloaks. The Bukojemskis protested at once against the assistance of Jacek in this, but he told them:

"And what would you gentlemen have done, had you wounded me? Would you have left me without any assistance? This is a noble's service to another that should not be refused."

They fell silent, for he had ingratiated himself to them to a certain degree with these words, and after a while they were lying on straw in the broad sleigh, where they immediately felt warmer.

"Where to?" asked the peasant.

"Wait. You will take one more person," replied Cyprianowicz.

And turning to Jacek:

"Well, sir!" he said. "It is time for us."

But Taczewski glanced at him with an almost friendly look.

"It's better if we drop this. God knows why this has happened, and you took my side, sir, when these gentlemen attacked me in a group. Why should we fight?"

"We will and must fight," replied Cyprianowicz coldly. "You insulted me, and even if you had not, my reputation is at stake now—do you understand? Though I were to lose my head, though this were to be my last hour—we have to fight!"

"Ha! Let it be so, though it is against my will!" replied Jacek.

CHAPTER 6

AND they began the duel. Though he was not as strong as the Bukojemskis, Cyprianowicz was more skilled. It was evident that he had been taught by better masters and that his practice had not been limited to markets and inns. He charged more sensibly, and parried with greater accuracy and adroitness. Taczewski, in whose heart there was no more rancor, and who would have preferred to stop after the lesson given the Bukojemskis, began to praise him.

"With you, sir, it is quite another matter," he said. "No ordinary fellow trained your hand."

"Too bad it wasn't you!" replied Cyprianowicz.

And he was doubly gladdened: first, at the praise, and then because he had given an answer, for only the most masterful of swordsmen permitted themselves to talk during a duel, and, moreover, polite conversation was considered the hallmark of courtliness. All this raised Cyprianowicz in his own eyes.

So he pressed forward again with renewed vigor. But after engaging Taczewski several times, he was forced to acknowledge his opponent's superiority. Taczewski defended himself with what seemed reluctance, but with the greatest ease—and in general acted as though he were engaged in a fencing exercise rather than a duel. Apparently he had wanted to determine what Cyprianowicz knew and how much better he was than the Bukojemskis, and having done precisely that, he was completely sure of himself.

Pan Stanislaw understood this also, and because of that, his joy left him and he began to attack with greater passion. Suddenly Taczewski made a face, as if he had had enough of playing around, deflected a blow with a feint, pressed on, and then sprang to the side.

"You've been wounded, sir!" he said.

Cyprianowicz did feel something cold on his arm, but replied:

"It is nothing! Continue!"

And he cut at him again, but at that moment the end of Taczewski's saber laid open his lower lip and the skin under it. Pan Jacek sprang aside once again.

"You are bleeding!"

"It is nothing!"

"If it's nothing, then glory to God!" said Taczewski. "But I have had enough, and here is my hand. You have acted like a real cavalier."

Cyprianowicz was greatly wrought, but won over by Jacek's words at the same time. He stood for a moment, as if undecided whether to make peace or fight on. Finally, he sheathed his saber and extended his hand.

"So be it. In truth, it appears that I am bleeding."

Saying this, he touched his chin with his left hand and began to look, with what seemed amazement, at the blood that had profusely stained his palm and fingers.

"Hold snow on the wound or else it will swell!" said Pan Jacek. "And go to the sleigh."

Saying this, he took him under the arm and led him to the Bukojemskis, who glanced at him in silence with an astonished but also dejected look. They felt real respect for Pan Jacek, not only as a master of the sword, but also as a cavalier of "lofty manners," precisely the manners that they were lacking.

After a moment or two, Mateusz turned to Cyprianowicz:

"How are you, Stas?"

"Fine. I could walk, but prefer to ride on the sleigh to hasten the journey."

Taczewski sat sideways next to him and called out to the driver:

"To Wyrabek!"

"To where?" asked Cyprianowicz.

"To my house. You gentlemen will not be too comfortable there, but it can't be helped. At Belczaczka the ladies would get frightened, and Father Woynowski is at my place. He will take care of your wounds, for he is quite knowledgeable in handling them. Your horses can be sent for, and then you can do whatever you want. I will also ask the priest to ride to Belczaczka to relate tactfully what has occurred."

Here Jacek thought for a moment, then said:

"Oh! Now there will be trouble for certain! . . . God knows that you gentlemen insisted on this duel."

"True, we insisted!" said Cyprianowicz. "I will testify to this, as will the Bukojemskis."

"I will testify, though my arm pains me terribly," said Marek, groaning. "Oh, but you've feasted on us. May you be shot!"

It was not far to Wyrabek. Shortly, they entered the main lane, in the middle of which they met Father Woynowski wading through the snow. Anxious about what might happen, he could not stay put and had to go out.

Taczewski sprang from the sleigh upon seeing him, while the priest advanced with great speed to meet him, and seeing that he was sound and uninjured, called out:

"Well, what happened?"

"I've brought you these gentlemen," replied Jacek.

The old man's face brightened up momentarily, but became serious as soon as he saw the blood-smeared Bukojemskis and Cyprianowicz.

He clapped his hands.

"All five!" he cried out.

"Five. . . ."

"An offense to God!"

And turning to the wounded:

"How are you?"

They touched their caps in greeting, except for Marek, who, having a cut collarbone, could move neither his right nor left hand. So he merely groaned, and said:

"Ha, he worked over us well, that can't be denied!"

"It's nothing!" the others said.

"We hope in God that it is nothing," replied the old man. "Straightaway to the house! As quickly as possible! I'll take care of you in a moment."

And he had the sleigh move forward, while he and Taczewski followed with the utmost possible haste. For a moment, however, he stopped. Joy gleamed in his face, and he suddenly grabbed Taczewski by the neck, and said:

"Jacek, let me embrace you! You brought a sleighful of them, like so many sheaves of wheat."

Taczewski kissed his hand, and replied:

"They wanted it, reverend father."

The priest put his hand on Taczewski's head, as if wanting to bless him, but all of a sudden checked himself, for he thought that joy was not befitting a man of the cloth, so he looked sternly at the young man, and said:

"Just do not think that I am praising you. It is fortunate for you that they themselves wanted this duel, but it is still a scandal!"

And they entered the courtyard, after which Jacek jumped onto the sleigh to assist the driver and the sole house servant in getting the wounded off.

But they got off by themselves, with the exception of Marek, who had to be supported by the arms, and in a moment they found themselves inside the house. Straw was already awaiting them, and Taczewski's own bed had been covered with a white, slightly worn horse skin, with a thick felt serving as a pillow. On a table near the window could be seen bread kneaded with a spiderweb, excellent for stopping the flow of blood, as well as Father Woynowski's superior balsams used for healing.

Removing his cassock, the old man proceeded to dress the wounds with the skill of an old soldier who has seen thousands of such wounds and who from many years of practice knew how to handle them better than many a surgeon. The work went quickly, for excepting Marek, the others were just lightly cut up. Marek's collarbone needed considerably more work, but when finally it was set, Father Woynowski breathed freely and wiped his blood-smeared hands.

"Well," he said, "thanks to the Lord Jesus, nothing serious has occurred. For sure you gentlemen are feeling better now."

"I'm thirsty!" said Mateusz Bukojemski.

"A drink wouldn't hurt! Jacek, tell my man to bring some water."

Mateusz raised himself up from the straw.

"Water?" he asked in a broken voice.

And Marek, who was lying on his back on Jacek's bed and moaning a bit, spoke up unexpectedly: "Surely the reverend father is going to wash his hands."

Jacek glanced with real despair at the priest, who began to laugh, saying:

"Ah, real soldiers! Very well, you can have some wine, but not too much."

Taczewski, however, drew him by the sleeve into an alcove.

"Reverend father," he whispered, "what can I do? The pantry is empty, the cellar, too; I have had to tighten my belt more and more. What can I give them?"

"There's something, there's something!" the old man whispered back. "When I was leaving, I made arrangements, and they've brought it here already. And if that shouldn't suffice, I will request something from the brewers at Jedlinka. I'll say it's for myself, of course, for myself. Have them given one glass right now, so that they may be cheered up after their adventure."

Hearing this, Jacek set to work with great dispatch, and soon the Bukojemskis were comforting each other. And their good feeling toward Jacek increased with every minute.

"We fought, for that happens to every man," said Mateusz, "but I thought from the start that you were a worthy cavalier."

"That's not true: I was the one who thought so first," put in Lukasz.

"You? You thought something? Have you ever been able to think?"

"Yes, and I think that you are a simpleton; so I am able to think, but my mouth hurts me."

And they began to quarrel. Meanwhile, a mounted man darkened the window.

"Someone has arrived," said the priest.

Jacek went to see who it was, and returned in a moment, disconcerted.

"Pan Pagowski has sent a man," he said, "with notice that he is waiting for us at dinner."

"Let him eat it alone," stated Jan.

"What shall we say to him?" inquired Jacek, looking at the priest.

"It's best to tell the truth," replied the old man. "But it will be best if related by me."

And going out to the servant, he said:

"Tell Pan Pagowski that neither Pan Cyprianowicz nor the Bukojemskis can come, for all have been wounded in a duel to which they challenged Pan Taczewski. But do not forget to tell him that they are not badly wounded. Now go!"

The servant was off like a shot, while the priest, returning to the house, began to calm Jacek, who was quite perturbed. He did not fear meeting five men in a duel, but he feared Pan Pagowski, and even more what Panna Sieninska would say and think.

But the priest said:

"Well, it happened, and there's nothing that can be done about it. Let them find out as soon as possible that it was not your fault."

"Will you testify to this, gentlemen?" asked Jacek, turning once again to the wounded.

"We're thirsty, but we will testify," replied Mateusz Bukojemski.

Jacek's concern increased more and more, however; and soon after, when a sleigh with Pan Pagowski and the starost, Pan Grothus, stopped by the porch, his heart froze completely. Nevertheless, he jumped to greet Pan Pagowski, bowing down to the knees, but the latter did not even glance at him, as if he had not seen him, and with a gloomy, severe face, he entered the room.

Inside, Pan Pagowski bowed to the priest with solemnity, but with reserve, for since the day when the old man reproached him from the altar for his excessive severity toward the peasants, the stubborn noble could not forgive him, so that now, after the cold bow, he turned immediately to the wounded, looked at them for a moment, and then said:

"Honorable gentlemen! After what has happened, I would verily not have passed the threshold of this house if I did not wish to tell you how deeply hurt I am by the wrong that has been done you. See what has become of my hospitality! This is the reward that my rescuers have received in my house! But I will tell you this, that whoever has wronged you has wronged me, that whoever has spilled your blood has done worse than spill mine, for the man who challenged you under my roof has dishonored me—"

Mateusz interrupted him suddenly:

"We challenged him, not he us!"

"That is so, honorable sir," added Stanislaw Cyprianowicz. "This cavalier is not to blame for what has happened; the blame lies with us, for which we humbly beg forgiveness."

"It would have been better for the judge to examine the witnesses before he passed judgement," said Father Woynowski with gravity.

Lukasz wanted to say something also, but since his cheek and gum were cut to the teeth, the pain was terrible when he moved his chin, so he only put his palm over the salve, which was already starting to dry, and mumbled aloud:

"May the devil take the judgement and my jaw!"

Pan Pagowski became somewhat disconcerted by those voices, but did not yield. On the contrary, he rolled his severe eyes, as if wanting in this way to express silent rebuke against Jacek's defenders, and said the following:

"It is not for me to offer pardon to my rescuers. No blame is attached to you, gentlemen. On the contrary, I understand everything, for I see perfectly well how you were intentionally insulted. Indeed, that same jealousy, which could not catch up to living wolves on a dying horse, gave impetus later to vengeance. I was not alone in noting how that 'cavalier,' whom you defend so magnanimously, gave occasion and did everything from the first moment of meeting to bring you to take such action. But the fault is mine that I indulged him and did not tell him to find suitable company for himself at the market or the inn."

Upon hearing this, Jacek's face turned as pale as a sheet, while Father Woynowski's face, in contrast, became red.

"He was challenged!" he cried out. "What was he to do? Be ashamed of yourself, sir!"

But Pan Pagowski looked down up him, and replied:

"These are worldly matters in which the laity are as *periti* as the clergy, even more so; but I will answer your question, so that no one here will accuse me of injustice. 'What was he to do?' As a younger to an older man, as a guest to his host, as a man who ate my bread so many times when he had none himself, he should have, above all, informed me of the matter, and I would have settled it with my authority as host and not let it come to this, that my rescuers, and such worthy cavaliers, are lying here in this hut in their own blood on straw, as if in a pigsty."

"But, sir, you would have thought that I had turned coward!" cried Jacek, wringing his hands and shaking as if in a fever.

Pan Gideon did not answer him at all, for from the beginning he had pretended not to see him, and so he turned instead to Cyprianowicz.

"Sir Cavalier," he said, "the starost, Pan Grothus, and I are going *eo instante* to your father, to Jedlinka, to offer him our condolences. I do not doubt that he will accept my hospitality at Belczaczka, so I invite you, together with your companions, to return to my house. I also remind you that you find yourselves here just by chance, and that you are really my guests, to whom I wish to show my gratitude with all my heart. Your father, Pan Cyprianowicz, cannot, after all, visit the man who has caused your wounds, and under my roof you will have greater comfort and will not die of hunger, which may easily happen here."

Cyprianowicz became greatly troubled and for a moment hesitated to answer, not only out of regard for Taczewski, but, because, being a very handsome young man, he was concerned with how he would look if he accepted the invitation, for his lip and chin, which had already swollen beneath the plaster, disfigured him considerably.

"We would not feel hunger or thirst here," he said, "as has been already *probatum fuit,* but at the same time we are your guests, Honorable Sir, and my father, not knowing what has occurred, may not want to come here. But how could we appear before those ladies, your grace's relatives, with such unsightly mugs that could only rouse abhorrence?"

Saying this, he twisted his face, for his lip hurt him from being moved during speech—and, in truth, he did not look too handsome at the moment.

But Pan Pagowski replied:

"Do not trouble yourself about that. Those ladies will feel abhorrence, but not for your wounds, and after your wounds heal your previous good looks will return. Soon three sleighs will arrive here with servants, and in my house comfortable beds are already waiting. Meanwhile, good-bye and keep well, for it is time for Pan Grothus and me to go to Jedlinka. Farewell!"

And he bowed to Cyprianowicz and the Bukojemskis, separately to the priest, and not at all to Jacek. When he was near the door, the priest came up to him, and said:

"You have too little compassion and too little justice, sir."

And Pan Pagowski replied:

"I only confess my sins at Holy Confession."

And he went out, followed by Pan Grothus.

Jacek stood for the entire time, suffering torment. His face had altered. At moments he did not know whether to throw himself at the feet of Pan Pagowski with a plea for forgiveness or at his throat for the humiliation he was enduring. He remembered that he was in his own house, nevertheless, and that standing before him was the guardian of Panna Sieninska. So when Pagowski and Grothus exited, he sprang after them, not realizing at all what he was doing, but because of custom which mandated that guests be conducted out, and in some kind of blind hope that perhaps at the very point of departure the obstinate Pan Pagowski would at least bow to him. But even this hope failed him; only Pan Grothus, who one could see was a kind and forbearing man, pressed his hand on the porch, and whispered:

"Despair not, cavalier, his initial rage will pass and everything will be all right."

But Jacek did not think this would be so, and would have been certain that everything was lost forever, had he not known that Pan Pagowski, though truly outraged and angry, feigned anger far more than he felt it. In truth, Cyprianowicz and the Bukojemskis were his rescuers, but Taczewski had not, after all, killed them, and the duel of itself was too common to elicit such implacable stubbornness.

But Pan Pagowski, from the moment that Grothus told him that old people marry and sometimes even have children, looked with different eyes upon Panna Sieninska. That which he had never previously thought, suddenly became possible to him and alluring at the same time. At the thought of the charms of that girl, beautiful like a rose, his soul became warm, and his pride was affected even more. He could marry and the Pagowski family tree might bloom again, and—what's more—issuing forth from such a patrician as Sieninska, who was not only related to all the great houses in the Commonwealth, but the last offspring of her line, from whose fortune rose, in great part, the Zolkiewskis, the Danilowiczes, the Sobieskis and many others. Pan Pagowski almost became dizzy at this thought, and he felt that it was important not only for him but for the entire Commonwealth that such Pagowskis be born. So immediately thereafter came the fear that perhaps this would not come to pass, because the young lady could possibly love someone else and give her hand to another man. He did not see a worthier candidate in the region than himself, but there were younger ones. But who? Cyprianowicz? Yes! He was young, polished and quite rich, but only a third generation noble from the Armenian nobility. That such a *homo novus* could actually hope to attain Panna Sieninska was beyond the realm of possibility in Pan Pagowski's mind. As for the Bukojemskis, though they were of a solid noble line and claimed kinship with Saint Peter, it was laughable to think of any one of them with Panna Sieninska. Only Taczewski remained—a true Lazarus, as poor as a church mouse, but from an ancient line of renowned knights from Taczewo of the Powala escutcheon, one of whom, a real giant who had taken part in the terrible defeat of the Germans at Grunwald, had been famous not only in the Commonwealth, but in foreign courts as well. Only Taczewski could stand up to a comparison with the Sieninskis, and, besides, he was young, courageous, handsome, melancholic (a trait that frequently moves a woman's heart), and felt at home in Belczaczka, and was like a friend—or even a brother—to the young lady. So Pan Pagowski began to recollect various things: their supposed disputes and sulkings, then their reconciliations and friendship, their various glances and words, and mutual sorrow, joy and laughter. And everything that he had paid little attention to previously, seemed suddenly suspicious to him. Yes! Danger could threaten only from this side. The old noble even thought that Panna Sieninska could have been the cause, at least in part, of the duel, and he became alarmed. Therefore, to prevent this danger, he tried, above all, to present the dishonor of Jacek's action to the young lady in the strongest possible manner and arouse in her due anger, and then, by feigning greater anger than he felt and than the case called for, burn all bridges between Belczaczka and Wyrabek, and by humiliating Jacek mercilessly, close the doors of his house.

And he was realizing his goal. Jacek, returning from the porch, sat by the table, fingers dug in his hair, head propped up by his elbows, and was silent, as if struck dumb by pain.

Finally Father Woynowski approached him and placed a hand upon his shoulder.

"Jacek, suffer what you must suffer," he said, "but your foot should not pass the threshold of that house."

"It will be so," replied Taczewski in a dull voice.

"But do not surrender to pain. Remember who you are."

And the young man clenched his teeth: "I remember, and it is precisely for that reason that I'm burning!"

Suddenly Cyprianowicz spoke up:

"No one here applauds Pan Pagowski for what he did, for it is one thing to reprimand someone, and another to trample a man's honor!"

This set the Bukojemskis in motion, and Mateusz, whom speech troubled least, said:

"I will not say anything in his house, but when I get better and meet him on the road or at a neighbor's, I will tell him simply to go jump in the lake."

"Oh, my!" added Marek. "To insult such a cavalier! The time will come when this will not be forgiven him."

Meanwhile, three sleighs strewn with carpets arrived and, aside from the drivers, three servants who were to transport the wounded. Taczewski did not dare to detain the wounded because of the expected arrival of the older Cyprianowicz, and because they were, in truth, Pagowski's guests, while they, hearing of Jacek's great poverty, would not have remained, lest they burden him. They began, however, to bid him farewell and thank him for his hospitality with as much sincerity as if nothing had happened between them.

But when Cyprianowicz was about to take his place in the last seat, Pan Jacek suddenly sprang forward, and said:

"I am going with you, sirs! I cannot just stay here! I cannot! Before Pan Pagowski returns, I must—for the last time! . . ."

And Father Woynowski, though knowing Jacek and that any arguments would be useless, pulled him to the alcove, and began to plead:

"Jacek, Jacek! Once again a *mulier*! God grant that a still greater wrong not befall you. Remember, Jacek, the words of Ecclesiastes: *'Virum de mille unum reperi, mulierem ex ominibus non inveni!'* [In a thousand I found one man, among all I found not one woman.] Remember this, and have pity on yourself."

But these words were of no avail. In a moment Taczewski was already sitting in a sleigh by Cyprianowicz's side, and they started off. Meanwhile, an easterly wind twisted the mist and drove it into the wilderness, and a bright sun appeared in a blue sky.

CHAPTER 7

PAN Gideon did not lie when he spoke of the abhorrence that both ladies at Belczaczka would feel for the victor. Jacek found that out himself with one glance at them. Pani Winnicka came out to meet him with an indignant face, and she slipped her hand away when he tried to kiss it in greeting, while the young lady, without compassion for his distress and confusion, did not answer his bow and occupied herself completely with Cyprianowicz. She spared neither tender looks nor solicitous questions, and pushed her concern to such a degree that when Cyprianowicz rose from the chair in the dining room to go to the room set apart for the wounded, she supported him under the arm, and though he recoiled from this and voiced his opposition, she led him up to the door.

At the sight of this, Jacek's heart cried out in despair and jealousy: "There is nothing for you here; all is lost!" His pain was the greater in that he had not supposed until now that this same girl, who had shown such changing humors toward him and who had for one kind word given him ten cold or even downright malicious ones, could be sweet, kind and angelic to a man whom she really loved. That Panna Sieninska loved Cyprianowicz the unfortunate Jacek had no doubt whatsoever. He would have suffered not only such a wound as Cyprianowicz had, but would have gladly shed all his blood to have her, at least once in her life, speak to him in such a voice and look upon him with such eyes. So, aside from the pain he felt, he was gripped at the same time by a boundless sorrow, which sent a torrent of tears to his eyes that, if it did not gush out and flow down his cheeks, flooded his heart and suffused his entire being. Thus did Jacek feel his breast fill with tears, and to make matters worse, Panna Sieninska had never seemed to him so incredibly beautiful as she did now, with her pale face and her crown of flaxen hair slightly disheveled from emotion. "She is an angel," his sorrow cried out within him, "but not for you! Beautiful, but another will take her!" And he wanted to fall at her feet and confess all his suffering and love, but felt at the same time, and particularly after what had occurred, that it would not be proper to do so, and that if he did not control himself and stifle his inner turmoil, he would tell her something quite different from that which he wanted and sink himself utterly in her estimation.

Meanwhile, Pani Winnicka, as an elderly person and one skilled in medicine, went with Cyprianowicz into the other room, while Anulka returned from the doorway. Jacek, realizing that he must use the opportunity, drew near her.

"I would like a word with you, gracious lady," he said in a trembling voice that sounded unfamiliar to him, trying to control himself.

She looked at him with cold astonishment:

"What do you wish, sir?"

Jacek's face was lighted by such a pained smile that it almost seemed like that of a martyr.

"What I wish for will not come to pass, though I were to give the salvation of my soul for it," he said, shaking his head; "but I ask for one thing, dear lady: do not fault me, do not bear a grudge toward me, have a little compassion, for I am not made of wood or iron. . . ."

"I have nothing to say to you, sir," she replied, "and the time is not right to do so."

"There is always time to say a kind word to a man for whom it is hard in the world!"

"Should I say a kind word to you because you have wounded my rescuers?"

"No, because God stands by the innocent. The attendant who came for those cavaliers to Wyrabek should have said what Father Woynowski told him to, that I did not challenge them. Did you know about this?"

She knew. The attendant, being a simple man, did not repeat, in truth, the exact words of the priest and announced only that "the young man from Wyrabek cut up everybody"; but Pan Pagowski, returning from Wyrabek, dropped by the house and explained what had happened. Quite simply, he feared that the news that it was Jacek who had been challenged would come from someone else's lips and weaken her anger, so he wanted to relate what happened himself, not forgetting to add that Taczewski had forced the challenge by malicious insults. He also counted on this: that Panna Sieninska, taking things in a woman's way, would always be on the side of those who had suffered the most.

Still, it seemed to Jacek that her beloved eyes looked at him with less severity, so he repeated his question:

"Did you know about this, lady?"

"I knew," she replied, "but I remembered what you would not have forgotten had you had even a little goodwill toward me; namely, that I owe my life to these cavaliers. I also know from my guardian that they had to challenge you."

"I do not have goodwill toward you? Let God, who looks into men's hearts, be the judge."

Suddenly the girl's eyes began to blink repeatedly. She shook her head, till a tress fell onto the other shoulder, and said:

"Yes! . . ."

And he continued on, in a breathless and deeply sad voice:

"But it is true! True! I should have allowed myself to be chopped to pieces rather than have you be distressed. That blood which is dearest to you would not have been shed. But nothing can be done about this now! Nothing can be done about anything now! Your guardian told you, my lady, that I forced them to a challenge. Let God judge this also. But did he say that, under my own roof, he insulted me without mercy and measure? I came here because I knew that I would not find him present right now. I came so that my unfortunate eyes could take in for one last time the sight of you. I know that it doesn't matter to you either way, but I thought, that perhaps . . ."

Here Jacek broke off, for tears choked his voice. Panna Sieninska's lips also began to quiver and take on more and more the shape of a little horseshoe; pride, together with a girlish timidity, fought inside her with force. She checked it, nevertheless, perhaps because she did not believe that he would indeed leave and never return. More than once there had been misunderstandings between them, more than once had Pan Pagowski caused him great pain, and yet after brief periods of anger came silent or spoken apologies, and everything went back to the way it was.

"So it will be this time also!" thought Panna Sieninska.

Because it was sweet for her to listen to him and sweet to look on that great love, which, though it did not dare to express itself in clear words, issued forth from him with equal amounts of submissiveness and strength. She wanted him to speak to her in his wonderful voice for the longest time, and for the longest time lay his young, loving and aggrieved heart at her feet.

But he, inexperienced in matters of love and blind like all who love, did not notice and understand what was happening inside her. He read her silence as hardened indifference—and bitterness began to gradually fill his soul. The calmness with which he had spoken at first, began to desert him; his eyes began to take on a different light, and cold drops of sweat pearled his temples. Something was tearing and breaking in his soul. He was seized by that despair in which a man questions nothing and is ready to scratch with his own hands his own real wounds.

He spoke again, seemingly in a calm tone, but his voice already sounded different—harder, harsher.

"Yes!" he said. "Not one word?"

Panna Sieninska merely shrugged her shoulders.

"Ha! The priest did not lie when he said that a greater wrong would meet me here!"

"How have I wronged you?" she asked, hurt by the unexpected change that had come over him.

But he blundered along blindly:

"If I had not seen how you were with Cyprianowicz, I would have thought that you had no heart. You do have a heart, but only for him, not for me! One look from him, and that was enough."

And suddenly he seized the hair on his head with both hands.

"Would to God that I had cut him to pieces!"

It seemed that a flame flashed through Panna Sieninska immediately. Her cheeks flushed, her eyes blazed with anger, both at Jacek and also at herself, since a moment earlier she had been ready to weep. A deep and sudden resentment seized her heart.

"You have lost your senses, sir!" she cried out, raising her head and shaking back her tresses.

She wanted to leave, but this very act drove Jacek completely mad. He grabbed both her hands and detained her:

"You will not leave, but I!" he said through clenched teeth. "But I will tell you this, that though I have loved you more than health itself, more than life, more than my own soul, I will never come back here. I will chew my own hands from pain, but I will not come back—so help me God!"

And leaving behind his dilapidated Magyar cap on the floor, he sprang to the doorway, and in a moment flashed by the windows, turning to the garden, through which it was a shorter distance to Wyrabek, and disappeared.

Panna Sieninska stood motionless for some time, as if a thunderbolt had struck her. Her thoughts scattered in all directions like a flock of birds, and for a moment she did not know what had happened. But when they returned, her anger disappeared, it disappeared without a trace of offense, and in her ears resounded nothing but Jacek's words: "I loved you more than health itself, more than life, more than my own soul—I will never come back! . . ." Now she felt that he would not, in truth, return, precisely because he loved her so greatly. Why had she not given him at least one kind word, for which, before madness seized him, he had begged as if for alms or for a piece of bread for the road? She was seized both by boundless sorrow and fear. He had rushed off in pain and in madness—perhaps he would fall somewhere along the road, perhaps, in desperation, he would harm himself, while, after all, only one heartfelt word could have calmed and corrected everything. Would he perhaps still be able to hear her voice?

And snapping to, she ran to the garden. Deep snow lay on the middle path, but Jacek's tracks were visible, so she ran after them, sinking at times to her knees, losing her rosary along the way, her handkerchief, a little bag with thread inside. Finally she reached the garden gate, panting.

"Pan Jacek!"

But the meadow beyond the garden was already empty. Besides, the same wind that had blown the morning mist made now a great noise among the pear and apple branches. Her weak voice was completely lost in this noise. Then, ignoring the cold and her light, indoor clothing, she sat on a bench near the gate and began to cry.

Tears as large as pearls flowed down her rosy cheeks, and she, not having anything to wipe them away with, started to remove them with her tresses.

"He will not come back."

The wind, meanwhile, sounded louder and louder, and shook down wet snow from dark branches.

CHAPTER **8**

WHEN Taczewski rushed into his manor house at Wyrabek like a whirlwind, without his cap and with disheveled hair, Father Woynowski divined what had happened, and said:

"*Praedixi!* May God help you, Jacek, but I will not ask you anything until you regain your senses and calm down. . . ."

"It is over! It is all over!" replied Taczewski.

And he began to pace up and down the room like a wild beast in a cage. The priest did not speak and did not interrupt him at all; only after a long while had passed did he rise and put his arms around him, kissing him on the head; and then, taking him by the hand, he led him to the alcove.

There he knelt before a cross, which hung above Jacek's bed, and when the young man knelt beside him, he began to speak:

"Lord, you know what pain is, for you suffered for the sins of man on the cross. Therefore I bring my bleeding heart to you and place it at your pierced feet, so that you will have mercy on me. I do not cry to you to take my suffering, but I cry out: give me strength, so that I can endure it. Because I am a soldier at your command, oh Lord, and I want to serve you and my mother, the Commonwealth. But how can I do this when my heart is faint and my right hand is weak? Make me forget myself, and make me only think of your glory and the rescue of my motherland, for these things are greater than the pain of a wretched insect like myself. Strengthen me, Lord, in my saddle, so that in battle against the pagans I can ride to a glorious death and to heaven. By your crown of thorns, hear me! By thy wound in your side, hear me! By thy hands and feet pierced with nails, hear me!"

They kept kneeling for a long time, but already during the middle of the prayer, it was evident that the pain in Jacek's breast had broken, for suddenly he covered his face with his hands and began to sob. So when they stood up and went to the first room, Father Woynowski sighed out deeply, and said:

"My dear Jacek, I have gone through much in my years as a soldier and have met a worse misfortune than you have, of which I do not want to speak, but I will only tell you this, that at the moment of my greatest suffering I composed this very prayer and owe my salvation to it. More than once I have repeated it in times of misfortune since that day, and always with great relief. That is why I repeat it now. So tell me. Hasn't your pain lessened? Tell me!"

"I am still sorrowful, but it burns less," replied Taczewski.

"Ah, you see! Now drink some wine, while I tell you, or rather show you, something that should cheer you up. Look."

And bending his head down, he showed a terrible white scar beneath his white hair that ran along his entire skull; and he said:

"I almost perished from that. The wound pained me terribly, but the scar does not hurt. That is the way it always is, Jacek. Your wound will also stop hurting when, in time, it becomes a scar. Now, tell me what happened."

Jacek began to relate what happened, but it did not go well. It was not in his nature to invent, exaggerate or add, so that he wondered how everything that had hurt him so, seemed less cruel now as he spoke about it. Nevertheless, Father Woynowski, a man of experience who knew the world, said, after hearing him out to the end:

"I know that it is difficult to express in words looks or even gestures that could be quite plainly contemptuous and insulting. More than once just one glance or the wave of a hand has led to duels and the shedding of blood. The main thing is that you declared to that lady that you would never return there. Youth is fickle, and when effected by sadness, it changes as the moon in the sky. And love is also like a *luna mendax*, which appears to be decreasing precisely when it is growing and getting closer to being full. So tell me. Do you genuinely intend to keep your word?"

"I said: 'so help me God,' and if you want, father, I will take such an oath right now on the cross."

"And what do you plan to do with yourself?"

"Go into the world."

"I've been waiting to hear this, for I have advised such an action for a long time. I knew what kept you here, but now, when the cord has been severed, yes, go into the world. You will find nothing for you here, nothing good has met you here and nothing will. This has been a waste for you! Thankfully, I was nearby and at least taught you Latin and a little bit of swordplay—otherwise, you would have become a peasant here. Do not thank me, Jacek, for it arose from sincere affection. It will be sad for me without you, but I am not the issue. Go into the world, for, as I understand it, this means that you want to join the army. This is the straightest and most honorable path, particularly since war with the pagan is approaching. The pen and headquarters, they say, guarantee promotion more than the sword, but that does not suit someone of your blood. . . ."

"I gave no thought of any other service," replied Taczewski. "But I cannot join the infantry, after all, and cannot possibly join the higher banners, for I am a starveling."

"A noble who has Latin on his tongue and a sword in his hand will always be able to make his way," interrupted the priest, "but there is no question but that you must have a respectable retinue. We have to confer about this. Meanwhile, I will tell you something I never told you. I have for you ten red zlotys, which your dead mother left with me, and her letter, in which she asks that I not give you them, so that they wouldn't be frittered away, except in case of sudden need if the time came when you would be in desperate straits. Well, the time has come! You had an honorable, saintly, but unhappy mother, for when the poor dear was dying, the want in the house was already great, and that which she left me, she took away from her own mouth. . . ."

"Better that God give her eternal rest," replied Jacek. "Let these red zlotys be used for masses for her soul, and I will sell Wyrabek, even if not for much."

Hearing this, Father Woynowski was moved, so much so that a tear glistened in his eye, and he put his arms around Jacek once more.

"There is honorable blood in you," he said, "but you are not allowed to refuse your mother's gift, even for such a purpose. Masses will not be lacking for her, you can be certain of that, for though she has no great need of them, there are other souls, who are in purgatory, for whom they will be useful. As for Wyrabek, it would be better to mortgage it, for people always look upon a noble differently if he has even the smallest patch of ground left, rather than if he is *possesionatus*."

"But I am in a hurry. I would like to go even today."

"You will not go today, though the sooner the better. First I must write letters for you to my comrades and acquaintances. One will also have to talk to the brewers in Jedlinka, who have bags full of money and horses better than many a cuirassier. In my presbytery there is some kind of old armor and several sabers, not so much ornamented as tested on Swedish and Turkish necks."

Here the priest looked through the window, and said:

"Well, the sleighs are ready, so we must be off. . . ."

But an expression of pain flashed across Jacek's face anew; he kissed the priest's hand, and said:

"I have one more request, my father and reverence: let me go with you and remain in the presbytery until it is time for me to leave. From here I can see those roofs, and I am too close to . . ."

"Of course! I wanted to propose that myself; you have taken the words right out of my mouth. There is nothing for you here, and my heart will be glad to have you with me. Hey, Jacek, be of good cheer! The world does not end with Belczaczka; it stands wide open before you. Once you get on a horse, God only knows how far you will go. War awaits you! Glory awaits you! And what pains you today will be forgotten. I already see how the wings are growing out of your shoulders. Fly, O bird of the Lord, for you were created and predestined for this!"

And joy like a ray of the sun brightened up the worthy face of the priest. In soldierly fashion, he struck his thigh with his hand and cried out:

"Now, grab your cap and off we go!"

But small things frequently stand in the way of bigger ones, and the comic mixes with the tragic. Jacek glanced around the room, then gave the priest a perplexed look, and repeated:

"My cap?"

"Of course! You will not go with your head uncovered."

"Of course!"

"Well?"

"Ah! I left it at Belczaczka."

"That's love for you! What now?"

"What now? . . . Perhaps I could take a cap from my man, for I cannot go in a peasant's cap."

"In a peasant's cap you cannot go!" repeated the priest. "But send your man to Belczaczka for yours."

"For nothing in the world!" cried out Jacek.

The priest was beginning to lose patience.

"The devil take this! War, glory, and the wide world awaits—but a cap is needed!"

"At the bottom of a chest there is an old hat that my father took from a Swedish officer at Trzemesznia."

"Then take it—and let's go!"

Jacek disappeared into the alcove, and after a moment came back wearing a yellow reiter's hat that was too big for his head. Cheered up by this sight, Father Woynowski grabbed at his left side, as if looking for a saber, and said:

"It is fortunate that this is a Swedish hat and not a Turkish turban. What a real carnival!"

Jacek smiled back in reply, and said:

"There are some jewels in the buckle; perhaps they are worth something."

After which they took seats in the sleigh and were off. Immediately beyond the fence one could see, through the leafless alders, Belczaczka and its mansion like the palm of one's hand—so the priest carefully watched Jacek, but the latter only pulled down the large Swedish hat over his eyes and did not look, though he had left behind there more than his Magyar cap.

CHAPTER 9

"HE will not come back! All is lost!" thought Panna Sieninska at first.

And a strange thing! There were five bachelors in that house, and one of them was young and handsome; and besides the starost Grothus, the elder Cyprianowicz was to arrive. In a word, rarely had there been so many guests at Belczaczka. Meanwhile it seemed to the young lady that a vacuum had suddenly surrounded her and some great absence, that the house was empty, the garden empty, and that she was as alone as if she were on a deserted steppe—and would remain that way forever.

Therefore, her heart was wrung with great sorrow, as if she had lost the closest person to her. She was certain that Jacek would not come back, the more so that her guardian had offended him grievously. As the same time, however, she could not imagine how it would be without him, without his face, words, laughter, glances; she could not imagine what would it be like tomorrow, the day after tomorrow, in a week and in a month; she could not imagine why she would rise from her bed in the morning, why arrange her tresses, and for whom would she dress and comb her hair. Why live?

And she had a feeling as if her heart were a candle that someone had blown at and extinguished.

Nothing, only darkness and emptiness!

But when she entered the room and saw Jacek's Magyar cap on the floor, all these vague feelings gave way to a clear and immense longing for him. Her heart was stirred once again, and she began to call him by name. At the same time, a gleam of hope rose within her. Picking up the cap, she pressed it unwittingly to her bosom, after which she put it in her sleeve, and began to think the following:

"He will not come to Belczaczka every day as he used to, but before my guardian will arrive from Jedlinka with Pan Grothus and Pan Cyprianowicz, he must return for his cap, so I will see him and tell him that he was cruel and unjust, and that he should not have done what he has done."

But she was not being truthful with herself, for she wanted to say more to him, to find some warm, sincere word which would join again the threads severed between them. If this could happen, if they could meet without anger in church or, on occasion, at neighbors', then in the future some method would be found to turn everything for the good. . . . What method this would be and what this good would be exactly, Panna Sieninska did not reflect upon for the moment, for she was thinking, above all, about how to see Jacek as soon as possible.

Meanwhile, Pani Winnicka came out of the room in which the wounded men were lying, and seeing the agitated face and reddened eyes of the girl, began to calm her down:

"Do not worry, they will be all right. Only one of the Bukojemskis is seriously hurt, but he will also be all right. The others are barely hurt. Father Woynowski has dressed their wounds well, so there is no need to change them. They are also in good spirits."

"Thank God."

"Has Taczewski left? What did he want here?"

"He brought the wounded. . . ."

"Well, but who would have expected this of him?"

"They themselves challenged him."

"They do not deny that, but he hacked up all of them—five in number! One right after the other. And one would have thought that he could not deal with a clucking hen."

"Then you don't know him, auntie—no, no!" replied Panna Sieninska, with a certain pride in her voice.

But in Pani Winnicka's voice there was almost as much amazement as blame, for, born and raised in regions subject to continual Tartar attacks, she had learned from childhood to count courage and skill with the sword as the highest qualities of a man. So, after the first alarm for the guests had passed, she began to look upon this duel somewhat differently.

"Nevertheless," she continued, "I must confess that they are worthy cavaliers, for not only do they not feel animosity toward him, but they even praise him, particularly that Cyprianowicz. 'That man is a born soldier,' he says. They are even angry at Pan Pagowski, who, they say, overstepped his bounds at Wyrabek."

"Auntie did not receive Pan Jacek any better."

"He got what he deserved. You certainly received him much better!"

"I?"

"Yes, you. I saw how you pouted at him."

"My dear auntie . . ."

Here the girl suddenly broke off, for she felt that she was about to cry. The conversation resulted in Jacek being raised in her eyes. He had faced such trained men by himself—and had hacked up all, had vanquished all. In truth he had told her that he hunted boars with spears, but, after all, peasants living along the borders of the wilderness went hunting even with clubs, so that amazed no one. But to finish five knightly nobles a man needed to be more skillful and bold than they. Panna Sieninska was simply amazed that a person with such sad and gentle eyes could be so formidable in a fight. Therefore, it was only to her that he had surrendered so, only from her did he endure such things, only for her was he so sweet and conciliatory. Why? Because he loved her more than anything else—more than his health, happiness and the salvation of his soul. He had confessed so himself an hour ago.

And once again a yearning for him overflowed her heart. She felt, however, that something had changed between them, and that if she were to see him, and afterward see him frequently, she would not allow herself to play with him as she had formerly played with him, now plunging him into sadness, now cheering him up and giving him hope, now pushing him away, now drawing him near—she felt that, despite her will, she would look at him as if with greater respect, and would be more careful and submissive in dealing with him.

There were still moments when some voice inside her said that Jacek had indeed acted too impetuously, that he had spoken words more bitter and offensive than she had, but that voice became weaker and weaker, while the desire for reconciliation became greater and greater.

If only he would return before the others arrived from Jedlinka.

But, meanwhile, an hour passed, then a second and a third, and he did not return. Then she realized that it was already too late and that he would not come himself, but would send someone for the Magyar cap.

So she decided to send a letter along with the cap, and in that letter explain everything that weighed on her heart. Because the messenger could arrive at any moment and wanting to prepare everything in advance, she shut herself up in her small private chamber and went to work on the letter.

"May God forgive you for the sadness and worry that you have caused me, for if you could see into my heart, you would not have done what you did. That is why I am not only sending your Magyar cap, but also adding a kind word, so that you will be happy and forget . . ."

Here she saw that she was not writing what she thought and what she desired, for she in no way wanted him to forget, so she crossed out the note and began another, with greater emotion and rancor:

"I am sending back your cap, for I know that I shall never see you in Belczaczka again, and that you will not weep for anyone here, least of all for an orphan like me, as I shall not weep because of your injustice, no matter how painful it may be . . ."

But these words denied the facts, and big tears suddenly stained the paper. How could she send him such a proof, especially if he had thrown her completely out of his heart? After a while, another thought came to her, that perhaps it would be better not to write about his injustice and impetuous deed, for he would become more obstinate. With this in mind, she began to look for a third piece of paper, but there did not appear to be any in her room. In the face of this she stood helpless, for if she wanted to borrow paper from Pani Winnicka she could not avoid questions that she could not possibly answer. She felt, besides, that she was losing her head and that in no way could she accurately explain to Jacek all that she wanted to say, so she became greatly anxious and, seeking in a womanly way solace from her suffering, gave in to her tears once more.

Meanwhile it became dark outside; sleigh bells tinkled before the porch, and Pan Pagowski returned with his guests. The servants were lighting candles in every room, for the darkness inside had increased. The girl wiped away her tears and entered the guest chamber with a certain fear that all would see immediately that she had been crying and would think God knows what or else torment her with questions. But in the chamber there was only Pan Pagowski and Pan Grothus, without Pan Cyprianowicz, of whom she began to inquire straightaway, attempting to turn attention from herself.

"He went to his son and the Bukojemskis," replied Pan Pagowski, "but I already assured him on the road that nothing bad had happened."

Then he looked at her closely, but his usually gloomy face and severe gray eyes brightened up with an exceptional kindness.

Drawing close to her, he placed his hand on the girl's light hair, and said:

"And you should not worry yourself needlessly about this. In a couple of days all of them will be well. But, enough of this! We owe them gratitude—true!—and that is why I concerned myself with them; but the reality is that they are, after all, strangers and of rather lowly condition."

"Of lowly condition?" she repeated, like an echo, and for the purpose of merely saying something.

"Why, yes, for the Bukojemskis are starvelings, and Cyprianowicz a *homo novus*. But, ultimately, they do not matter to me! They will go on their way, and we will have peace and quiet as before."

Panna Sieninska thought to herself that there would even be too much quiet, for there would only be three people in Belczaczka, but she did not voice this thought.

"I will go to get the supper ready," she said instead.

"Go, housewife, go!" replied Pan Pagowski. "You bring joy to the house and are useful."

After which, he added:

"Have the silverware brought out, so that this Cyprianowicz can see that fine utensils are to be found not only among Armenians who have been ennobled."

Panna Sieninska hastened to the servant quarters, but wanting to settle before supper another affair of more importance to her, she called a serving boy and said to him:

"Listen, Wojtus, dash over to Wyrabek and tell Pan Taczewski that the young lady sends him her sincere greetings and returns this cap. Here is a silver coin for the road; now repeat to me what you are to say."

"That you send him your greetings and are returning the cap."

"Not that she send him greetings, but that she sends him sincere greetings, understand?"

"I understand."

"Then go! And take an overcoat, because at night the frost bites again. Take the dogs with you too. 'Sincere greetings' remember, and return straightaway, unless Pan Taczewski wishes to give a reply."

Thus settling the affair, she proceeded to the kitchen to get the supper ready, which it almost was, for the return of the master and his guests had been expected. Then, after she had changed her attire and smoothed her hair, she went down to the dining room.

The elder Cyprianowicz greeted her kindheartedly, for her youth and beauty had been greatly to his liking even in Jedlinka. Since he was completely at rest concerning his son, he began, when they sat to table, to converse with her joyously, even trying with the help of jokes to dispel the worry he saw written on her forehead, the cause of which he attributed to what had happened.

But the supper was not to end without incident for the girl, for right after the second course, Wojtus turned up at the threshold of the room, and cried out, as he blew on his frozen fingers:

"Madame, I left the cap, but Pan Taczewski is not in Wyrabek, for he has gone away with Father Woynowski."

Hearing this, Pan Pagowski was astonished; he knitted his brows and, fixing his iron eyes on the servant, asked:

"What is this? What cap? And who sent you to Wyrabek?"

"The young lady," the young servant replied in fear.

"I did," repeated Panna Sieninska.

And seeing that all eyes were turned on her, she became very confused, but not for long, as the evasive wit of a woman quickly came to her aid.

"Pan Taczewski brought the wounded here," she said, "but because both auntie and I received him badly, he became angry and rushed off to his home without his cap, and so I returned the cap to him."

"It is true, we did not receive him too gratefully," added Pani Winnicka.

Pan Pagowski took a breath, and his face became less threatening.

"You did well!" he said. "I would have sent the cap back myself, for he surely does not have another."

But the upright and forbearing Pan Cyprianowicz began to stand up for Taczewski.

"My son," he said, "does not have any bad feeling for him. They themselves forced him to do battle, and later he even took them to his house, dressed their wounds and entertained them. The Bukojemskis say the same thing, adding that he is a master at the sword who, if he had wanted to, could have notched them really good. Ha! They wished to teach a lesson but instead were taught one themselves. If it is true that His Royal Majesty is going to move against the Turks, such a man as Taczewski will be useful."

Pan Pagowski was not pleased to hear these words, and finally said:

"Father Woynowski taught him these tricks."

"I saw Father Woynowski only once, at a church fair," said Pan Cyprianowicz, "but I heard a lot about him during my days in the army. At the fair the other priests laughed at him, saying that his presbytery is like an ark and that, like Noah, he raises all the *animalia* there. I know, however, that his was a great sword, and now his virtue is great; if Pan Taczewski has also learned from him, then I would wish my son, when he recovers, not seek any other friendship. . . ."

"They say that the Diet will start to raise the armies straightaway," said Pan Gideon, attempting to change the conversation.

"That is so; everyone is already getting involved with this," confirmed the starost Grothus.

And the conversation turned to matters of war. But after supper, Panna Sieninska, choosing an appropriate moment, approached Cyprianowicz and, raising her deep blue eyes to him, said:

"You are kind, sir, very kind."

"Why do you say that?" asked Cyprianowicz.

"Because you took Pan Jacek's side."

"Whose side?" inquired Cyprianowicz.

"Pan Taczewski's. His name is Jacek!"

"But you rebuked him so severely! Why?"

"My guardian rebuked him even more. But I admit to you, sir, that we did not behave properly toward him, and I think that he is due some comfort."

"I am sure he would be glad to receive it from your hands."

But the girl shook her golden head in a sign of disagreement.

"Oh, no," she replied with a sad smile, "he is angry with us forever."

Cyprianowicz looked at her with a genuine fatherly kindheartedness.

"Who could be angry forever at such a charming flower as you?"

"Oh, he could! . . . But as to comfort, it would be best for him if you, sir, would tell him yourself that you feel no resentment toward him and that you believe in his innocence. Then even my guardian will be forced to render him some justice, which is due him from us."

"I see that you were not so severe with him, since you are now taking his part with such a warm heart."

"Because I feel remorse, and I do not wish wrong on anyone, and he is alone in the world and is very, very poor."

"Then I will tell you what I have already decided. Your guardian, as a hospitable neighbor, has declared that he will not let me go until my son has recovered, but I can take Stas and the Bukojemskis home as early as tomorrow. But in the meantime, I would certainly visit Pan Taczewski and Father Woynowski at their homes, and not because of any kindness, but because I understand that I owe them this. I do not say that I am bad, but I think that if anyone here is truly good, it is not I, but you, lady. Do not say no!"

She did say no, however, for she felt that she was concerned not merely about justice for Jacek, but about other things, of which Pan Cyprianowicz, unaware of her girlish considerations, could not possibly know. Gratitude toward him filled her heart, however, and when saying goodnight, she kissed his hand, which made Pan Pagowski angry at her.

"He is only a third generation noble, and before that his ancestors were merchants," he said. "Do not forget who you are!"

CHAPTER 10

TWO days later Jacek left for Radom with ten ducats for the purpose of dressing himself handsomely before his journey, while Father Woynowski remained in his presbytery brooding over where more money could be gotten for a complete soldier's outfit, for wagons, for horses, for a retinue and for servants—everything a "comrade in arms" had to have if he loved dignity and did not want to be called a bumpkin.

It was especially important for Taczewski to appear this way, since he bore a great and renowned name, though somewhat forgotten in the Commonwealth.

One day Father Woynowski sat down at his small table, knitted his brows, so that his white hair fell over his forehead, and began to calculate how much would be needed. His *animalia*, that is, the dog Filus, the domesticated fox and, thirdly, the badger, were rolling balls in play at his feet, but he paid them no attention, so greatly was he occupied and troubled, for his calculations were not working out well at all. They failed not only on minor matters, but major also. The old man rubbed his forehead with more and more force, and finally began to speak to himself loudly.

"He took ten ducats with him. Fine. Nothing will remain of that, for sure. Let us calculate further: five on credit from the brewer Kondrat, three from Slonka, that makes eight. Six Prussian thalers from Duda, and a saddle horse on credit. To be paid for in barley, if there is a harvest. So the total is eight red zlotys plus six thalers and twenty zlotys of my own. Too little! Even if I gave him the Wallachian as an attendant, that will only be, counting his own steed, two horses, and two more are needed for a wagon—and for Jacek's cart at least two more. *Pauca!* It is impossible to go with less, for if one horse falls, he will need others to replace it. And a livery for the servants, and reserves for the wagon, and kettles, and coverings, and cases! Pshaw! With such money he could only hope of joining the dragoons."

Then he turned to the animals, which were making a real ruckus.

"Be quiet, you changelings, or else I will sell your skins to the Jews."

And once again he began to talk to himself:

"Jacek is right in stating that Wyrabek has to be sold. But when someone asks him later where he is from, he will have nothing to say. Where are you from? From the Wind. From what Wind? From the Wind in the field. No one will take him seriously after that. It would be better to mortgage the property, if someone could be found to give money. Pagowski would be the best guarantor, but Jacek would not hear of such a thing, and I myself would not speak to him about this. Dear God! People wrongly say 'poor as a church mouse.' Man is sometimes even poorer than that. On Saint Szczepan's Day, when the people throw grain in church, a church mouse has a nice life, and wax is always there to be had. Lord Jesus, who multiplied bread and fish, multiply these several red zlotys and sundry thalers, for, Merciful Lord, it will cost you nothing, and you will help the last of the Taczewskis. . . ."

Here it occurred to him that the Prussian thalers, as coming from a Lutheran country, could only arouse abomination in heaven, but as to the red zlotys he hesitated whether to place them at the feet of Christ's figure for the night—what if he would find them multiplied tomorrow! He did not feel worthy of a miracle, however, and even struck himself several times on the breast for this impudent thought.

After a while the door opened and a tall, gray-haired man, with black eyes that looked out with wisdom and kindness, entered the room. The man bowed at the threshold and said:

"I am Cyprianowicz from Jedlinka."

"Why, yes, I saw you, sir, at the church fair at Przytyk, but only from a distance, for the crowd was great," called out the priest, advancing with liveliness toward his guest. "I greet you, sir, at my lowly threshold with gladness."

"I have come here also with gladness," replied Cyprianowicz. "It is a great and pleasant duty to bow to such a renowned knight and such a saintly priest."

Saying this, he kissed the old man on the shoulder and the hand, though the priest warded this off, saying:

"Pshaw, what kind of saintliness! It's possible these beasts here have more merit before God than I."

But Cyprianowicz spoke with such openness and sincerity that he immediately won over Father Woynowski; and so each one began to speak kind words to the other that came from the heart.

"I have met your son, sir," said the priest. "He is a worthy cavalier of lofty manners. Those Bukojemskis seem like servants beside him. I tell you, sir, that Jacek Taczewski conceived such an affection for him straightaway that he continually praises him."

"And the same is true of my Stanislaw. It happens frequently that men fight and then hold an affection for each other. None of us hold any offense toward Pan Taczewski, and we would want to establish a genuine friendship with him. I have just come from his house in Wyrabek. I thought that I would find him here. I wanted to invite him and you, reverend father, to Jedlinka."

"Jacek is in Radom, but he will be returning, and for sure will gladly accept your offer. . . . But, sir, see how they treated him at Belczaczka!"

"They themselves saw that," replied Pan Cyprianowicz, "and regret it already: not Pan Pagowski, but the women."

"Few are as hard as Pan Pagowski, and he will pay a great price for this before God; and as to the women, God be with them. . . . But why hide the fact that one of them was the cause of this duel."

"I divined that myself before my son told me. But the cause is innocent."

"All of them are innocent. . . . But do you know, sir, what Ecclesiastes says of women?"

Pan Cyprianowicz did not know, so Father Woynowski took down the Vulgate from a shelf and read a passage from Ecclesiastes, after which he said:

"What do you think?"

"There are women even like that," replied Pan Cyprianowicz.

"Jacek is going out into the world for no other reason. But I have not dissuaded him from this in the least. On the contrary!"

"How's that? He is going immediately? The war won't come until summer."

"Do you know this for sure?"

"Yes, for I have been inquiring about it, because I also will not hold my son back."

"He is a noble, that is why. Jacek is going as soon as possible because, truthfully speaking, it is painful for him to remain here."

"I understand. I understand everything. Haste is the best remedy for such things."

"He will stay in these parts only until Wyrabek is sold or mortgaged. It is not a large piece of land, but I am advising Jacek that it would be better to mortgage than sell it. Even if he were never to come back, he can always say he is from there, and this is proper for a person of his blood and name."

"Must he sell or mortgage it?"

"Yes. The man is poor, quite poor. You know, sir, how much each expedition costs, and he cannot serve in just any dragoon regiment."

Pan Cyprianowicz thought for a while, and then said:

"You know what, reverend father, perhaps I could take a mortgage on Wyrabek."

Father Woynowski blushed like a young lady when a young man confesses unexpectedly what she wishes above all else; but this blush passed over his face as quickly as summer lightning passes through the evening sky, after which he looked keenly at Cyprianowicz and asked:

"Why do you want it?"

But the other answered with the complete sincerity of an honest soul:

"Why do I want it? I wish to render a service to an honorable young man, without loss to myself, for which I will win his gratitude. Never fear, reverend father, I have my own interest in this. I will send my one son to serve under the same banner in which Pan Taczewski is to serve, and I anticipate that my Stas will find in him a worthy comrade and friend. You know how important a comrade is, and what it means to have a true friend by one's side both in camp, where altercations are easy to come by, and in war, where death comes even more easily. God has not begrudged me fortune, but has given me only one son. Pan Taczewski is courageous, sober, a master of the sword—as has been seen—and virtuous, for you have raised him! Let him and my Stas be like Orestes and Pylades. This is my motive."

Father Woynowski opened his arms widely to him.

"God has sent you, sir! I answer for Jacek as I do for myself. He is as of gold, and his heart is as grateful as a wheat field. God has sent you! Now my boy will be able to show himself as befits a Taczewski of Powala. More importantly, in seeing the wide world, he will forget about that girl for whom he has wasted many years and has suffered so much."

"Has he loved her that long?"

"Ha, to tell the truth, since he was a little child. Even now he doesn't say anything, he grits his teeth, but he squirms like an eel on a furnace. . . . Let him go as soon as possible, because nothing could have or will come from this."

A moment of silence followed.

"Yet we have to speak *accuratissime* about these matters," the old priest finally said. "How much can you lend for Wyrabek? It is a miserable piece of land."

"At least one hundred ducats."

"Fear God, sir!"

"But why? If Pan Taczewski pays me back one day, it will not matter how much I give, and if he will not be able to pay me back, then I will make out well, nevertheless, for though the land here is poor, the new soil beyond the forest must be good. Today I will take Stas and the Bukojemskis back to Jedlinka. Do us the favor of visiting us as soon as Pan Taczewski returns from Radom. The money will be ready."

"Sir, you have come from heaven with your fortune and your golden heart," replied Father Woynowski.

Then he had mead brought. He himself poured, and they drank with pleasure as men do who have joy in their hearts. With the third glass the priest became serious, and said:

"For your help, for the good word, for your kindheartedness, let me repay you, at least, with good advice."

"I am listening."

"Do not settle your son in Wyrabek. The girl is goodlooking beyond imagination. She may even be honorable in her own right, this I do not deny, but she is a Sieninski, of which not only is she so proud, but Pan Pagowski too; if someone were to ask for her hand, even, let's say, the king's son Jacobus, the old man would still not be satisfied. Guard your son; do not allow him to scratch himself on this haughty young heart, or even fatally wound himself against it, as Jacek has done. I say this out of sincere and warmhearted friendship for you, wanting to repay good for good."

Pan Cyprianowicz drew his hand across his forehead, and answered thus:

"They dropped in on us out of nowhere at Jedlinka because of what happened on the road. I once went to Pan Pagowski's on a neighborly visit, but he did not return the visit. Realizing how haughty he is, I have not sought his friendship or acquaintanceship since. I will not settle my son in Wyrabek nor will I allow him to flirt in Belczaczka. We are not such an old nobility as the Sieninskis or even, perhaps, the Pagowskis, but we are nobility, and nobility grown from war, from great pains, as Pan Czarniecki once said. We are able to preserve our dignity; my son is no less sensitive to this than I. It is hard for a young man to guard against Cupid's arrows, but I will tell you, gracious sir, what Stas said to me when I asked him just a while ago at Belczaczka about the girl: "I would rather," he said, "not pluck the apple from the tree, lest I jump too high for it and miss, which would be shameful."

"Ah, he has a good head!" exclaimed the priest.

"He has been so from childhood," replied Cyprianowicz with a certain pride. "He also said something else, that when he found out what that girl meant to Taczewski and what he had passed through because of her, he would not, for anything in the world, get in such a worthy cavalier's way. No, my dear sir, I do not take a lease on Wyrabek so that my son can be near Belczaczka. May God guard my boy and protect him from all evil!"

"Amen. I believe you as if an angel were speaking to me. As to that young lady, let some third man take her, even one of the Bukojemskis, who boast of such great relatives."

Cyprianowicz began to laugh, after which he finished his mead, bade farewell and departed. Father Woynowski went to the church to thank God for the unexpected help, after which he waited impatiently for Taczewski.

When Jacek finally returned, he ran out to him all the way into the yard, seized him by the shoulders, and began crying out:

"Jacek! For one crupper you can pay ten ducats. You have one hundred zlotys as good as on the table, and Wyrabek remains yours!"

And Taczewski fixed his eyes, sunken from suffering and sleeplessness, on him and asked with astonishment:

"What happened?"

CHAPTER 11

IN truth, a good thing had happened because it flowed from the heart of an honest man. Father Woynowski also noted with great pleasure that Jacek, despite his heavy distress and all his heartfelt torments, took on, as it were, a new spirit at the news of the agreement with Cyprianowicz. For several days he spoke and thought only of horses, wagons, the outfits of a soldier, and servants, so that it seemed that there was no place in his heart for anything else.

"Here is your medicine, here is your balsam, here is your cure-all," Father Woynowski repeated to himself, "for no matter how much a man is ensnared by a woman, no matter how much of a wretch he is, once he prepares to go to war he must make sure that he doesn't buy a horse whose breath is gone or whose hocks are enlarged; he must choose the right sword, try on armor, test his lance once, then twice, and through this the *animus* will immediately turn away from a woman, and the heart, taken up with more appropriate things, will find sure relief."

And he remembered how, in his younger years, he himself sought in war forgetfulness or death. But, now, since war had not blossomed yet, death was distant from Jacek in any case, and meanwhile he was completely absorbed by the expedition and the affairs related with it.

There was much to do.

Both of the Cyprianowiczes came again to Father Woynowski's, where Jacek was living. Then all went to the city to draw up the lease. There they prepared a portion of Jacek's outfit, the remainder of which the experienced and foreseeing Father Woynowski advised them to take care of either in Warsaw or Cracow. All this occupied several days, from morning to night, during which Stanislaw Cyprianowicz, whose slight wound had almost completely healed, eagerly helped Jacek, with whom he developed an ever deeper acquaintance and friendship.

The old men were pleased to see this, for both considered it very important. The honest Pan Serafin even began to regret that Jacek was to leave so quickly, and he tried to persuade the priest not to hasten his departure.

"I understand," he said. "I understand very well why you, reverend father, would want to send him away as soon as possible, but I have to tell you in all fairness that I do not think badly of this Panna Sieninska. It is true that after the duel she did not receive Jacek very nicely, but do not forget that Stas and the Bukojemskis had just snatched her and Pani Winnicka from the wolves' jaws. No wonder that at the sight of their wounds and blood, she was seized by anger, which, as I know, Pagowski had purposefully roused in her. He—he is a truly obstinate man, but the girl, when I was there, came to me completely remorseful: 'I admit,' she said, 'that we did not behave properly and that Pan Jacek is due some kind of comfort.' And her eyes immediately welled up with tears, so that I felt sorry for her, because she also has such a lovely face. But her soul is honest and she knows when an injustice has been done. . . ."

"For the love of God, do not let Jacek know of this, for his heart would be under penalty of death straightaway, and he has just barely begun to breathe better. He ran away from there without his cap, swore he would not return, and may God protect him from doing so. Women, you see, are like those will-o'-the-wisps that move over the rich marshes at Jedlinka. You chase one—it escapes; you escape—it chases you. . . . That is the way it is!"

"This is a wise dictum, which I must relate to Stas," said Pan Serafin.

"And let Jacek go as soon as possible. I have already prepared letters for him to various acquaintances and dignitaries whom I knew before they became prominent, and to the most illustrious soldiers. In these letters I also recommend your sire's son as a worthy cavalier, and when the time comes for him to go, then I will also give him separate letters, though these may be unnecessary, for Jacek will already have prepared the way for him. Let them serve together."

"I thank you, reverend father, from the bottom of my heart. Yes! Let them serve together, and may their friendship last to the end of their lives. You spoke of the company of the king's son, Alexander, which is under Zbierzchowski. It is a superior company, perhaps the best among the hussars, so I would be delighted if Stanislaw joined it, but he told me the following: 'The light cavalry is for six days a week, while the hussars are, as it were, for Sunday.'"

"*Generaliter* he spoke the truth," replied the priest. "In truth, the hussars are not sent out on scouting expeditions, and rarely do they get involved in single combat, as it is not fitting for such a soldier to meet just anyone; but when their Sunday comes, they slaughter and trample so, that others in six days are not able to spill so much blood. Anyway, war is not commanded, but commands, so it sometimes happens that even hussars perform ordinary work."

"You know this better than anyone, reverend father."

Father Woynowski closed his eyes for a moment, as if trying to remember the past exactly, then raised them, looked at the mead under the light, took one swig and then another, and said:

"That is the way it was when, toward the end of the Swedish war, we went to punish that traitor, the Elector, for his collusion with Carolus. Marshal Lubomirski took fire and sword right to Berlin. I was then a comrade in this very hussar company, in which Wiktor was the lieutenant. The Elector of Brandenburg countered us as best he could: now with the infantry, now with general militia in which were German nobles; and I tell you, sir, that for us hussars, as well as for the Cossacks of the court, our arms could barely move toward the end. . . ."

"So the work was that difficult?"

"It was not difficult, for at the mere sight of us the muskets and pikes of those poor devils trembled in their hands like branches in the wind— but from morning to night there was work. Whether a man thrusts his spear into a breast or a back, he will tire himself out. Oh, it was a nice expedition, for—as was said—there was plenty to do, but I have never in my life seen so many backsides of both men and horses as then. We devastated half of Brandenburg so thoroughly that even Luther wept in hell."

"It is pleasant to recall that treason was justly punished."

"Of course it is pleasant. Later the Elector came to Pan Lubomirski to ask for peace. I did not see this, but afterward soldiers said that the marshal walked around the parade ground with his hands on his hips, while the Elector tripped after him, bowing so low that his wig nearly touched the ground and embracing the marshal's knees—bah! they even say, that he kissed them at random, but I do not put much store in this, for the marshal, having a proud heart, liked to have the enemy bend, but was too diplomatic a man and would not have permitted something like that."

"God grant that what happened then at Brandenburg may happen now with the Turks."

"My experience is not lofty but it is long; so I will tell you sincerely that I think it will go as well, or even better. The marshal was an experienced soldier and particularly fortunate, but he cannot compare with His Majesty, who is, luckily, reigning over us."

Then they fell to talking about all the victories of the crown and the battles in which they themselves had taken part, and drinking to the health of the king and rejoicing that, under such a leader, the young people would not only taste war but acquire immense glory, particularly as the war was to be against the agelong enemy of the cross.

In truth, no one knew anything much about it.

It was not yet known if the Turkish power would turn first on the Commonwealth or the Emperor. The question of an alliance with the Austrian court was to be raised at the Diet. But already at the meetings of nobles and provincial dietines, there was talk only of war. Experts in Warsaw and at the court foretold it without reservation, and besides this, the entire nation was seized by a feeling that it was inevitable—a feeling almost stronger than certainty, and arising from the actions of the king, as well as the general desire and the destiny of a nation.

CHAPTER 12

ON the road to Radom Father Woynowski invited the Cyprianowiczes to the presbytery for a rest, after which he and Jacek were to visit them in Jedlinka. Meanwhile, three of the Bukojemskis appeared unexpectedly at his house. Marek, whose collarbone had been cut, could not yet move, but Mateusz, Lukasz and Jan came to bow before the old man and thank him for dressing their wounds. Though Jan had lost his little finger, and the older brothers had sizeable scars—one on the forehead, the other on the cheek, their wounds had healed completely and each was as sound as a bell.

Two days before, they had gone on a hunt in the wilderness and smoking out a sleeping she-bear in her den, pierced her with spears and took her cub as a gift to the priest, whose love for wild beasts was widely known.

The old man, who took the brothers to heart as "honest boys," was gladdened by them and by the young bear—and even shed tears of laughter when the cub, seizing one of the cups filled with mead for a guest, began to roar loud enough to arouse a good measure of fear, thus protecting his booty.

Seeing that no one was about to take his prize, the cub stood on his hind legs and drank down the mead as if he were a man, the sight of which elicited even greater joy among those present.

"I will not make him my cellarman or my beekeeper," said the amused priest.

"Ha!" exclaimed Stanislaw Cyprianowicz, laughing. "This little one was only a short time at school with the Bukojemskis, but he learned more in one day from them than he could his entire life in the forest."

"That's not true," replied Lukasz, "for this is a beast who by nature has great wit and knows what is good. We had barely brought it out of the forest when it drank down some vodka, as if he drank it every morning in the forest, and then he smacked a dog on the snout, as if to say, 'Take this! Don't sniff at me!' And then he went to sleep."

"Thanks to you, gentlemen, I will derive genuine pleasure from him," said the priest, "but I will not make him my cellarman, for though he knows his drinks well, he would stay around them with too much passion."

"A bear can do many things," noted Jan. "Father Glominski at Przytyk has a bear that, they say, pumps the organ. But some people are scandalized, for sometimes he also roars, particularly when he is teased with a pole."

"There is no scandal in that," replied the priest. "Birds build nests in churches and sing to the glory of God, and no one is scandalized by this. Every beast is a servant of God, and the Savior was born in a stable."

"They say, besides," said Mateusz, "that the Lord Jesus turned a miller into a bear, so perhaps there is a human soul in him."

Cyprianowicz replied to this:

"Then you have killed the miller's wife, and must answer for it. His Majesty the King is very protective of his bears and does not keep foresters to kill them."

Hearing this, the three brothers became genuinely anxious, and it was only after a long period of thinking that Mateusz, desiring to say something in defense of what they had done, said:

"Bah, are we not nobles? The Bukojemskis are as good as the Sobieskis."

But a happy thought came to Lukasz, and his face brightened up.

"We gave our knightly word," he said, "that we would not shoot bears—no? So we do not shoot them, we spear them."

"His Majesty the King is not thinking of bears nowadays," noted Jan, "and, besides, no one will tell him. Let any forester try. . . . Ha! It is a pity, nevertheless, that we boasted about this to Pan Pagowski and Pan Grothus, for Pan Grothus is on his way to Warsaw, and as he sees the king often, he may mention this accidentally."

"When did you meet Pagowski?" asked the priest.

"Yesterday. He was conducting Pan Grothus. Do you know, reverend father, where that inn called 'The Drinking Den' is? They arrived there to give their horses a rest and found us inside. Pan Pagowski began asking about many things, and about Jacek also."

"About me?" inquired Taczewski.

"Yes. He asked: 'Is it true that Taczewski is going to the army?'"

"We replied: 'It's true!'"

"'And when?'"

"'Soon.'"

"And Pagowski said: 'That is good, but he'll probably join the infantry.'"

"At this we all became angry, and Mateusz said: 'Sir, do not say such things, for Jacek is now our friend and we have to stand up for him.' And as we began to breathe heavily, he restrained himself, and said: 'I do not say this out of any special malevolence, but I know that Wyrabek is not a starosta.'"

"A starosta or not, it is home!" exclaimed the priest. "Let him not trouble his head over this."

But apparently Pan Pagowski was of another opinion on this matter, and he did trouble his head over Jacek, for an hour later the servant brought in, along with a new demijohn of mead, a sealed letter, and said:

"Sir, there is a messenger for you from Belczaczka."

Father Woynowski took the letter, broke the seal, opened it, struck the sheet with the back of his hand, and approaching the window, began to read.

Jacek paled from emotion and stared at the paper as if it were a rainbow, for his instinct told him that the letter concerned him. Thoughts flew through his mind like swallows—perhaps the old man was repentant? Perhaps this was an apology? That was the way it should be, and it could not be any other way. Pagowski did not have a right to still be angry about what had happened, no more than those who had suffered in the duel. So his conscience had finally spoken: he recognized the injustice of his conduct, he understood how grievously he had wronged an innocent man, and desired to correct an injustice.

Jacek's heart began to beat like a hammer.

"Oh, I will go," he said to himself. "Happiness is not for me, and even though I can forgive, I cannot forget; but if, before I leave, I could see Anulka but once, so cruel but so beloved, if I could but once have a good look at her, hear her voice—this, Gracious Lord, do not refuse me!"

And his thoughts flew even quicker than swallows, but before they had a chance to pass, something quite unexpected happened, for suddenly Father Woynowski crushed the letter in his hand and grasped at his left side, as if seeking a saber. Blood rushed to his face, his neck swelled, and his eyes flashed like lightning. Quite simply, he looked so fierce that the Cyprianowiczes and Bukojemskis looked at him with great astonishment, as if he had suddenly changed into another man through some bewitchment.

A deep silence prevailed in the room.

Meanwhile the priest leaned toward the window, as if looking at something through it, after which he turned around, glanced at the walls, then at the guests, but apparently he had already struggled with himself and calmed down, for his face had paled and the fire in his eyes was extinguished.

"Gracious gentlemen," he said, "this man is not only hotheaded, but quite simply evil. To say more than is proper in the heat of passion happens to everyone, but to obstinately continue to wrong someone and trample on the wronged party is not worthy of a noble or a Catholic."

Saying this, he bent down and picked up the crushed letter, and turned to Taczewski:

"Jacek, if there is any splinter still remaining in your heart, then take it out with this knife. Read, poor boy, read aloud, for you should not be ashamed, but the person who wrote such a letter. Let these gentlemen known what kind of a man is Pan Pagowski."

Jacek grabbed the letter with trembling hands, unraveled it, and read:

"My dear Gracious Reverend Father, etc., etc.

Having learned that Taczewski of Wyrabek, who used to frequent my house, is joining the army at this time, I, in memory of the bread I fed him because of his poverty, and for the services in which I was able to use him at times, am sending him a horse and ducat for horseshoes, with the recommendation that he not spend it on other, useless things.

I am gladly sending at the same time my ardent services, yours sincerely, etc., etc.,"

After reading the letter, Jacek paled to such a degree that those present became frightened for him, especially the priest, who was not certain if that paleness did not a herald an outburst of madness, and he knew how terrible that young man was in anger, though he was usually quite mild.

"Pagowski is old and is missing an arm," he said quickly, "so he cannot challenge him!"

But Taczewski did not explode, for a boundless and painful amazement took precedence within him over all other feelings.

"I cannot challenge him," he repeated like an echo, "but why is he still stepping on me?"

The elder Cyprianowicz then rose, took both of Jacek's hands, shook them strongly, after which he kissed him on the forehead, and said:

"Pagowski has only injured himself, not you, and if you desist from seeking revenge, the more everyone will be impressed with your exceptional soul that is worthy of the blood you possess."

"Those are wise words," exclaimed the priest, "which you surely deserve!"

Stanislaw Cyprianowicz embraced Jacek in turn.

"Truthfully speaking," he said, "I love you more and more."

But for the Bukojemskis, who had not ceased gnashing their teeth since the letter was read, such a turn of events was not to their liking. Following Stanislaw's example, they began to embrace Jacek.

"Let it be as you want," Lukasz finally said, "but if I were in Jacek's place, I would act differently."

"How?" inquired the two other brothers with interest.

"That's just it; I do not know how, but I would think of something and not forgive such a thing."

"If you don't know how, then you shouldn't speak up."

"So, you know how?"

"Be quiet, sirs!" said the priest. "I will not leave the letter unanswered, but to desist from vengeance—this is a Christian and Catholic act."

"Bah! The first thing your reverence did was to reach for a saber at your side."

"For I carried a saber for too long. *Mea culpa!* But as I said, there is the circumstance that Pagowski is old and without one arm. Iron rules are useless here. . . . And I will tell you, gentlemen, that I am disgusted to the highest degree by this obstinate fellow precisely because he takes such a shameful advantage of this with impunity."

"Our neighborhood will be too confining for him," said Jan Bukojemski. "We're determined to see that not one person steps into that house. . . ."

"In the meantime an answer must be given," interrupted the priest, "and immediately."

For a while, however, they thought about who should respond: Jacek, to whom the letter was aimed, or the priest, to whom it was sent. It was determined that the priest would respond; Taczewski himself settled the matter, saying:

"For me that entire house and the people living in it are as if dead, and it is fortunate for them that I have said so in my soul."

"Let it be so! The bridges are burned!" added the priest, looking for pen and paper.

Jan Bukojemski responded:

"It is well that the bridges are burned, but it would be better if Belczaczka went up in smoke too! In the Ukraine when some straggler would settle down and not know how to live with people, he was cut up and his property went up in smoke."

No one, however, paid attention to these words, except the elder Cyprianowicz, who impatiently waved a hand, and retorted:

"You, gentlemen, have arrived in these parts from the Ukraine, I from Lwow, and Pan Pagowski from Pomerania, so according to your wit, Pan Taczewski might consider all of us as intruders; but know this, that the Commonwealth is one big house, in which lives a family of nobles and in which a noble is at home in every corner. . . ."

Silence ensued, broken only by the scratching of a pen from the alcove and half-spoken words pronounced by the priest, who was dictating to himself.

Taczewski rested his forehead in his palms and sat for some time without movement; suddenly he straightened up, glanced at those present, and spoke:

"There is something here that I cannot understand."

"We also cannot understand it," replied Lukasz Bukojemski, "but if you drink some mead, we will drink it also."

Involuntarily, Jacek poured mead into cups, while at the same time following the course of his own thoughts, he continued speaking:

"Because the duel began at his house, Pagowski could have been offended, though such things take place everywhere. But now he knows that I did not issue the challenge; he knows that he unjustly offended me under my own roof; he knows I've become reconciled with you, he knows that I will not show my face at his house anymore—and he still goes after me, he still attempts to step on me. . . ."

"It's true that there is some type of special obstinacy in this," said the elder Cyprianowicz.

"Ha! Then you also think there is something in this?"

"In what?" asked the priest, who, emerging from the alcove with the finished letter, had heard the last words.

"In this special hatred toward me."

The priest looked at the shelf on which stood, among a number of other books, the Holy Bible, and he said:

"I will tell you what I've told you a long time ago: there is a *mulier* in this."

He turned to those present.

"Gentlemen, have I quoted to you what Ecclesiastes says about woman?"

But he could not finish, for Jacek sprang up as if burned by a live fire, dug his fingers into his hair, and began to cry out in boundless pain:

"The more so I do not understand, for if there is one person in the world—for if I have in this world—for if there is such a person—then with my entire soul. . . ."

And he could not continue, for sincere pain gripped his heart as if in a vice and brought forth two big bitter and burning tears, which flowed down his cheeks.

The priest understood him perfectly.

"My Jacek," he said, "it is better to cauterize your wound, though it may pain you terribly, than to let it fester. That is why I do not spare you. Why, in my time I was a lay soldier, so I understand many things. I know that no matter how far a man travels, memories and sorrow trail after him like dogs and howl in the night, making him unable to go to sleep. So what is to be done? Better to kill them straightaway. At this moment you feel that you would have given all your blood for her, and because of this it seems strange and horrible that it is precisely from her that vengeance comes. This seems impossible to you, but it is possible, after all. . . . For if you have wounded a woman's pride and a woman's self-love, if it was expected that you would whimper and you did not whimper, if you did not fawn when you were beaten, but pulled on your chain and broke free of it, then know that this will never be forgiven you, and that the fury of a woman, more than a man's, will always pursue you. There is only one remedy for this: break the love, even if against your own heart, and hurl it far away from you like a broken bow—that is what you must do!"

And once again there was a moment of silence. The elder Cyprianowicz nodded his head in agreement with the priest, surprised, as a man of experience himself, by the wisdom of his words.

Jacek repeated:

"It is true that I pulled on my chain and have broken free of it. . . . Yes, it is not Pagowski who is pursuing me!"

"I now know what I would do," Lukasz Bukojemski spoke up suddenly.

"Speak, don't hold anything back!" exclaimed his two brothers.

"Do you know what a rabbit says?"

"What rabbit? Are you drunk?"

"That rabbit in the neighboring fields."

And apparently in a merry mood, he stood up, put his hands on his hips, and began to sing:

> *A rabbit sits on the ridge,*
> *on the ridge,*
> *The hunters do not know he's there*
> *they do not know*
> *He sits, lamenting*

*and writing his testament
on the ridge.*

Here he turned to his brothers and asked:
"And do you know what is the *tenor* of this testament?"
"We know, but it's pleasant to hear it!"
"Then listen:

*Kiss me all of you,
horsemen and hunters,
on the ridge . . .*"

"That's what I would write to everyone in Belczaczka, if I were in Jacek's place; and if he will not do this, let the first Janissary disembowel me, if I do not write it in my own name and yours to Pagowski in farewell."

"Oh, as God is dear to me, that is a splendid idea!" exclaimed Jan with joy.

"Both imaginative and to the point!"

"Let Jacek write him back!"

"No," said the priest, made impatient by the brothers' talk. "The letter will be written by me, not Jacek, and it is not appropriate for me to borrow your expressions."

He turned to Cyprianowicz and to Jacek:

"The task was difficult, for I had to bend down the horns of his malice without abandoning diplomacy, and show him that we understood from where the sting originated. Listen, therefore, and if anyone of you gentlemen have any polite comment to make, please do so."

And he began to read:

"Dear sir and brother . . ."

Here he struck the letter with the back of his hand, and said:

"Notice, gentlemen, that I do not write 'Honorable sir,' but rather 'Dear sir.'"

"He will have enough!" said Pan Serafin. "Read on."

"It is known to all citizens living within our Commonwealth that only those individuals who have either kept the company of diplomatic men since youth, or who, coming from great blood, have brought diplomacy into the world with them, know how to *conservare et applicare* proper diplomacy in every way. Neither one nor the other situation has befallen Your Lordship, while the Honorable Pan Jacek Taczewski, who has, *ex contrario*, inherited excellent blood and soul from renowned ancestors, forgives you your common words and also sends back your common gifts. If, like the *caupones* who maintain inns in the towns or along the roads, you wish to bill the Honorable Pan Jacek Taczewski for the hospitality that he found at your home, the Honorable Taczewski is ready to pay for any expenses, and add such a *supplementem* as befits his generous nature. . . ."

"Oh, as God is dear to me!" interrupted the elder Cyprianowicz, "Pagowski will burst a blood vessel!"

"Ha! It was necessary to humble his pride; and if bridges are burned—Jacek wanted this himself."

"Yes, yes!" exclaimed Taczewski passionately.

"And now listen to what I add from myself: 'Bearing in mind his forgiving nature, I have disposed the Honorable Taczewski to the view that though the bow is yours, the poisoned arrow with which you wanted to strike this worthy youth probably did not come from your own quiver. Since reason as well as strength weaken with the years and impotent old age, it is easy to surrender to the suggestions of another, and one is deserving of more forbearance. I end with this last thought, adding, as a priest and a servant of God, this observation: the older one is and the closer to life's end, the less a man should serve pride and hatred while the more should he think of his soul's salvation, a thing I wish your Grace. Amen. I remain yours, etc, signed, etc.'"

"Everything is written *accurate*," said Pan Serafin. "Nothing to be added, nothing to be cut."

"Ha!" said the priest. "So you think he deserves this letter?"

"Oh, even my blood boiled at certain passages."

"And mine," added Lukasz Bukojemski. "For sure, when a man hears such things he wants to drink as if it were a hot day."

"Attend to these gentlemen, Jacek, while I seal the letter and send it off."

Saying this, he removed the signet ring from his finger and went to the alcove. But while sealing the letter another thought apparently came to his head, for when he returned, he said:

"It is done. The affair is over. But do you think the letter is too cutting? He is an old man; what if the letter costs him his health? Written words that are *vulnera* do not hurt less than those wounds given by a sword or a bullet."

"True! true!" replied Taczewski.

And he gritted his teeth.

But it was precisely this involuntary exclamation of pain that settled the matter. The elder Cyprianowicz said:

"Reverend father, these are honorable scruples, but Pagowski does not possess them. His letter aimed straight for the heart, while yours aims only at pride and hatred; I am of the opinion, therefore, that it should be sent."

And the letter was sent, after which preparations for Jacek's departure increased in pace.

CHAPTER **13**

BUT Taczewski's friends did not foresee that the priest's letter would be useful in some respects in the hands of Pan Gideon Pagowski and serve his own ends.

In truth, he did not receive it without anger. Jacek, who so far had been merely an obstacle to him, became henceforth an object of hatred, though he did not write the letter himself. That hatred blossomed in his obstinate old heart like a poisoned flower, but his ingenious mind determined to profit from the priest's response.

So Pan Gideon restrained his fierce rage, assumed an expression of contemptuous pity, and went with the letter to Panna Sieninska.

"For good works one gets paid with bad," he said. "I did not want to do this, for I am a person of experience and I know people; but when you began to clasp your hands and say that a wrong had been done him, that I had been too severe, and that you had been too severe—that he ought not to leave in anger—I yielded. I sent him some monetary relief; I sent a horse; I sent a polite letter. I thought he would come, bow down, give us thanks, and bid farewell as befits a man who has spent so much time under our roof. Meanwhile, take a look at the answer I have received!"

Saying this, he drew the priest's letter from his belt and handed it over to the young lady.

She began to read, and soon her dark brows knitted in anger, but when she reached the place where the priest stated that Pan Pagowski wished to humiliate Jacek thanks to the suggestion of another, her hands shook, and her face turned a momentary scarlet, then became white as a sheet, and stayed that way.

Though Pan Gideon saw all, he pretended otherwise.

"May God forgive them what they write about me *ad personam*," he said after a moment of silence, "for He alone knows whether the

Pagowskis are so much lower than the Taczewskis, of whose greatness more fables than truth are heard. But what I cannot forgive them is that they have paid you, my poor dear, for your kind, angelic heart with such ingratitude."

"It was not Pan Jacek who wrote this letter, but Father Woynowski," replied Panna Sieninska, as if grasping at a last ray of hope.

The old noble sighed at this, and asked:

"Do you believe that I love you?

"Yes," answered the girl, bending down and kissing his hand.

And he began to stroke her bright hair with great tenderness.

"Though you believe it," he said, "you still do not know how much I love you. You are my entire comfort. Rarely do I permit myself words such as these, and rarely do I express what my heart feels, for there is an old wound closed up within it. But you should know that I have only you in the world. I would want to see that you have joy and happiness every hour of your life, rather than worries and anxieties and, even more so, pain. I do not wish to ask what began to spring up in your heart, but I will tell you that if it was, as I suspect, a purely sisterly feeling, or something more, that young man, who has given us ingratitude in return for sincere friendship, is unworthy of it. My Anulka, you would be deceiving yourself if you thought that the priest wrote this letter without Taczewski's knowledge. They drew up the letter together, and do you know why they replied with such arrogance? I have heard Taczewski received money from that Armenian in Jedlinka. Well, he needed money, and now that he has it, he cares for no one anymore. This is the truth—and you yourself must admit in your soul that to think otherwise would be willing self-deception."

"I admit it," whispered the young lady.

Pan Gideon thought for a moment, as if he were considering something, and then said:

"No! People say that it is a bad habit of old people to praise the old days and condemn the new. But no! It is not a bad habit! . . . The world is getting worse, people are getting worse, and in my day no man would have acted as has Taczewski. Do you know what was the cause of all this? That night in the tree, which exposed the cavalier to the ridicule of people. He supposedly was hurrying to help someone, but wound up climbing a tree in fear. This can happen, but it is better in such a case not to boast of it, for if it is a laughable thing, it is a laughable thing. I do not hold up the Bukojemskis or Cyprianowicz as any kind of heroes: they are drunkards, idlers and surly people—this I know! They were more interested in wolf skins than in us. But in Taczewski resides this *invidia*, so that he could not even forgive them this unrequested help. From this arose the duel. May God judge me if I did not have just cause to get angry. Ha! They made up afterwards, for it is apparent that the cavalier understood that he could get money out of Cyprianowicz, and so preferred to direct his anger at us. Pride, anger, greed and ingratitude—this is what he has shown is inside him. And nothing more! He has wronged me—may God forgive him! But why did he attack you, my flower? Years of being a neighbor, years of being our guest, daily visits! Under such conditions a gypsy would become attached, a swallow become accustomed to a thatched roof, and a stork lay out a nest; but he spat on our house as soon as he felt an Armenian coin in his pocket. . . . No! no! No one would have acted that way in my day!"

Panna Sieninska listened to this with her palms against her temples and her eyes staring straight ahead of her, so Pagowski paused and, glancing at her once, then twice, asked:

"What are you thinking about?"

"I am not thinking about anything," she said, "but I am so sad that words have deserted me."

And not finding words, she found tears. Pan Gideon let her cry her fill.

"It is better," he finally said, "that this sadness flow out with your tears rather than fester in your heart. Oh, well, it can't be helped! Let him go, let him use other men's coins, let him drag his horse through the mud, let him feign being a lord and charm Warsaw idiots. But we will remain here, my girl. Surely it is not a great comfort, but a comfort nevertheless, when I think that no one will deceive you here, no one will offend you, nor wound your heart; that you will always be the apple in the eye of everyone here, and that your happiness will be the primary concern and, at the same time, the last thought of my life. Come. . . ."

He stretched out his arms to her, and she fell on his breast, embittered, but at the same time grateful, like a daughter is grateful to a father who tries to comfort her in a moment of suffering. Pan Pagowski began once again to stroke her flaxen hair with his one hand, and for a long time they sat thus in silence.

Meanwhile, it was growing dark. Later the frosted windows glittered in the moonlight, and outside, dogs were heard here and there barking away.

The warmth of the girl's body penetrated Pan Gideon's heart, which began to beat with more vigor, but because he feared to betray himself prematurely, he did not want to expose himself further to temptation.

"Rise, my child," he said. "You will not cry anymore?"

"I will not," she replied, kissing his hand.

"You see! There you have it! Always remember where you have certain refuge and where it will be peaceful and cosy for you. Every young man is glad to go where the wind takes him, but for me you are the only one. Keep this well in mind! Perhaps you have thought now and then: 'My guardian casts severe glances like a wolf, he is glad to find someone to shout at, and he has no understanding of my youthful ways.' But do you know what this guardian has thought of and thinks about? Often of his bygone happiness, often of that pain which is stuck like an arrow in his heart—true, but aside from this, only about you, only of your future lot, only about how to increase everything good for you. Pan Grothus and I talked many hours about this, until he laughed at times at what he said was the only thing on my mind. But I was concerned about one thing: securing for you at least a peaceful and sufficient life after my death."

"Heaven forbid that time should come!" exclaimed the young lady, bending again to Pan Gideon's hand. And there was so much sincerity in her voice that the stern face of the old noble brightened up momentarily in genuine joy.

"Do you love me even a tiny bit?"

"Oh, guardian!"

"God reward you, my child. My age is not yet so advanced, and my body would be sufficiently vigorous if not for the wounds in my heart and flesh. But, as they say, death is always close by and can knock at one's door anytime it wants. In such a case, you would be left alone in the world with Pani Winnicka. Pan Grothus is a good and powerful person who would always respect my last will and testament, but as for the other relatives of my deceased wife—who knows? And I received Belczaczka through my wife. What if they wanted to contest the will? What if they raised a lawsuit? One has to anticipate everything. Pan Grothus gave me advice on this matter. Of course it is effective, but strange—and that is why I will not mention it to you. . . . I would like to have an audience with His Majesty the King, so that I could commend you and my will to him. But the king is now occupied with the Diet and the upcoming war. Pan Grothus said that if war comes, the armies under the hetmans will move first, and His Majesty will join them at Cracow. Perhaps then . . . perhaps both of us will go together. . . . But whatever happens, know this, my child, that everything that I have is, and will be, yours—though I would have to follow Pan Grothus' advice as the last resort. Bah! Even if an hour before death! So help me God. After all, I am not a wind in the field, nor empty-headed, nor a person who hulls shells, nor am I Taczewski."

CHAPTER 14

PANNA Sieninska returned to her room full of gratitude toward her guardian, who up until then had never spoken to her so warmly; yet she was also resentful, full of bitterness and disillusioned with the world. At first she could not and knew not how to think calmly; she only had the feeling that a great wrong had been done her, a great injustice and that a cruel, painful disappointment had befallen her.

For her love, for her sorrow, for her yearning, for all that she had done to bind again the severed threads, she was paid only in hateful suspicion. And there was no remedy for it now. She could not, after all, write to Jacek a second time, explaining and justifying herself. At the very thought of this a blush of humiliation and shame came over her face. Besides, she was almost certain that Jacek had already left. . . .

And then war would come; perhaps they would never see each other again, perhaps he would perish—and perish with the conviction that in her breast beat an evil and deceitful heart. Suddenly she was seized by boundless sorrow: Jacek appeared before her eyes as if he were there, with his swarthy face and those sad eyes, which she had laughed at on occasion as being the eyes of a maiden.

The thoughts of the girl flew like a swift swallow after the traveler and called to him:

"Jacek! I did not wish to do you any harm! Jacek, God sees my heart!"

Thus she called out to him, but he pays no heed. He rides on straight ahead, and when he thinks about her, he only frowns and spits.

And again pearls appeared on her eyelids. A certain weakness came over her and a moment of emotion, and a moment of resignation, in which she began to say to herself: "It cannot be helped! May God forgive him and lead him, and never mind about me!"

But her lips quivered like a child's, her eyes looked like the eyes of a wounded bird, and somewhere, in a hidden little corner of her soul, as pure as a tear, she silently blamed God for that which had befallen her.

Now she was certain that Jacek had never loved her, and she could not understand why he had not, even a little.

"My guardian spoke truthfully!" she thought.

But later came a consideration.

"No, that could not be!"

Immediately she recalled those words Jacek spoke that were etched in her memory like stone: "You will not leave, but I. But I will tell you this, that though I have loved you more than health itself, more than life, more than my own soul, I will never come back here. I will chew my own hands from pain, but I will not come back—so help me God!" He was as pale as a sheet when he said this, and nearly crazed from anger and pain.

He did not return—true! He did not show up again, he renounced her, he made his complaint, left her, wronged her with an unjust accusation; he composed that horrible letter with the priest—everything was true and in this her guardian was right. But that he had never loved her, that after receiving money he was to leave with a light and joyful heart, that he had stopped thinking about her altogether, that was simply impossible to believe.

A guardian's solicitude could imagine such a thing, but the reality was different. He who has no love does not grow pale, grit his teeth, gnaw his fist from pain and rend his soul. . . .

If that was the case, she thought, there is only the difference that now two were suffering instead of one, and a certain comfort came to her, and even a kind of hope.

The days and months ahead appeared perhaps sadder to her, but less bitter. The words of the letter ceased to burn her like red-hot iron, for though she doubted not that Jacek had assisted in the writing, it is one thing to act through sorrow and pain, and another through deliberate malice.

So once again a great compassion for Jacek took hold of her with new strength, so great, and particularly so ardent, that it could not be simple compassion. Her thoughts began to weave and turn into some kind of gold thread that disappeared in the future, casting, at the same time, a glitter of joy on her.

The war will end, so will the separation.

"Surely, that cruel Jacek will not return to Belczaczka," she thought. "Oh, no! Once such a stubborn man says something, he keeps to it. But he will return to these parts, to Wyrabek. He will live close by, and whatever happens then is in God's hands. He went away in tears perhaps, or in pain, perhaps wringing his hands—may God comfort him!"

One always returns home with an overflowing heart and with joy, and particularly after having achieved great glory in war. . . .

Meanwhile, she will wait quietly here in Belczaczka, where her guardian is so good to her. She will explain gradually to that guardian that Jacek is not so bad as other young men, and she will continue to spin that golden thread which began to wind once again around her heart.

The bullfinch in the Gdansk clock in the drawing room whistled out a late hour, but sleep had completely deserted the young lady.

Lying now in her bed, she fixed her bright eyes on the ceiling and pondered how to deal with her cares and troubles in the meantime. If Jacek had already gone away, it was only because he was running away from her, for according to what she had heard, war was still far off. Because her guardian had not mentioned that the young Cyprianowicz and the Bukojemskis were to go also, she thought that she ought to speak with them, find out something about Jacek and say some kind word which might reach him through them, even if in distant camps during the war.

The young lady did not have much hope that they would come to Belczaczka. It was apparent to her that they had gone over to Jacek's side and that for some time they had looked with disapproval on Pan Pagowski, but she counted on something else.

Simply, in several days, the Feast of Our Lady would occur and there would be a great fair at the parish church in Przytyk, where all the neighboring nobility, together with their wives and children, would arrive. There she would meet Cyprianowicz and the Bukojemskis, if not at the church, then at dinner in the house of the priest, who on that day received everyone.

She also expected that, in the crowds, she would be able to talk freely with them and that she would not meet any kind of resistance from her guardian who, though not too well-disposed toward them recently, could not, because of the memory of the service they had rendered him, completely make a break with them.

The road from Belczaczka to Przytyk was quite long, and Pan Gideon, who did not like to rush, usually made it in conjunction with a night's stay at Radom, or else Jedlinka, if he chose the road through the Jedlinsk district.

This time, because of the floods, they took the longer, though safer, Radom road, and they started on the day before the fair—on wheels, not on runners, for winter had broken suddenly and completely. They were followed by two heavily laden wagons with servants and provisions, and also bedding and carpets for some type of adornment of the rooms they would be staying at.

When they started, the stars were still twinkling, and the sky had barely begun to pale in the east. Pani Winnicka began to sing the canonical hours in the darkness, and the young lady and Pan Gideon chimed in with still very drowsy voices, for the evening before they had gone to bed late because of the preparations for the journey. Only beyond the village and the small forest, in which thousands of crows had their night's lodging, did the ruddy dawn light up the equally ruddy face and sleepy eyes of Panna Sieninska. Her mouth was set to yawn yet again, but when the first ray of the sun struck, lighting up the fields and woods, she began to rouse herself from drowsiness and look around with more alertness, for the clear morning filled her with a certain good hope and gladness in her soul. The day promised to be wonderful indeed, as it was sunny and warm. In the air one could smell the first breath of early spring. After the unparalleled frosts and snows, came days of sun and warmth all at once, to the amazement of the people. It was said that from the New Year the winter had been "cut as if by a knife," and herdsmen foretold from the mooing of cattle longing in cowsheds that the winter would not come back again. Somehow, spring had already arrived. In furrows, in forests, at the north side of woods and along brooklets, sizeable amounts of snow still lay, but the sun was warming them from above, and from beneath them streams and currents flowed out, forming broad overflows in lowlands in which were reflected, as if they were mirrors, wet leafless trees. The damp ridges of fields shone like golden belts in the rays of the sun. At times a strong wind rose, but filled with joyous warmth as if it came directly from the sun; and it blew over the fields, rippling waters and dislodging at the same time thousands of pearls from slender, dark branches.

Because of the thaw and the muddiness of the road, and also because of the weight of the coach, drawn by six horses with no little difficulty, they moved at a very slow pace. As the sun rose higher and higher, it became so warm that Panna Sieninska untied the ribbons of her hood, pushed it back from her head, and began to unbutton the front of her weasel-skin shuba.

"Are you so warm?" inquired Pani Winnicka.

"Spring, auntie! A real spring!" she answered.

And she was so beautiful with her bright, somewhat disheveled hair, pushed out of her hood, with her laughing eyes and rosy face, that Pagowski's stern eyes also became mild. For some time he looked at her, as if seeing her for the first time in his life, after which he said, as if half to himself, half to her:

"Well, well, you are no less pretty than the weather! Upon my word!"
And she smiled at him in answer.

"Oh, how slowly we are moving!" she said after a while. "The road is quite bad. Is it not true, sir, that one should wait until the roads dry up a little if one has a long journey before one?"

Pan Gideon's face darkened; he did not respond to the question, but merely looked out of the coach and said:

"Jedlinka."

"Perhaps we can go to the church there?" inquired Pani Winnicka.

"No we cannot; firstly, because the church is sure to be closed, for the priest has undoubtedly gone to Przytyk also, and secondly, because he has offended me greatly and I will not give him my hand if he approaches me."

After which he added:

"And I request that neither you nor you, Anulka, engage in any type of conversation with him."

A moment of silence followed. Suddenly the tramping of horses was heard behind the coach and the gunshot-like sounds made by the mounts as they pulled out their feet that were stuck in the mud here and there. Then came loud words at either side of the coach:

"Greetings! Greetings!"

It was the Bukojemskis.

"Greetings!" replied Pan Pagowski.

"Are you riding to Przytyk, sir?"

"I go every year. I suppose you gentlemen are going to the fair also?"

"Of course," replied Marek. "One has to be absolved of one's sins before going off to war."

"Isn't it too early for that?"

"Why should it be too early?" asked Lukasz. "The sins that one has will fall off one's shoulders after indulgence, for that is the purpose of indulgence; and the priest will absolve future sins when one faces the enemy, *in particulo mortis*."

"You wish to say: *in articulo*."

"It is all the same, as long as the penance is real."

"How do you explain that?" inquired an amused Pan Pagowski.

"How do I explain that? Father Wior, after our confession the last time, had us give ourselves thirty lashes, and we gave ourselves fifty. For our thinking was thus: if it pleases the heavenly powers—well, let them have their fill!"

Even the serious Pani Winnicka laughed at this, while Panna Sieninska covered her entire face in her muff, as if wishing to warm her nose in it.

Lukasz noticed, as did his brothers, that his answer had aroused laughter, so somewhat offended, they became silent, and for some time the only sounds heard were the grating of chains in the coach, the snorting of the horses, the lapping of mud under the hoofs and the cawing of crows, great flocks of which bathed in the sunlight, flying from the little towns to villages to forests.

"Hey, they sense already that there will be grub in profusion!" said the youngest Bukojemski, following them with his eyes.

"Ha, war is a harvest to them!" noted Mateusz.

"They do not sense it yet, for it is far off," said Pan Pagowski.

"Far off or near, but certain!"

"How do you know, sir?"

"Why, we all know what the talk was about at the local council and what instructions will be given to the Diet."

"True, but it is not known what the other regional dietines decided on."

"Pan Przylubski, who has traveled through much of the land, said that everywhere it was the same."

"What Pan Przylubski?"

"From Olkusz. . . . He recruits for the bishop of Cracow."

"So the bishop of Cracow has already commanded recruitment before the Diet is to adjourn?"

"You see, sir! That is the way it is! This is the best proof that war is certain. The bishop wants a considerable light cavalry regiment. Well, and Pan Przylubski came to these parts on purpose . . . he has heard a bit about us."

"Ho! Ho! Your fame has spread wide throughout the world. . . . Have you enlisted?"

"Of course!"

"All of you?"

"Why not? It is good to have friends at one's side during wartime, and still better brothers."

"Well, and young Cyprianowicz?"

"Cyprianowicz will serve with Taczewski."

Pan Pagowski glanced quickly at the young lady sitting in front, and saw a sudden redness flash across her cheeks, and inquired further:

"Are they confidants already? Under whom will they serve?"

"Under Pan Zbierzchowski."

"What, in the dragoons?"

"In God's name, what are you saying, sir? This is the hussar company of Prince Alexander."

"Well, well! That is no common company."

"Taczewski is no common man."

Pan Gideon was about to say that such a flunky in the hussars could only be a mail deliverer, not a comrade-in-arms, but he checked the comment, fearing that it might come out in the open that his letter was not so diplomatic and his assistance not so considerable as he had told Panna Sieninska, so he merely frowned and said:

"I heard about the leasing out of Wyrabek. How much was given on it?"

"More than you would have given," answered Marek curtly.

Pagowski's eyes flashed momentarily with fierce anger, but he checked himself for the second time, for it occurred to him that further conversation might serve his purpose.

"All the better," he said. "The cavalier must be pleased."

The Bukojemskis, though by nature rather slow-witted, began to brag, trying to outdo each other, just to show Pagowski how little Taczewski thought of him and everyone at Belczaczka.

"Of course!" said Lukasz. "When he was leaving he almost went mad with joy. He sang so that the candles at the inn toppled over. It is true that we had something to drink at parting."

Pan Pagowski glanced again at Panna Sieninska and noticed that her face, usually rosy and full of life and youth, had turned to stone. Her hood had fallen entirely off her head, her eyes were closed as in sleep, and only from the movement of her nostrils and the slight quivering of her chin could one tell that she was not asleep, but was listening, and listening intently.

She was a pitiful sight, but the implacable noble thought:

"If there still is a splinter in your heart, I will tear it out."

And he said aloud:

"I expected as such. . . ."

"What did you expect, sir?"

"That you gentlemen would take to drink at the parting, and that Pan Taczewski would depart singing. Ha! He who chases after fortune must hurry, and if it smiles on a person, perhaps that person can get it."

"Of course!" repeated Lukasz.

Marek add:

"Father Woynowski gave him a letter to Pan Zbierzchowski, who is a known acquaintance and friend, and there, in Zbierzchowa, the soil is such that you could sow onions anywhere you like—and his daughter is there, just fifteen years of age. Don't worry about Taczewski, sir. He will manage and without your help, and without these sands at Radom."

"I do not worry about him," said Pagowski dryly, "but perhaps you gentlemen are also in a hurry, while my coach moves along this mud like a turtle."

"Very well, then, good day!"

"Good day, good day. I am at your service."

"We are likewise!"

Saying this, the brothers moved their horses on with greater impetus, but when they had ridden an arrow's shot from the carriage, they slowed down and began to talk with animation.

"Did you see?" asked Lukasz. "Twice I said 'of course!' and twice I thrust a sword into his heart. He almost burst."

"I did better," said Marek, "for I gave it to the old man and the girl."

"How? Speak, don't hide anything!" exclaimed his brother.

"Didn't you hear?"

"We heard, but repeat it again."

"What I said about Panna Zbierzchowska. Did you notice that the girl paled immediately? I was looking: her hand was on her knee—and she opened it, and closed it, opened it and closed it! Just like a cat who wants to scratch. One could see she was seething with anger."

But Mateusz reined in his horse, and said:

"I felt sorry for her, though. Such a little flower. And do you remember what old Cyprianowicz said?"

"What?" asked with great curiosity Lukasz, Marek and Jan, reining in their horses also.

And he looked at them momentarily with his protruding eyes, after which he said, as if in sorrow:

"Why, I've forgotten."

Meanwhile, in the coach, not only Pagowski, but even Pani Winnicka, who generally knew little of what was happening around her, turned their attention to the changed face of the young lady, and Pani Winnicka asked:

"What is the matter, Anulka? Are you cold?"

"No," replied the girl in a somewhat sleepy, strange voice. "Nothing is the matter, only the air has taken hold of me in a strange way."

And though her voice broke suddenly, she did not have tears in her eyes. On the contrary: In her dry pupils there shone some peculiar, unusual sparks, and her face seemed older.

Seeing this, Pan Pagowski said to himself:

"Would it not be better to strike while the iron is hot?"

CHAPTER 15

NUMEROUS nobles arrived at the fair from near and far places. Present were the Kochanowskis, the Podgajeckis, Silnickis, the Potworowskis, the Sulostowickis, Cyprianowicz and his son, the Bukojemskis and many others. But the greatest interest was roused by the arrival of Prince Michael Czartoryski, the voivod of Sandomierz, who stopped at Przytyk on his way to the Diet at Warsaw and, awaiting the fair, had passed several days in devotion. Everyone was glad of his presence, for he added splendor to the occasion, and at the same time it was possible to learn something about public matters. He himself spoke willingly. He told of the injustice the Porte had committed against the Common-wealth in demarcating Podolia, and of the Tartar forces that had, in defiance of the treaty, devastated Russian lands once again—and he predicted that war was certain. He claimed that an alliance with the Emperor would be concluded and that even supporters of France would not show open opposition to it, since the French court, though *gener-aliter* unfriendly toward the Empire, understood the danger in which the Commonwealth found itself. Whether the Turks would move on Cracow first, or on Vienna, this Prince Michael could not say. But he knew that the enemy was *parat virosque arma* at Adrianople and that aside from these, which were already with Tekeli at Koszyce, nay, in all of Hungary, thousands were assembling from Rumelia, from Asia, and from as far away as the Euphrates and the Tigris, and also from Africa, from the shores of the Red Sea to the waves of the boundless ocean. The Polish nobles listened to this eagerly: the older men, who knew how enormous was the pagan's power, with worry on their faces; the younger men—with fire in their eyes and furrowed brows. But hope and enthusiasm predominated, for the memory of Chocim was fresh, where the present ruling gracious king, at the time a hetman, besieged a Turkish force greater than his own, and routed the enemy with sword and hoof. They were comforted by the thought that the Turks, who rushed with unbridled courage at the armies of all other nations, felt their hearts weaken when they had to stand eye-to-eye in an open field against the terrible Polish cavalry. Still greater hope and great enthusiasm was aroused by Father Woynowski's sermon. Pan Pagowski was somewhat afraid that the sermon would contain, perhaps, references to sins and certain reproaches which could be applied to him and his treatment of Taczewski, but there was none of that. The priest's entire heart and soul had been swept by the war and the mission of the Commonwealth. "Christ," he said, "has chosen you among all nations. He has placed you on guard over others. He has commanded you to stand before His Cross and defend the faith to the last drop of blood, life's *fundamentem*, and to the last breath in you. Before you are the fields of glory, so though blood were to flow at your sides, though arrows and javelins were to be stuck inside you, rise, lion of God, shake your mane and roar so that from that roar fear will strike the very heart of the pagan, and crescents and horsetail ensigns will fall like trees in a tempest."

Thus did he speak to the knightly gathering, because he was an old soldier who had experienced war all his life and knew how it was on the field of battle; so when he began to speak about war it seemed to those present that they were looking at the canvases in the king's castle at Warsaw, on which various battles and Polish victories were painted as if real:

"The companies are starting. Their spears are already in line with their horses' ears, they lean forward in the saddle—a cry of fear among the pagans, and joy in heaven. The Most Holy Mother rushes to the window and calls out: 'Come, my Son, and see how the Poles are attacking!' The Lord Jesus blesses them with the holy cross: 'Good heavens!' He cries, 'Those are my nobles! Those are my soldiers! And their reward is ready for them!' And the holy Archangel Michael strikes his palms against his thighs: 'At them, the bastards! Strike!' That is the way they rejoice there, while these here cut and cut, pommel people, horses, standards, go over the bellies of Janissaries, captured cannon, trampled crescents—they advance to glory, to service, to an accomplished mission, to salvation and to immortality. . . ."

And so when he finally closed with the words: "And now Christ calls to you, and now is the time for your field of glory!" there erupted a shout in the church and a rattling of sabers; and during the religious service, when at the evangelical part of mass every blade grated in its scabbard and steel glittered in the sunlight, it seemed to tender ladies that war had started already, and they began to sob, commending their fathers, husbands and brothers to the Most Holy Lady.

At that point the Bukojemski brothers, whispering among themselves, made a vow not to take to their lips water, milk, or even beer, from right after the fair until Easter, but only contenting themselves with drinks that maintain the warmth of blood and, therefore, courage.

The widespread enthusiasm was so great that even the stern and cold Pan Pagowski could not resist it. He thought for a moment that, though his left arm was missing, he could manage to hold reins in his teeth, and with his right hand take revenge one last time for the wrongs he had suffered from the cursed pagan tribes while at the same time gilding anew his former services to the Commonwealth.

But he did not make any vow, leaving the matter for further thought.

Meanwhile the service proceeded splendidly. From the cemetery were fired cannon lent by the Kochanowskis for important occasions. From the belltowers pealed swinging bells; a tame bear in the gallery pumped the organ with such vigor that the lead pipes almost flew from their mountings; the church filled with incense smoke and shook from the voices of people. The high mass was celebrated by the prelate Tworkowski from Radom, a learned priest, full of maxims, quotations, proverbs and parables, but at the same time merry and thoroughly knowledgeable of the world, because of which he was sought out for advice on all affairs.

Pan Pagowski likewise sought him out, the more so that he was a friend. On the eve of the fair he went to him during confession, but when, in the confessional, he began to explain his intentions regarding Panna Sieninska, the priest postponed the discussion to a later, separate date, saying that he had barely enough time to hear the sins of people. He told him to send the women to Belczaczka on the return trip following the fair and stay with him at Radom, where he could listen to his *procul negotiis* at liberty.

And that is the way it happened—a day later they both sat down before a demijohn of fine Hungarian wine and a plate of roasted almonds, which the prelate happily partook of with his wine.

"*Conticeo*," he said, "*intentumque os teneo*—speak, sir!"

Pan Gideon took a draught from his glass, and his iron eyes glanced at the prelate with a certain dislike—because the latter had not eased his conversation with a proper beginning.

"Hmm! For some reason this is not easy, and I see that it will be more difficult than I imagined."

"Then I will help you, sir. Do you wish to speak of a holy thing?"

"Of a holy thing?"

"Yes. A holy thing that has two heads and four legs."

"What holy thing is that?" asked Pan Gideon in amazement.

"It is a riddle. Solve it, sir!"

"My dear prelate, he who has serious matters in his head has no time for riddles."

"Bah, think a bit, sir!"

"A holy thing that has two heads and four legs?!"

"Yes!"

"Upon my word, I do not know."

"Well! The holy state of matrimony. Is it not so?"

"As God is dear to me, true! Yes, yes, I want to talk to you precisely on this topic."

"This concerns Anulka Sieninska."

"Exactly. You see, reverend father, she is not my relative, or if she is, she is so distant a relative that no one could prove it. . . . But I have become attached to her, for I have brought her up and owe her family gratitude, for what the Pagowskis had in Russia, the same things the Zolkiewskis, the Danilowiczes and the Sobieskis had from the Sieninskis or through the Sieninskis. . . . I would like to leave the orphan what I have, but, in truth, the Pagowski fortune has vanished through Tartar incursions, and only my wife's wealth has remained. . . . This wealth is mine, for it had been willed to me, but there are many relatives on my wife's side. First, there is Pan Grothus, the starost of Rajgrod. Well! I have no fear on this point yet, for the man is good and rich beyond need. It was he, as a matter of fact, who suggested the idea to me, which, to be honest, occurred to me on occasion before, for the desire slept in the bottom of my heart . . . but he awoke it. . . .

"Still, besides Pan Grothus, there are the Sulgostowskis, the Krzepeckis, the Zabierzowskis. . . . Even today these people look with disfavor upon the girl, and what will it be like after my death! If I make a will and leave her my fortune, they will go to court; there will be lawsuits, this tribunal, that tribunal—how will she, poor thing, manage? I cannot leave her like this. There is attachment, there is compassion, there is gratitude—these are strong links, because of which I ask with a clear conscience: should I not secure her even in such a way?"

The priest bit an almond in two and showed the second half to Pan Gideon.

"Sir, do you know why I find this almond tasty? Because it is good! If it were pithy, I would not eat it."

"And so?"

"So Anulka is tasty for you, for she, too, is an almond. And what an almond! But if she were fifty years old, it is certain that your conscience, sir, would not be so troubled about her future."

Pan Pagowski became confused by this, while the priest continued:

"I do not take this ill of you in any way, for there must be a good reason for everything and God has ordained that every man prefers a young turnip to an old one. Only with wine is it different; that is why we willingly reconcile ourselves in regard to wine to the decrees of Providence."

"Yes, true! With the exception of wine, what is young is always better, and Pan Kochanowski wrote humorously that an old man—like an old oak—is taller than a young one. But this is the only question for me: If I leave my wealth to her as my wife no one will dare to even lift a finger, but if I leave it to her as a ward there will be litigation, lawsuits, and perhaps even attacks, and who will defend her from these? Certainly not Pani Winnicka!"

"This is true. . . ."

"But, not being a frivolous person or a simpleminded one, I do not want to decide this alone, and that is why I have come to you, so that you could tell me if I am acting wisely and throw some light on the matter."

The priest thought a while, and then said:

"You see, sir, advice is difficult in such things, and afterward one frequently repeats to oneself what Boethius said: '*Si tacuisses, philosophus mansisses*' [If you remain silent, you will be a philosopher] or what Job said: '*Stultus quoque si tacuerit, sapiens reputabitur*' [Even a fool if he remain silent will be considered a wise man]. Your intention, in so far as it arises from warm affection, is justified, and in so far as it also arises from concern about the girl's welfare, is even praiseworthy. But will not some wrong be done the girl by this, will not one have to use threats or fear to lead her *ad altare*? For I have heard that she and Jacek Taczewski are in love, and speaking sincerely and without mincing words, I have seen this, and not just once, as a frequent guest at your place."

"What have you seen?" asked Pagowski suddenly.

"Nothing sinful, but *signa* through which one recognizes intimacy and love: I have seen more than once how they held each other's hands longer than necessary, how they followed each other with their eyes; I have seen how once he sat in a tree and dropped cherries down to her apron, and how they were so taken up with each other that the cherries fell past the apron to the ground; I have seen how, when she was looking at flying storks, she leaned fully on him, seemingly unintentionally, and then (women are always cunning) scolded him for getting too close to her. And what else? Various other such *experimenta* which prove hidden cravings. You will say, sir, that this is nothing. Of course it is nothing! But that she felt an urge toward him as much, or even more, than he did toward her, only a blind man could not see, and I am surprised that you, sir, did not see it, and even more so, that if you did see it, you did not stop it in view of your own intentions."

Pan Pagowski had seen and known this, but the prelate's words still made a harsh impression.

It is one thing when something painful is hidden in one's heart, and another thing when the hand of another takes that pain and exposes it to the surface. So now his face reddened, his eyes became bloodshot; thick, knotty veins stood out on his forehead, and he began to suddenly gasp and breathe so quickly that the alarmed prelate asked:

"What is the matter, sir?"

He gave a sign with his hand that it was nothing, but he did not reply.

"Drink some wine, sir," cried the priest.

Pagowski stretched out his arm, took the glass with a trembling hand and raised it to his lips, then drank, snorted and whispered:

"I became a bit muddled."

"Because of what I told you?"

"No. This has been happening to me for some time, and now I am *fatigus* with the fast, the journey and this early, unexpected spring."

"Then perhaps it is better not to wait for May to be bled."

"I agree, but right now I need to rest a moment and then we will return to the subject at hand."

A long period of time passed, however, before Pagowski completely recovered; finally, however, he cooled down; the veins on his forehead subsided, his heart began to beat with a regular rhythm, and he said:

"I will not say that I lack strength, and if I were to squeeze this silver goblet with my remaining hand I believe I could crush it easily. But health and strength are not the same thing, though one and the other are in God's hand."

"Man's life is precarious!"

"It is precisely because of this that one has to act promptly. You speak, reverend father, of Taczewski and the affection that the young people may have felt for each other. I will say openly: I was not blind to this. I also saw what was developing, but only recently. For, do not forget, that until recently this was a green berry, which even now has barely ripened. He came every day, this is true! But perhaps because he had little to eat at home; besides, I received him, as it were, through compassion. Father Woynowski taught him Latin and how to use a saber, and I gave him something to eat. And that was all. Do not forget also that it was only a year ago that he grew into a young man. I looked upon them as children who felt like playing various games and pranks; I considered this a normal thing. But that such a pauper should dare to think—and of whom? of Panna Sieninska—this, I admit, never came to my head, and only lately have I even thought of such a thing."

"Bah! A pauper is a pauper, but Taczewski. . . ."

"The starveling! No, reverend father, he who licks another's plate can invite a dog for company. When I realized the situation, I began to look at him with more care, and do you know what I found out? That not only is he a fop and starveling, but also a venomous reptile ever ready to bite the hand that feeds it. Thank God that he is not around—he has left—but upon leaving he bit not only me, but the innocent maiden."

"Is that so?"

And Pan Pagowski began to relate to him what had transpired, painting Taczewski's deed with such blackness that one could immediately call the executioner.

"Have no fear, reverend father," he said finally. "The Bukojemskis drank to the full to Anulka during our drive to Przytyk. Ha! So much so that it overflowed, and now the situation is such that that girl will never feel such an abhorrence for any creature of God as for that whippersnapper, that degenerate, that rascal!"

"Restrain yourself, sir, or your blood will boil again."

"True. And I did not wish to speak of him, but of this, that I do not want to wrong the girl in any way, nor force her either. Persuasion is another thing. But this should be done by a outside individual, a friend of hers and mine, and at the same time a man renowned for his dignity and great wit, who can use urbane phrases and touch the heart and convince the mind. That is why I want to ask that you do this, my noteworthy reverend father. You will not refuse me, not only *per amicitiam* for me, but also for this reason, that the affair is just and honorable."

"It is a question of her good and of yours, so I will not refuse," said the prelate. "But I would like to have time to decide how best to accomplish this."

"Then I will go straightaway to the barber and have myself bled, so as to return home with a clear mind, while you think out a plan. It will not be difficult for you, and I think that on the other side there will be no obstacle."

"There could only be one obstacle, my brother."

"What obstacle?"

"Friendship should tell the truth, so I will speak openly. You are an honorable person—this I know!—but a bit stubborn. You have this reputation, and you have it because everyone who depends on you fears you tremendously. Not only the peasants, concerning whom you have quarreled with Father Woynowski, not only retainers and clerks, but your household staff. Taczewski feared you, Pani Winnicka fears you, and also the girl fears you. Usually two matchmakers arrive; therefore I will do what I can, but I cannot guarantee this other one will not ruin my labor."

For a moment Pagowski's eyes flashed with anger, for he did not like to have the truth told in his presence, but puzzlement overcame anger, so he asked:

"Of what are you talking about? What other matchmaker?"

And the priest replied:

"Fear."

CHAPTER 16

BUT they were not able to leave that same day for Belczaczka, as Pagowski weakened considerably after being bled and said himself that he needed rest. The following day, however, he felt more levelheaded, as if rejuvenated, and neared his home in good spirits, though with a certain unease. Taken up entirely with his thoughts, he spoke little along the way with the priest, but when they were entering the village and he felt his unease increasing, he said:

"It is strange to me. I always used to return to my home as the master of the house, and others were concerned with what face I would greet them, and now I am concerned about how they will greet me."

The priest responded:

"Virgil said *'amor omnia vincit'* [love conquers everything], but he forgot to add that it also *mutat*, changes everything. This Delilah will not cut your hair, for you are bald, sir, but it is certain that I will see you spinning at her feet, as Hercules spun at the feet of Omphale."

"Well, that is not my nature! I always knew how to keep both my servants and my family in hand."

"So people say, but it is precisely for that reason that you deserve someone to keep you on a short leash."

"A pleasant leash," replied Pagowski with atypical joy.

They drove very slowly, for in the village the mud was terrible; and since they had started without haste from Radom at midday, night had already fallen. In the cottages to their sides light from dying-out fires in hearths issued from windows and stretched across the road in red strips. Here and there near the fence loomed some human form, a woman or a man, who, seeing the travelers, quickly removed any head covering and made a deep bow. It was immediately evident from these excessively low bows that Pagowski knew how to keep his people in hand, indeed, even more in hand than necessary, and that not without cause did Father

Woynowski reprimand him for his excessive severity. But at the moment the old noble felt softer in his heart than usual, so, looking at the bowed figures and the sunken windows of the cottages, he said:

"I will grant some favor to these subjects whose part she always takes."

"Oh, do so, do so!" replied the prelate.

And they became silent. Pan Gideon was occupied for a while with his own thoughts, after which he spoke again:

"I know, reverend father, that you need no advice, but you have to tell her that the good deed is being done for her benefit and that I am above all thinking of her; and in case of some resistance—which I do not expect, but who knows?—perhaps you could scold her. . . ."

"Sir, you said that you did not want to force her."

"I said so, but it is one thing when I threaten and scold, and another thing when someone else reproaches her for ingratitude, particularly someone who is a man of the cloth."

"Leave the matter to me, sir, since I've undertaken it and will add my efforts to carrying it out in the best way. Nevertheless, I will tell you that I will speak to the girl *delicatissime*. . . ."

"Good, good! Just one more word. She feels great abhorrence for Taczewski, but if his name would be brought up, it would be well to say something more against him."

"If he has acted as you have said, then that is not needed."

"We are arriving. Well! In the name of the Father, the Son . . ."

"And the Holy Ghost. Amen!"

They arrived, but no one came out to meet them, for the wheels made no rattle because of the mud, and the dogs did not bark at people or horses they knew. In the hall it was dark, for the servants apparently were sitting in the kitchen, so when Pan Pagowski first called out, "Is anyone here?" no one showed up, and when he called out again, this time in a sharper voice, the young maiden herself appeared.

She came holding a candle in her hand, but since she was in its light while they were in darkness, she did not see them immediately and stopped by the door. They did not speak for a moment: firstly, because it seemed to them that it was a special omen that she was the first to appear before them and, secondly, that her beauty stunned them as if they had never seen her before. The fingers that grasped the candle seemed rosy and transparent; the light flickered over her bosom, lighting up her lips and small face, which seemed a little drowsy and sad, perhaps because her eyes remained in deep shadow. Her forehead and wonderfully bright hair, forming a sort of crown over her, were bathed in the light. And so she stood, surrounded by darkness but herself luminous and quiet, and seeming, quite simply, like an angel created from the rosy brightness.

"Oh, as God is dear to me, a perfect vision!" said the prelate.

And Pagowski exclaimed:

"Anulka!"

Then she ran over to them and, leaving the candle on the mantle of the hearth, fell to greeting them with joy. Pagowski pressed her to his heart with affection, commanded her to rejoice at the arrival of such a distinguished guest, one who was renowned as an adviser in all matters, and when they entered the dining room after finishing their greetings, he asked:

"Is supper over already?"

"No. The servant is to bring it in from the kitchen, and that is why no one was in the hall."

And the priest glanced at the old noble and asked:

"Should we not wait?"

"No, no," said Pagowski quickly. "Pani Winnicka will bustle in here momentarily."

Somehow or other, Pani Winnicka did indeed rush in soon—and fifteen minutes later they sat down to heated wine and scrambled eggs. Father Tworkowski ate and drank well, but at the end of supper his face became serious and, turning to the young maiden, he said:

"My gracious young lady! God knows why people call me a counselor and why they so frequently seek my advice, but since your guardian does so, I must speak with you on a certain serious topic that he has entrusted to my poor wit."

When Pan Pagowski heard this, the veins on his forehead swelled again, while the young maiden paled somewhat and rose anxiously, as she suspected, for some unknown reason, that the priest would talk to her about Jacek.

But the prelate said: "Let us speak privately in the other room!"

And they left.

Pan Pagowski sighed deeply once and then a second time, drummed the table with his fingers, then rose, and feeling the need of talking away, with whatever words, his internal emotions, he said to Pani Winnicka:

"Have you ever noticed how all the relatives of my deceased wife hate Anulka?"

"Especially the Krzepeckis," replied Pani Winnicka.

"Ha! They almost gnash their teeth when they see her, but soon they will gnash their teeth even harder!"

"Why so?"

"You will also find out soon enough, but meanwhile one has to get a bed together for the prelate!"

After a while Pan Pagowski was alone. Two servants entered to clear the dishes after supper, but he sent them away with a sudden burst of anger, and it became quiet in the dining room, with the exception of the great Gdansk clock that repeated loudly and with gravity: ticktock, ticktock, ticktock! . . . Pagowski placed his hand on his bald head and began to pace the room. He approached the door behind which the prelate was conversing with Panni Sieninska, but he only heard murmurs in which he did indeed distinguish the prelate's voice but not his words. So, in turns, he walked and stopped. He went to the window, for it seemed to him that it would be less stuffy there, and for a time he looked with vacant eyes at the sky, across which the wind was driving scattered spring clouds with illuminated crests, over which the pale moon appeared to rise higher and higher. Whenever the moon became hidden, Pan Pagowski was seized by evil forebodings. He saw through the window the black branches of nearby trees swinging in the wind as if in torment, and his thoughts swung the same way—wandering, evil thoughts, resembling pangs of conscience and dull feelings that something bad would happen for which he would suffer punishment soon. . . . But when it grew bright outside, once again a better spirit entered him. Everyone, after all, has a right to think of his own happiness—and as to Taczewski, what does it matter what such people do! What was at issue here? The future peace and well-being of a girl. And if life smiled on him a little in his old age, he was deserving of this. Only this was real, and the rest is wind, wind! . . .

Once again he felt his head reel and black spots danced before his eyes, but this lasted very briefly. He began to walk again and approached the door, behind which his fate hung in the balance. Meanwhile the wicks of the candles on the table lengthened, and the room darkened. At times the voice of the priest carried, so that words would have reached Pagowski's ear, if not for the loud and continual ticktock of the clock. It was easy to understand that such a conversation could not end quickly, but nevertheless, Pan Gideon's nervousness grew and grew, evolving into certain odd questions joined with the past, with memories of not only old sufferings and adversity, but also old unexpiated faults, grievous old sins—and recent wrongs inflicted not only on Taczewski, but on other people.

"For what and why should you be happy?" asked his conscience.

And at that moment he would have given God knows what if even Pani Winnicka would return to the room so that he would not have to be alone with his thoughts. But Pani Winnicka was occupied somewhere else, in another part of the house, and in this room only the clock repeated ticktock! ticktock! and his conscience asked:

"For what should God reward you?"

Pan Pagowski felt now that if that girl, similar to a flower and to an angel at the same time, should pass him by—then a darkness would descend over his life that would last until that hour in which the night of death would arrive. . . .

And suddenly the door opened and Panna Sieninska entered the room, pale, with tears in her eyes, and behind her was the priest.

"Are you crying?" asked Pan Pagowski in a hoarse, stifled voice.

"From gratitude, guardian!" she exclaimed, stretching her hands to him.

And she fell at his knees.

CHAPTER 17

THAT evening, though it was late in the night, Pani Winnicka went to the room of her relation and, finding the young lady still dressed, began to talk to her.

"I cannot recover from my astonishment," she said, "for I would have sooner expected death than that such an idea should have come to your guardian's head."

"I also did not expect this."

"How is it so? Is it true? I myself do not know what to think—should I be glad or not? For, of course, as a spiritual person, the prelate has better judgement than the laity, and he is right when he says that you will have a roof over your head until death, and a roof that will be yours and not another's; but, on the other hand, your guardian is advanced in years" —here Pani Winnicka lowered her voice— "are you not a little afraid of him?"

"It has happened, and there is no purpose in thinking about it!" replied Panna Sieninska.

"What do you mean?"

"I mean that I should be grateful to him for shelter, for a piece of bread, and that it is a poor payment—my person, whom no one else would want—but since he wants it, then, that too, is a favor on his part."

"He wanted this a long time ago," said the old woman mysteriously. "He called me over today after he had spoken with you; I thought that there had been something wrong with the supper and that he would scold me—but this was not so! I saw that he was rather cheerful—and suddenly he told me the news. My legs almost gave way. So he says: 'Why have you turned into a pillar of salt like Lot's wife? Am I such an old fogey?' 'No!' I replied. 'Because this is so unexpected!' And he said: 'I've had this idea for a long time, but it was like a fish at the bottom of the river before someone helped it to swim to the surface. And do you know who it was, my dear lady?' I was certain that it was the prelate Tworkowski, but he said: 'It wasn't Father Tworkowski at all, but Pan Grothus. . . .'"

A moment of silence followed.

"But I thought it was Pan Taczewski," said Panna Sieninska through set teeth.

"How's that? Why Taczewski?"

"To show that he doesn't care for me."

"But certainly you know that Taczewski did not see your guardian?"

And the other began to repeat feverishly:

"Yes! I know! He had something else on his mind! No matter! I do not want to know anything. I do not, I do not! It has happened, and it is good that it has happened!"

Dry, convulsive sobbing shook her breast. After a while she repeated again: "It is good that it has happened!" Then she suddenly knelt down to pray, something which both women usually did together every day.

The following day Anulka came down to the dayroom with a calm face. But something had changed in her, something remained unexpressed; something had shut itself up in her. She was not sad, but she looked several years older and had inside her a certain quiet dignity, so that Pan Pagowski, who thus far had taken into account only himself, began unconsciously to consider her also. In general he was unable to comprehend all this, and it particularly appeared strange to him that he felt a certain dependence on her. He began to fear those thoughts which she did not express but which she could have hidden in her heart—and he tried to prevent them and put in their place other thoughts, thoughts that he wished she would have. Even the silence of Pani Winnicka weighed on him and seemed suspicious, so he improvised, talked to no end, joked, but at times a flash of impatience flew across his steely eyes.

Meanwhile news of his engagement spread through the neighborhood. He made no secret of this; on the contrary, he sent letters announcing the engagement to Cyprianowicz in Jedlinka and his closest neighbors; and likewise wrote letters to the Kochanowskis, the Podlowiskis, the Sulgostowskis, to Pan Grothus and to the Krzepeckis, and even to the distant relatives of his wife, with an invitation to the betrothal, after which the marriage would immediately take place.

In truth, Pan Pagowski actually would have preferred to receive a dispensation from the banns, but unfortunately the Lenten season was upon them and one had to wait until Easter would come and pass. So he took both women to Radom where the young lady was to arrange her wedding outfit, and where he would buy horses more splendid than those in the Belczaczka stables.

Reports came to him that among the relatives who had expected to inherit everything not only after his deceased wife's death, but even after his own, there was as much activity as in a beehive. This made him glad, however, for he despised them to the depth of his soul and was always planning ways he could do them mischief. These tidings of meetings, counsels and secret conferences made his stay in Radom seem short, and when finally the wedding outfit was finished and team of horses bought together with new horse-collars, they returned to Belczaczka right on Easter eve. Guests began to arrive almost at the same time, for the betrothal was to take place on the third day after Easter.

First came the Krzepeckis, who were the nearest relatives and neighbors: the father, an old man almost eighty years old, with a vulturine face and renowned as a miser; his three daughters, of which the youngest, Tekla, was a pretty and merry girl—and the older ones, Agnieszka and Joanna, past their prime, hotheaded, with constantly flushed cheeks; and finally the son, Marcian, nicknamed Stump in the neighborhood.

He bore the name justly, for at first sight he did, indeed, look like a thick stump. His chest and shoulders were massive, but his legs were bandied and so short that he almost looked like a dwarf. His arms, moreover, reached his knees. Some thought him a hunchback, but he was not hunchbacked; his head was just so deprived of a neck and placed so low over his body, that his high shoulders almost reached his ears. Protruding, lustful eyes peered out of that head, and his face was like that of a billy goat; and this resemblance was strengthened by the small beard he wore, as if purposefully defying popular custom.

He never served in the military, for he had been laughed out of service, as a result of which he had had many duels in his time. In his short, squat body resided uncommon strength, and people feared him, for he was a brawler and an idler, always on the lookout for a fight, and exhibiting a type of animal fierceness in any incident. Once, in Radom, he seriously wounded his cousin's brother, a handsome and worthy young man who almost died of his injuries. His sisters feared him, and even his father, while he himself felt respect only for Jacek, whose skill at the saber was known to him, and for the Bukojemskis, one of whom—namely, Lukasz—once threw him over a fence in Jedlinka like a bundle of straw.

He had the reputation of being a great lecher—and this was deserved. Pan Pagowski threw him out of his home several years ago because he had looked too much in a goatlike way at Panna Sieninska, still a young girl at the time. But since several years had passed since that incident and, as they saw each other in Radom, and in the houses of neighbors, he invited him now, together with the entire family, to the celebration.

Immediately after the Krzepeckis came the Sulgostowskis, twin brothers who so resembled each other that when they put on identical garments no one could tell them apart; then three remote Sulgostowskis from beyond Przytyk—and the numerous and handsome Zabierzowski family, formed of nine people. From nearby came Pan Cyprianowicz, but alone, for his son had gone already to the cavalry; Pan Podlodowski, the starost, once the plenipotentiary of the powerful lord in Zamosc; Pan and Pani Kochanowski, priests from Przytyk, the prelate Tworkowski from Radom, who was to bless the rings—and many lesser nobles from near and distant places; some even without invitations, in the correct notion that a guest, even if a complete stranger, will always be greeted with open arms—and if there is a chance of eating and drinking, one should not miss it.

So the courtyard of Belczaczka teemed with carts and coaches, the stables with horses, the outbuildings with servants of all types, and the mansion with colorful robes, sabers, shaved heads; and there was much Latin spoken, the chattering of women, a profusion of trimmings, laces, and various ornaments. Maids were flying around with hot water, tipsy servants with demijohns of excellent wine. From morning till night the kitchen was smoking like a tar pit, while the windows of the mansion were lit up and glowed so that the entire area thereabout was visible. And amid all this confusion Pan Pagowski went from room to room, a bit haughty, grave, but at the same time rejuvenated, decked out in a robe and a saber that glittered with jewels, which Panna Sieninska had inherited as her only dowry from once wealthy ancestors. He went about, entertaining; at times when he became dizzy, he supported himself with his hand against the arms of chairs, and then once again would move about, seeing to guests and personages, shuffling his feet as he approached older women. But above all he followed "his Anulka" with eyes that were more and more enamored. And she, in that colorful crowd, amid glances there were frequently filled with animosity and jealousy, and at times lascivious, blossomed as pure as a lily, sweet, perhaps somewhat sad or conscious only of the significance of what was to meet her, and lost in thought.

Then on the third day of the holiday, on Tuesday, the cannons of the house thundered in the yard, announcing to the guests and the estate that the moment of the betrothal had arrived.

Then, all the guests arranged themselves in a half circle in the parlor: both the women and the men, in splendid costumes changing like the colors of the rainbow in the light of glowing candles; and opposite them stood Pan Pagowski and Panna Anulka Sieninska. Silence descended, and the eyes of all were fixed on the bride, who, with downcast eyes, with concentration and dignity in her face, neither smiling nor sad, seemed as if asleep. The prelate Tworkowski, dressed in a surplice, with Tekla Krzepecka by his side holding a silver tray with rings on it, advanced from the half circle and began to address the future couple. He spoke learnedly, long and eloquently, explaining what the *sponsalia de futuro* were and what a great worth the Church placed on betrothals since the first days of Christianity. He quoted Tertullian and the Council of Trent, and the opinions of various learned canonists, after which he turned to Pan Pagowski and Panna Sieninska and began to expostulate on how wise their decision was, what a great testimony they were giving to each other, and how their future happiness depended solely on themselves. Those present listened to this with admiration, but at the same time with impatience, for as relatives from whom an inheritance was slipping they looked at the union with displeasure. Even Pan Gideon, who had become dizzy from standing too long, began to shift from one leg to the other and give signs with his eyes to the prelate to finish. The prelate was slow to pick up on this, but finally blessed the rings and put them on the fingers of the betrothed. At that point the cannon thundered once again in the courtyard, and from the gallery in the dining room was heard a loud band of five skilled Jewish musicians from Radom. The guests now came in turn to congratulate their host and the young lady—for the most part sourly and insincerely. The two old maids, the Krzepeckis, simply curtsied with a sneer before their "aunt," and Pan Marcian, upon kissing her hand, commended himself to her future graces with such a goatlike glance that Pan Pagowski should have driven him out of the mansion a second time for good measure.

But others—more distant relatives who were better people and less greedy—gave sincere and warm wishes. Meanwhile, the door of the dining room was thrown wide open. Pan Pagowski gave his arm to his betrothed, and other couples moved after them amid the flickering and wavering of the candles caused by a sudden cold gust coming into the hall. From this hall flowed the servants, already half drunk, bearing an immeasurable amount of food and demijohns of wine. Because of the constant opening of doors, the air became so cold in the dining room that the banqueters, when they sat to table, were seized with shivers from the first moment, and due to the continual flickering of candles the entire room, despite the exquisite service, seemed to them rather dark and gloomy. But it was to be expected that the wine would quickly warm the blood, and Pan Pagowski did not begrudge wine. He was a rather stingy person in everyday life, but on special occasions he liked to show off so that people would long talk about him. So it happened now. Behind every banqueter stood an attendant with a mossy demijohn, and under the table were even hidden a number of servants with bottles, ready to refill a glass at once should a guest, unable to drink more, place his glass between his knees. Large drinking glasses, goblets, cups glittered before every tablesetting, but before the ladies were smaller Italian or French glasses.

The guests did not, however, occupy the entire table, for Pan Pagowski had more plates set than the banqueters present. The prelate cast his eyes on those empty places and began to praise the hospitality of the house and the host, but since he always had a very resonant voice and, besides, had risen somewhat from his chair, wishing to rearrange the folds of his soutane, those present supposed that he wanted to offer the first toast, and all became silent.

"We're listening!" several voices were heard.

"Well, there is no reason," replied the priest merrily. "This is no toast yet, though the time will soon come for that, for I see how some of you gentlemen are knocking your heads together in time, and Pan Kochanowski is already whispering to himself and counting something on his fingers. It can't be helped, my dear sirs! From whom can we expect rhymes if not from Kochanowski. I only wanted to say that it is a praiseworthy old Polish custom to leave a place for unexpected guests."

"Bah," said Pan Pagowski, "as the house is lit up in the night someone may come in from the darkness. . . ."

"Who might come?" spoke up Pan Kochanowski.

"Perhaps Pan Grothus?"

"No . . . Pan Grothus is at the Diet. If someone comes, it will be someone completely unexpected."

"But we will not hear him, for the ground is soft."

"Not true! The dog is barking by the window. Someone will show up."

"No one will come up from this side, for the windows face the orchard."

"Truthfully speaking, the dog is howling, not barking."

And it was so. The dog barked once, twice, a third time, then the barking turned into a low, dreary howling.

Pan Pagowski gave a start despite himself, for he remembered how many, many years ago, in another place, at his manor which stood a mile from the Pomeranian castle in Ruthenia, dogs had howled in the same way before a sudden Tartar attack.

And the thought came to Panna Sieninska that she had no right to expect anyone anymore, and that whoever should arrive out of the darkness at the lit-up house would come too late.

But to the other participants this seemed somewhat strange, the more so that a second dog joined in with the first—and a double howling was heard near the window.

So, despite themselves, they listened in awkward silence, broken after a while by Marcian Krzepecki.

"What matters to us a guest at whom a dog howls?" he said.

"Wine!" cried out Pan Pagowski.

But the wine cups were full, so there was no need to refill them. Old Krzepecki, Marcian's father, rose ponderously from his chair, apparently wishing to speak. All turned their eyes to him, while the old people began to cup their ears to hear better what he would have to say; but he only managed to move his lips for a long moment, causing his chin to almost touch his nose, for he was completely toothless.

Meanwhile, despite the fact that a thaw had set in and the ground was soft, from the other side of the manor came a dull rattle—and it was heard rather long, as if someone had ridden two times about the area. So old Krzepecki, who was about to raise his glass, set it down on the table again and began to look at the door.

All followed his example.

"See who has come!" said Pan Pagowski to an attendant.

The attendant dashed out and returned immediately.

"There is no one," he said.

"That's strange," replied the prelate Tworkowski. "The sound could be heard clearly."

"We all heard it," said one of the Sulgostowski twins.

"And the dogs have stopped howling," added the other twin.

Suddenly the door to the hall, evidently not closed well by the attendant, opened by itself and such a strong gust of wind came in that it extinguished a dozen or so candles at once.

"What is that? Shut the door! The candles are going out!" several voices cried out.

But along with the wind came, as it were, fear. Pani Winnicka, a timid and superstitious person, began to cross herself loudly:

"In the name of the Father, the Son, and the Holy Ghost. . . ."

"Quiet, woman!" said Pan Pagowski.

After which, turning to Panna Anulka, he kissed her hand.

"My joy cannot be lessened by an extinguished candle," he said, "and may God grant that I be as happy until I die as I am at this moment—is that not right, my Anulka?"

"Yes, guardian," she said.

"Amen!" finished the prelate.

And rising, he began to speak:

"Honorable Ladies and Gentlemen! Since that unexpected sound apparently nipped the king's cupbearer Pan Krzepecki's thought process, let me be the first to speak of the affection which warm our *corda* for the future newlyweds. So, before we cry out 'O Hymen, O Hymenaios,' before we, in Roman fashion, begin to call Thalassius, that fair youth (and may God grant that this happen as soon as possible), let us raise *ex imo* this first toast to their prosperity and future happiness: *Vivant, crescant, floreant!*"

"*Vivant, vivant!*" thundered all the guests.

The Radom band was heard, and outside the windows the drivers began to crack their whips in the darkness. The servants also raised a shout throughout the entire house, and in the dining room, amid endless cheers and the gulping down of wine, was heard:

"*Vivant, crescant, floreant!*"

Long lasted these cries, the stamping of feet, the sounds from horns and the cracking of whips—and it only quieted down when Pan Pagowski stood up, raised his glass, and said in a loud voice:

"My most gracious and most dear guests and relatives! Before I express with inadequate words my complete gratitude, first let me thank you for the brotherly and neighborly goodwill that you have shown me by coming in such numbers under my poor roof. . . ."

But the words "under my poor roof" were uttered with a strange, subdued and almost submissive tone, after which he sat down again and bent his head, so that his forehead actually rested on the table—while the guests were amazed that a man usually so cold and proud would speak with such sincerity.

They thought, however, that great happiness melts even the hardest of hearts—and waiting for what he would say further, they looked at his gray head, which continued to rest on the edge of the table.

Voices were heard: "Silence! We are listening!"

And indeed a deep silence fell on the gathering.

But Pan Pagowski did not move at all.

"What is the matter, sir? What is it? Dear God!"

"Speak, sir!" cried out the prelate.

But Pan Pagowski answered only with a terrible wheezing, while his neck and arms began to shake all of a sudden.

Panna Sieninska jumped up from her seat, white as a sheet, and began to cry out in a horrified voice:

"Guardian! Guardian!"

At the table arose dismay and confusion. Cries and questions resounded. Pagowski was surrounded by a circle; the prelate grabbed him by the shoulders and leaned him back in his chair; some began to throw water on him, others yelled to take him to bed and have him bled as quickly as possible. Some of the women knelt down, some ran about the room as if crazy, lamenting shrilly and wailing—while Pan Pagowski, his head thrown back, the veins in his forehead swollen like cords and his eyes closed, was wheezing and rattling louder and louder.

The unexpected guest had arrived indeed from the darkness, and entered his manor—a guest terrible and merciless.

CHAPTER 18

AT the command of the prelate, the servants picked up the sick man and bore him to the other end of the manor, to the chancellery, which also served Pan Pagowski as a bedroom. The village blacksmith was sent for, as he knew how to bleed and bled people as well as animals. After a moment it was found out that he was in front of the manor, together with the rest of the crowd gathered there for the food and drink—but unfortunately he was completely drunk. Pani Winnicka remembered that Father Woynowski was renowned in the area as being an excellent doctor, so a carriage was sent with all speed for him, though it seemed clear that all this would be for naught and that the sick man was past any help.

So it was. With the exception of Panna Sieninska, Pani Winnicka, the two Krzepeckis, and Pan Zabierzowski, who dabbled a bit in medicine, Father Woynowski did not allow anyone into the chancellery, in case a crowd might hinder help. But all the other banqueters, the women as well as the men, gathered in the neighboring guest chamber where beds had been prepared for the men, and all stood there like a flock of timid sheep, filled with worry, fear, curiosity, and watching the door, they waited for news, while some spoke quietly of the terrible occurrence and the omens which had announced the misfortune.

"Did you notice how the candles quivered, and how the flames were somewhat blackish? One can see that Death had covered them," said one of the Sulgostowskis in a whisper.

"Death was among us and we did not know."

"Dogs howled at it."

"And that clatter? Perhaps that was Death arriving?"

"One can see that God did not want to let the marriage happen, which would have been an injustice to the family."

Further whispering was interrupted by the appearance of Pani Winnicka and Marcian Krzepecki. She went quickly through the room, hurrying to get a reliquary which warded off evil spirits, while he was surrounded immediately by a crowd.

"What is happening? How is he?"

Marcian shrugged his shoulders, raising them so that his head nearly touched his chest, and said:

"His is still rattling."

"There is no hope?"

"None!"

All of a sudden through the open door came the distinct solemn words of the prelate Tworkowski:

"*Ego te absolvo a peccatis tuis — et ob omnibus censuris, in nomine Patris et Filii et Spiritus Sancti. Amen.*"

Everyone knelt and began to pray. Pani Winnicka passed between the kneeling people, holding the reliquary with both hands. Marcian followed her inside the chancellery and closed the door.

But it did not remain closed for long, for a quarter of an hour later Marcian appeared at the threshold and called out in his squeaky, clarinetist voice:

"He's dead!"

Then with the words "Eternal rest," they moved one after the other into the chancellery to bid their last farewell to the deceased.

Meanwhile, at the other end of the house, in the dining room, heinous things began to happen. The servants of Belczaczka had hated Pagowski as much as they feared him, so it seemed to them that with his death would come a time of relief, joy and unpunished licence. For the visiting servants an opportunity arose for revelry, so all of the servants, those of the house as well as those from outside, drunk since the afternoon, more or less, threw themselves now at the food and wine. Attendants raised to their lips whole flagons of Gdansk vodka, Petersburg wine, malmsey and Hungarian wine; others, more greedy for food, seized pieces of meat and cake. The snow-white tablecloth became stained in a twinkling of the eye with pools of manifold liquids. In the commotion, chairs and table candlesticks were overturned. Ornamented cut glasses slipped from drunken hands and broke with a crash on the floor. Here and there quarrels and fights arose; some stole the service outright. In a word, an orgy began, the sound of which reached the other side of the house.

Marcian Krzepecki, followed by the two Sulgostowskis and one other guest, rushed to the source of the outcries, and seeing what was happening, they seized their sabers. In the first moments the commotion increased even more. The Sulgostowskis went no further than striking the drunks with the flat of their sabers, but Marcian Krzepecki was seized by mad fury. His protruding eyes projected even more, his teeth flashed under his mustache, and he began to simply cut up whoever was before him. Several servants were covered with blood, others took shelter under the table, while the rest crowded together in disorderly flight through the door, and he cut at the throng, crying out:

"Rascals! Sons of bitches! I am lord here! I am the master of the house!"

He drove them out into the hall, from where his shrill voice was still heard:

"Sticks! Lashes!"

And those that stood in the room, as if amid rubble, looked at each other with shocked expressions and shook their heads.

"I have never seen such a thing in my life," said one of the Sulgostowskis.

And the other said:

"A strange death and strange circumstances. If you look at this, you would say that the Tartars have invaded."

"Or evil spirits," added Zabierzowski. "A terrible night."

They commanded, however, those hiding under the table to come out to bring some sort of order to the dining room. The servants came out, sobered completely from terror, and they swiftly went to work, and in the meantime Marcian returned.

He was calmer now, only his lips still trembled from anger.

"They won't forget that for a long time!" he said, addressing those present. "But I thank you, gentlemen, for helping me to punish those scoundrels. It will not be easier for them here than when the deceased was around! My head on this!"

Both of the Sulgostowskis glanced at him sharply, and one said:

"You do not have to thank us for anything, just as we don't have to thank you."

"What do you mean?"

"Why have you placed yourself as the sole judge here?" asked one of the twins.

And he immediately began to jump up and down on his short bowlegs, as if wanting to reach their eyes, and replied:

"Because I have the right! I have the right! I have the right!"

"What right?"

"A better one that yours!"

"What? Have you read the will?"

"What is a will to me?" Here he blew on the palm of his hand. "This? Wind! To whom has he willed his property? His wife? But where is there a wife? Well? I am the next of kin here. We—the Krzepeckis—not you!"

"We will see. May you die!"

"May you die! Get out of here!"

"You goat, you stump! Just wait and see! You tell us to get out of here? Take better care of your goat head!"

"Are you threatening me?"

Here Marcian shook his saber and advanced toward the brothers, while they also grasped their hilts.

But at that moment the outraged voice of Father Tworkowski was heard behind them:

"Honorable gentlemen! The dead man's body is not cold yet."

The Sulgostowskis became terribly ashamed, and one of them said:

"Father prelate, nothing concerns us here, for we have our piece of bread and do not desire that of others. But this viper is beginning to stab and wants to throw people out of this house."

"What people? Whom?"

"Whomever. Today us, whom he has told to get out, and tomorrow perhaps those women orphans living under this roof."

"That is not true! That is not true!" exclaimed Marcian.

And, winding himself into a ball all of a sudden, he laughed, began to rub his hands, bowing and saying with some venomous kindness:

"On the contrary, on the contrary! I invite all to the funeral and the funeral banquet; I invite most humbly, both my father and I; and as far as Panna Sieninska is concerned, she will always find a roof and protection here—always, always!"

Saying this, he continued to rub his hands with great joy.

CHAPTER 19

MARCIAN decided to tell Panna Sieninska himself that she should always consider Belczaczka as her own, but he put off this conversation until after the funeral ceremonies, for he first wanted to speak to his father, who, because of the lawsuits which he had been conducting all his life, was skilled in law and knew how to prevent in advance any difficulties. Both were convinced, anyway, that their case was good, so on the second day following the incident, just at the moment when Pan Gideon was being placed in his coffin, they locked themselves in a side room and began to take counsel in an equally good mood.

"Providence is above us," said the old man, "nothing but Providence, and Pagowski will answer dearly for the wrong he intended to do us."

"Well, let him answer for it," replied Marcian. "Our luck that he only intended to do it, but did not make it in time, for now we will take everything in our hands. Already the Sulgostowskis have quarreled with me, but I will tear out their hearts before they will get one field from Belczaczka."

"Ha, the scoundrels! Those sons of bitches! May they be cursed! But I do not fear them, only the will. Have you questioned Father Tworkowski? If anyone knows, it is he."

"I had no opportunity yesterday, for he caught me quarreling with the Sulgostowskis and told us: 'The dead man's body is not cold yet.' Then he went for a coffin and for priests—and today there was no time."

"What if Pagowski has willed everything to that she-goat?"

"He had no right to do so, for the property belonged to his deceased wife, our closest relative."

"Then the testament will be thrown out, but there will be expenses, rides to tribunals . . . God knows what!"

"Father is accustomed to lawsuits, but I have figured out something so that there will be no need of lawsuits. Meanwhile, *beatus qui tenet* [happy is the man in possession], for this reason I will not leave Belcza-czka and have already sent for our servants. Let the Sulgostowskis or Zabierzowski drive me out later."

"What of the girl, if it is willed to her?"

"But who will take her side? She is all alone in the world: no relatives, no friends—a simple orphan. Who will wish to expose his head for her, open himself up to disputes, duels, expenses? What concern is she to anyone? Taczewski was in love with her, but Taczewski is not here; he may never come back, and even if he were to return, he is just a poor beggar—and knows as much about lawsuits as my horse. To tell the truth, the situation is such that if instead of Pagowski her own father had left her Belczaczka, we could still come here and rule the place any way we wanted to, under the pretext of guarding the orphan. I think that Pagowski only intended to make an endowment in the marriage articles, so either no testament will be found at all, or if one is found, it will be so old that it has a bequest for Panna Sieninska as ward."

"Such a will can be overturned," said the old man. "My head on this! Though a lawsuit will not be avoided."

"How so? I hear what you say, but I think it will be avoided."

"Speaking between us, since Pagowski's wife (she was foolish. . . . Lord, shine on her soul!) left everything to her husband, he had a right to leave it to whomever he wanted."

Old Krzepecki uttered these last words almost in a whisper, while looking around on all sides, though he knew that there was no one in the room except him and Marcian.

But his son asked:

"How could she have left it to him when she died suddenly?"

"It was dated a year after their marriage. It can be seen that Pagowski wrested this out of her because they lived in dangerous places and no one could know when the Tartars would start howling his requiem. They bequeathed to each other and the wills were drawn up in the stronghold in Pomerania, and Pagowski brought the wills here. I wanted to initiate a litigation at the time, but I knew that I could not win. Now it is different. . . ."

"And now I think we can circumvent everything without any type of lawsuits."

"If we can, so much the better, but we must be prepared."

"Oh, there is no need!"

"So, how is it to be?"

"I will be able to deal with this myself."

Hearing this, the old Pan Krzepecki became incensed.

"You will be able to deal with it yourself? What? How? Just don't ruin my work. He will be able to deal with it himself! Didn't you advise me to leave the Silnickis in peace concerning Drazkow? There was no way out, you said. Why? They had witnesses that could swear for the land—a big thing! I had men put earth into their boots from my yard, and then what happened? They went to the Silnicki's land and no one took a false oath when he said: 'I swear that the earth I am standing on belongs to Pan Krzepecki!' You would have thought a whole year and never have come up with such an idea. You will be able to deal with this yourself? Look at him!"

And in his anger he began to move his toothless mouth, as if he were chewing on something; besides which, his beard effortlessly touched his nose, hooked like the beak of a bird of prey.

And his son said:

"Recover your breath, father, and listen. When it is a question of *lege agere cum aliquo*, then I yield to you and your abilities in lawsuits, but when the issue touches wenches, my experience is greater, and I trust my own counsel more."

"Well?"

"So if it comes to a procedure against Panna Sieninska, then it will not be dealt with before any tribunal."

"What are you thinking?"

"It is not difficult to divine. Is this not the perfect opportunity? You will not able to find another such wench in this entire region."

Saying this, Marcian craned his neck upward and began to look into his father's eyes, while his father looked at him, too, but with a questioning glance, chewing his gums, and then he asked:

"So that's it, eh?"

"Why not? I've been thinking about this since yesterday!"

"Hmm! Why not? Because she is as poor as Lazarus."

"But I will come to Belczaczka singing, and without any impediments. She is poor, but a wench from a great line. Does father remember what Pagowski said—that if one were to look through the papers of the Sieninskis, one would be able to sue to get half of the province? Why, the Sobieskis grew great from them, so there would be royal protection. The king himself ought to think of a provision. . . . And the wench has pleased my eye for a long time, for she is a tasty titbit, tasty, tasty!"

And he began to jump up on his short legs, licking his mustache at the same time, and looked so unsightly, that old Krzepecki said:

"She will not want you."

"And did she want old Pagowski? Well? Are there too few girls who have wanted me? Many young men have gone to the army, so one can buy dozens of wenches like so many shoe nails. Old Pan Pagowski knew why he ran me out of his house—and he would not have run me out, if he had been certain of the wench."

"But supposing that she does not want you, then what?"

Evil twinkles flashed in Marcian's eyes.

"Then," he replied emphatically, "a man can behave with an unprotected girl so that she herself will ask him to go to church with her."

But the old man became frightened by these words.

"What?" he asked. "You know that this is a hanging offense?"

"I know that no one will take her side!"

"And I tell you: hands off! As it is, there are voices against you. Whether you win or lose a lawsuit for the property, you will not become infamous, but this is a criminal act—do you understand?"

"Ah, it will not come to that unless she herself wants it. But do not hinder me, just do what I say. After the funeral let father take Tekla home, and if any excuse can be found take old Winnicka also, while I will stay with the wench, and with Agnieszka and Joanna. They are reptiles, spiteful of any woman who is younger and more good-looking than they. Already yesterday they began to prod her with their stings, and what will happen when they live under one roof with her? They will poke her, and bite her, and treat her like dirt, and claim that they are giving her the bread of compassion! I see all this as if it were in the palm of my hand—and this is water for my mill."

"And what will you grind with it?"

"What will I grind? This, that I will get into frequent quarrels with them on purpose and rail against those vipers, and once in a while smack one in the face: 'Take that!' And her? I will kiss her on her hands, bah, and on her knees, saying: 'I am your *defensor*, I am your brother, I am your real friend—you are the real mistress here!' And do you not think, father, that her heart will melt, that she will love that person who will be her shield and protection, and who will wipe her tears, who will watch over her day and night? And if in her bitterness, grief and tears she comes to some extraordinary act of confidence, then so much the better, so much the better, so much the better!"

Here Marcian rubbed his hands and looked at his father with such goatlike eyes, that the old man had to spit.

"Pish! Pagan! You have only one thing on your mind."

"For I get tingly when I look at her. Not for nothing did Pagowski drive me out of his house."

A moment of silence followed.

"So you will tell Joanna and Agnieszka to act as you want?"

"Them? One doesn't have to tell or teach them anything, for their natures will suffice. Only Tekla is a dove, while they are hawks."

Marcian was not mistaken, for his sisters had begun, each in their own way, to look after Panna Sieninska. The third sister took her in her arms continually and wept with her, while Joanna and Agnieszka comforted her also, but in another way.

"What could not be, could not be," the older one said, "but you should calm down. You will not be our aunt, for the Lord God did not want this, but no one here will do you any harm or begrudge you a piece of bread."

"And no one will impel you to do any work," the other one continued, "for we know that you are not used to it. Once you recover, and if you wish so yourself, that is another thing, but wait on this, until your sorrow passes, for, indeed, you have met with a great misfortune. You were to be the mistress of the house here, you were to have a husband, and now you have no one aside from us; but believe us: although we are not your relatives, we will be like relatives to you."

After which, Joanna spoke again:

"Reconcile yourself to God's will. God has put you to the test in this, but He will pardon your other sins as a result. For if, perhaps, you have trusted too much in your beauty, or desired riches and splendid clothing (we are all sinners—that is the only reason I'm saying this), one is counted against the other."

"Amen," concluded Agnieszka. "Give some trimming or small jewel to the church for the deceased's soul, for you have no need of your wedding things, and we will ask our father to permit you to do this."

Thus speaking, they began to glance with sharp eyes at the robes lying on the table and on the chest, inside of which was the trousseau. They were seized by such an overpowering curiosity to see what was within, that finally Joanna said:

"Perhaps we might help you in selecting something?"

And after these words, both threw themselves at the chests, boxes and baskets in which lay robes still unpacked after the return from Radom, and began to take the robes out, to spread them, examine them in and under the light, try them on.

And Panna Sieninska sat, as if stunned, in the arms of the sweet Tekla—hearing and seeing nothing of what was happening to her and around her.

CHAPTER 20

WHEN she was betrothed she felt as if something in her life was growing dark, expiring, and was being cut and closed off, so the betrothal had not roused in her heart any joy. She had only consented to it because such was Pagowski's will and because her gratitude for his guardianship compelled her to do so, but even more so because, after Jacek's departure, there remained in her heart only bitterness and sorrow and resentment, and the painful thought that aside from this guardian she had no one, and that if not for him, she would be like a traveling orphan, wandering among unfriendly strangers. But suddenly a thunderbolt had struck the hearth beside which she was supposed to sit with some kind of peace, even if a sad one, and not one person was left standing who was important to her. Not strange, then, that the thunderbolt had stunned her at first and that all her thoughts became jumbled in her head, and that a feeling of sorrow for that sole close individual was fused in her heart with a feeling of shock and terror.

Therefore, the words of the two elder Krzepecki sisters, who had begun to pillage her dresses, struck her ears as noise without any meaning. Later Marcian came, bowing, rubbing his hands, jumping about, saying something at length; but she understood him no more than she did all the other guests, who, according to custom, approached her with words of sympathy that were more elaborate the less they were heartfelt. It was only when Pan Cyprianowicz put his hand on her head in a fatherly manner, and said: "God will watch over you," that something touched her all of a sudden, and tears rushed to her eyes. For the first time the thought came to her that she was like a poor leaf at the mercy of a strong wind.

Meanwhile, the funeral ceremonies began. Owing to the fact that Pan Pagowski was a man of prominence in the neighborhood, these ceremonies lasted, according to custom, around ten days. At the betrothal, with few exceptions, only invited guests were present, while at the funeral arrived every near and distant neighbor, so that the mansion was swarming with people; and receptions, speeches, trips to services and return trips from church followed one after the other. During the first days the general attention was turned exclusively toward the would-be widow, but later, as people saw that the Krzepeckis had completely taken over the house and were presenting themselves as the hosts, this regard ceased, and toward the end of the funeral ceremonies she was not paid more attention than if she were an ordinary resident of the house.

Only Pan Cyprianowicz, moved by her tears and touched by her fate, thought of her. The servants had already begun to whisper that the two Krzepecki maids had snatched away her entire trousseau and the old lord had hidden "jewels" in a casket, and that in the house they were already beginning to ill treat the "young lady." When these reports reached Pan Serafin's ears, they moved his good heart and he determined to talk about these things with Father Woynowski.

But Father Woynowski was greatly prejudiced against Panna Sieninska because of Taczewski, and right at the beginning of the conversation, he said:

"I am sorry for her, for she is a poor thing and in need, and I will help her in any way I can, but—speaking between us—it is certain that God punished her for what she did to my Jacek."

"But Jacek has left, as has my Stanislaw, and she is an orphan now."

"Of course he is gone, but how did he go? You saw him at the moment of departure, but I accompanied him farther—and I will tell you, sir, that the boy had his teeth set, and his heart was bleeding so much in his breast that he could not speak. Oh! He loved that girl as only people in olden times knew how, but which these days they do not."

"He is still able to move his hands, though, for I heard that just beyond Radom he had an altercation, and that he cut up a passing noble, or even two."

"Bah, because he has a girlish face every loafer thinks that he can have an easy time with him. Some drunks were looking for an excuse, so what was he to do? I will censure him for this, I will, but do not forget that a person with a heart torn apart by love is like *leo, quarens quem devoret* [a lion looking to devour someone]."

"That is true. But as to the girl—well, reverend father—God knows if she is as much at fault as we think."

"*Mulier est insidiosa.*"

"*Insidiosa* or not *insidiosa*, as soon as I heard that Pagowski wished to marry her, it occurred to me immediately that perhaps he was the principal author of everything, for it was most important for him to get rid of Jacek forever!"

But the priest shook his head.

"No. We realized *expedite* from his letter that it was written at her instigation. I remember that perfectly and could repeat every word to you."

"I also remember, but we could not know what Pagowski had told her and how he presented Jacek's actions. For example, the Bukojemskis admitted to me that when they met her and the deceased on the road to Przytyk, they said on purpose that Jacek had left for abundant rewards, and was laughing, merry and extraordinarily curious about the daughter of Pan Zbierzchowski, the man to whom you had written a letter."

"They lied! But what for?"

"Well, to show the girl and Pagowski that Jacek did not have them in his mind at all. But mark this, my grace, that if the Bukojemskis spoke thus out of friendship for Jacek, what then would Pagowski have said out of hatred."

"It is certain that he did not spare him. But even if she were to be less at fault than we had supposed, tell me, sir, what of it? Jacek has left and he may never return at all, for, as I know him, he will spare his life less than Pan Pagowski spared his reputation."

"Taczewski would have left in either case," replied Pan Cyprianowicz.

"And if he does not return I will not tear the cassock on my body. Death for the motherland and against Mohammedan wickedness is a worthy end for a Christian knight, and a worthy end for a great family. But I would have preferred to see him go without such a painful arrow in his heart—that is all."

"And my only son has not known any special happiness in life, and he also went and also may not come back," stated Pan Cyprianowicz.

And both became thoughtful, for both loved these youths with their entire hearts.

The prelate Tworkowski came upon them in this condition, and learning that they had been talking about the fate of Panna Sieninska, he said:

"I will tell you, gentlemen, but let this be a secret, that the deceased did not leave a will and the Krzepeckis had a right to take the property. I know that he wanted the marriage articles to be of benefit to his wife and leave her everything, but he did not do this in time. Just do not mention this in front of the Krzepeckis!"

"You have said nothing to them then?"

"Why would I? These are hard people, and I do not want them to be too hard toward the young lady, so not only did I not tell them, but I said: 'Not only does God test a man, but man tests man at times too.' Upon hearing this, they became greatly worried and began to ask: 'How is it? Have you heard something?' I replied: 'What will be revealed will be revealed; remember one thing, though, that the deceased had a right to will his entire property to whomever he pleased.'"

Here the prelate began to laugh and, placing his hands behind his violet belt, he continued:

"I will tell you this, gentlemen, that old Krzepeckis's legs trembled when he heard this. He began to object: 'Oh,' he said, 'that cannot be! He had no right. Neither God nor men would agree to that.' And I looked severely at him, and said: 'You do well to mention God, for at your age it is proper to be concerned about His mercy, but do not appeal to earthly tribunals, for it may well be that you will not have enough time to await their decision.' He became terribly frightened, and I added: 'And be kind to the orphan, lest God punish you sooner than you think.'"

At this, Father Woynowski, whose compassionate heart was moved at the fate of the girl, embraced the prelate.

"Reverend father," he exclaimed, "with such a head you should be a chancellor! I understand! I understand! You said nothing, you did not tell a lie, and you have alarmed the Krzepeckis, who assume that perhaps the testament is, yes, even in your hands; they have to count with this, and be careful as to how they deal with the orphan."

The prelate, happy with the praise, knocked on his head with his knuckles, and said:

"Not quite an empty nut is it?"

"Bah, there is so much wisdom there that it can barely fit in."

"Ha! If God wills it, it will burst, but meanwhile I think that I have indeed protected the orphan. On the other hand, I have to admit that the Krzepeckis spoke of Sieninska with greater humanity and with more kindness that I would have expected. The old ladies have apparently grabbed some trifles, but the old man said he would have them returned."

"Though the Krzepeckis were the worst people alive," stated Pan Cyprianowicz, "they would not dare to do harm to an orphan over whom the eyes of such a wise and good priest are watchful. But I wanted to ask your reverence something else: do me this favor and come now to Jedlinka; let me have the honor of entertaining under my roof such a notable *persona* with whom conversation is like the honey of politics and wisdom. Father Woynowski has already promised to visit me, so the three of us can talk about affairs *de publicis et privatis.*"

"I know about your hospitality, sir," replied the prelate courteously, "and to refuse it would be a real mortification, and since the time of fasting is over, which is sometimes mortification, I will gladly visit you. Let us go to take farewell of the Krzepeckis, but firstly of the orphan, so that the Krzepeckis see in what esteem we hold her."

And they went and, finding her alone, spoke words of kindness and concern, raising her spirits and courage. Pan Cyprianowicz stroked her bright head exactly as would a mother who wishes to calm an upset child; the prelate Tworkowski did the same, while the kindhearted Father Woynowski was so moved by her drawn face and sad beauty, which reminded him of a flower in a field cut down too early by a scythe, that he pressed her temples in a fatherly way, and always having Taczewski in his thoughts, said, half to her, half to himself:

"How can one wonder at Jacek, since you are such a beautiful picture. . . . The Bukojemskis lied when they said that he left in a joyful mood. Oh, how they lied!"

And she, hearing this, suddenly placed her lips to his hand and for a long time she could not tear them away. A genuine sobbing began to shake her bosom—and they left her like this, in a great, inconsolable fit of weeping.

An hour later they found themselves in Jedlinka, where good news awaited them. A messenger had arrived bearing a letter from Stanislaw. The young Cyprianowicz reported that both he and Jacek had joined the hussars of Prince Alexander, that both were in good health, and that Jacek, although always sad, had taken on a little good cheer and that he was not so self-absorbed as in the first days. Besides words of filial love, there was one more bit of information in the letter, which Pan Serafin received with astonishment:

"If my most beloved and most noble father [wrote Stanislaw] sees the Bukojemskis on their return, be not surprised and save them with your kindness, for they have met strange adventures, in which we cannot assist them anymore; and they, if they could not go to war, would probably die from anxiousness, which even now has almost destroyed them."

CHAPTER 21

DURING the following months Pan Cyprianowicz visited Belczaczka repeatedly, wishing to learn what was happening with Panna Sieninska. He did not do this from any personal motives, for Stanislaw, his son, was not in love with her, and her relationship with Jacek had been completely severed; he did this solely from the goodness of his heart, and a little from curiosity, for he wanted to ascertain in what manner and by how much the girl had contributed to breaking the bonds of that friendship.

This met with difficulty, however. The Krzepeckis respected his great wealth, so they received him hospitably, but this hospitality was a strangely watchful one, so diligent and close that Pan Cyprianowicz could not find himself alone with the girl for a second.

He understood that they did not want him to ask her how she was being treated, and that gave him pause to think, even though he had not noticed that she was being treated badly or made to serve unnecessarily. It is true that he saw her once or twice using a crust of bread to clean white slippers of such size that they could not be for her feet, and darning stockings in the evening; but the Krzepecki women did the same, so there could not be in this a desire to humiliate the orphan with domestic work. The old ladies were at times as sharp and stinging as nettles, but Pan Serafin soon noticed that such was their nature and that they could not at times restrain from nettling even their brother, whom they feared to such an extent that it was enough for him to look at one for her to immediately hide the half-drawn sting. Marcian himself was polite and affable to Panna Sieninska, but without obtrusiveness, and after the departure of old Krzepecki and Tekla, he became even more affable.

This departure was not to Pan Cyprianowicz's liking, however, though it was clear that the old man, somewhat disabled in walking, could not be without a woman's care, and that because of the two properties, the Krzepecki household had to be divided. Pan Serafin would have preferred that Tekla remain with the orphan, but when he once casually mentioned the most suitable age of the two girls, the two elder sisters met his words in the harshest manner:

"Panna Sieninska," said Joanna, "has already shown the world that age means nothing to her, the proof of which is our deceased uncle and Pani Winnicka, so we are not too old for her."

"We are as much older than she, as Tekla is younger, and I don't know if even this is true," the other sister added. "Anyway, it is our business how to rule this household."

But Marcian broke into the conversation, and said:

"Tekla's service is dearest to my father; he loves her more than anyone, which is not surprising. We were considering sending Panna Sieninska together with them, but she is accustomed to this house—and I think that it will be best for her here. And as to our care, I will do what is within my power to make it not too burdensome for her."

Saying this, he approached the young lady, his feet scraping along the floor, and tried to kiss her hand, which she withdrew quickly as if in fear. Pan Serafin thought that it was not proper to take Pani Winnicka from this home, but not wishing to interfere in a matter that did not concern him, he kept this opinion to himself.

He noticed more than once that, aside from sorrow, fear was what was reflected on Panna Sieninska's face, but he was not too surprised by this, for her fate was indeed very heavy. This orphan, without a living close soul nearby, without her own roof over her head, forced to live on the good will of people she did not care for and who had, in general, a bad reputation, had to be pained by the bygone promise of a brighter future and frightened of the present. A person who is in the worst of straits, however, will have a little comfort if only there is some hope of a better future. But she could not hope, and did not hope, for anything. Tomorrow would be the same for her as today, and the endless years to come the same lengthy orphanhood, loneliness, and living on the bread provided by a stranger's kindness.

Pan Serafin spoke of this frequently with Father Woynowski. They saw each other almost every day, for it was pleasant to them to talk about their young men. But Father Woynowski, however, shrugged his shoulders in sympathy, and praised the politics of Father Tworkowski, who, having hung the threat of a will over the heads of the Krzepeckis like a Damocles sword, had at least protected the orphan from bad treatment.

"What a crafty fellow!" he said. "Now you have him in your hands, now you don't. Sometimes I think that he did not tell us the whole truth and that there is a will in his hands, which he will reveal unexpectedly."

"I also thought the same, but why should he hide it?"

"I don't know; perhaps to test human nature. But I only know this, that the late Pagowski was a very farsighted man, and I cannot believe that he did not make some sort of provision a long time ago."

After a certain time the thoughts of both old men turned in another direction, for the Bukojemskis had arrived, or rather walked, from Radom. They turned up one evening at Jedlinka, with sabers, it is true, but in torn zupans, boots falling apart, and with such downtrodden faces that if Pan Serafin had not been expecting them for a while now, he would have been greatly terrified, thinking that they were bringing news of the death of his son.

In succession, the brothers embraced his knees and kissed his hands, while he, seeing their poverty, slapped his thigh and exclaimed:

"Stas wrote me that things had gone badly for you, but dear God!"

"We have sinned, your grace!" replied Marek, beating his chest.

After his example, the other began to repeat:

"We have sinned, we have sinned, we have sinned!"

"How so? Well? How is Stas? He wrote me that he had saved you. What happened?"

"Stas is well, grace, and both he and Taczewski shine like two suns."

"Praise God! Praise God! Thanks for the good news. You don't have a letter?"

"He wrote it, but did not give it to us because, he said, it could get lost."

"Are you not hungry? Dear God! It is as if I had four ghosts before me."

"We are not hungry, for the hospitality of every noble is ready, but we are unhappy."

"Sit down. Drink something warm, but tell me what happened while it is being heated up. Where have you been?

"In Warsaw," answered Mateusz, "but it is a horrible city."

"How so?"

"It is swarming with surly people and drunkards. On Long Street and in the Old City, and wherever else you turn, there are places selling wine."

"And?"

"And one son of a bitch persuaded Lukasz to play dice with him. Would to God that pagans had impaled him before this!"

"And he took his money?"

"He won what Lukasz had, and then, what we had. Desperation took hold of us, and we wanted to win back what we had lost, but then he won one of our horses—with the saddle and the pistols in the holsters. I tell you this, your grace, we thought that Lukasz would stab himself with a knife. . . . What could we do? How could we not help cheering up our brother? So we sold the second horse, so that Lukasz would at least have a companion to walk with."

"I understand now what happened."

"Yes, your grace. . . . But when we sobered up, we had a greater worry: the two horses were gone. So we were in need of greater comfort. . . ."

"And so you comforted yourselves until the fourth horse was gone. . . ."

"Until the fourth horse was gone! We have sinned, we have sinned!" the four repentant brothers repeated.

"Was that at least the end?" asked Pan Cyprianowicz.

"Of course not, our father and benefactor! We met a surly person, a certain Poradski, who began to shower us with abuse. 'So this is the way they fleece fools!' he said. 'But since you are big fellows, I will take you as foot soldiers, since I am gathering a levy for the army.' Lukasz cried out that he was holding us up to ridicule, and when he did not stop, Lukasz fell on him! Poradski's friends sprang to help him, and we to help Lukasz, and we cut up people until the marshall guards arrived and came at us! Then the others began to shout: 'Honorable gentlemen, they are attacking freedom and harming the entire Commonwealth in our persons—let us restore order!' This is what happened, and God blessed us immediately, for we chopped up eight soldiers in no time, and three of them fatally, and the rest, five in all, took to their heels!"

Hearing all this, Pan Cyprianowicz held his head, while Marek continued:

"Yes, now we know! God was looking upon our innocence, until people began to shout that we were right by the king's palace and it was a crime, a hanging offense—then we became worried and sought escape. They tried to get hold of us, but when we dealt a blow to this one and that one over the head, or across the neck, we escaped. Stanislaw saved us with his attendants' horses, but even so we barely got away with our heads, for the chase lasted as far as Sekocin—and if the horses had been any shoddier, it would have been the end of us. Thankfully, no one knew our names, so there will be no repercussions."

A long moment of silence followed, after which Pan Serafin asked:

"Where are Stanislaw's horses?"

And for the third time the brothers repeated:

"We have sinned, your honorable grace! We have sinned!"

Cyprianowicz began to stride broadly about the room.

"Now I understand," he said, "why you did not bring Stas's letter. He wrote me that you had met up with various sad adventures, and predicted that you would return needing money for horses and equipment, but he could not have foreseen how this would end."

"That is so, your honorable grace," replied Jan.

Meantime, heated wine was brought in. The brothers fell to drinking it with great eagerness, as they were tired from the road. They were worried, however, about the silence of their host, who continued to pace about the room with a distressed and severe expression.

"Your grace asked about Stanislaw's horses? Two of them foundered before we reached Grojek, for we rode at a gallop and during a time of terrible wind. We sold them to Jewish wagoners for whatever we could get, for they were useless by then and we didn't have even a cent to our name since, because of our sudden escape, Stanislaw did not have time to help us. Fortified a bit, we then rode further, two to a horse. You understand, grace! Coming the opposite way on the road was some noble and he seized his sides immediately. 'What kind of Jerusalem nobles are these?' he asked. Because of our terrible grief we were ready for anything. We had constant altercations and fights! Until finally we came to Bialobrzegi, where in desperation we sold the last two jades. Whoever wondered at our traveling on foot, we replied that we were doing so because of a religious vow. . . . So now, your grace, forgive us like a father, for you will not find more unfortunate men in the world."

"True! True!" cried Lukasz and Mateusz.

And the oldest, Jan, moved by the memory of these bad occurrences and by the wine, raised his hands in the air, and cried out:

"We are God's orphans! What is left for us in this world now?"

"Nothing but the love of brothers," replied Marek.

And they began to embrace one another, shedding bitter tears; afterward, they turned to Pan Serafin.

Marek was the first to embrace his knees.

"Father," he said, "our first protector, do not be angry at us. Lend us enough once more for the recruitment, and we will give it back, God grant, from booty; if you do not lend it to us—that is fine also, only be not angry, just forgive us! Forgive us out of the great friendship we have with your Stas, for I tell you sincerely that if anyone even touched a hair on his head we would make mincemeat of him with our sabers! Is that not true, brothers? With our sabers!"

"Give him here, that son of a bitch!" exclaimed Mateusz, Lukasz and Jan.

But Pan Cyprianowicz stopped before them, placed his hand on his forehead, and began to speak:

"I am angry, it is true! But less angry than sad. For when I think that there are many men such as you in this Commonwealth, my heart is pained, and I ask myself: how will this mother of ours be able to withstand all the onslaughts that threaten her with such children? You wish to apologize and receive my forgiveness? But—dear God!—it is not a question of me or my horses here, but of something a hundred times more important, for it concerns the public well-being and the future of this Commonwealth. The fact that you do not understand this, that even such a thought has not entered your heads, and that there are thousands like you—the heavier is the sorrow, the more severe the concern, the greater the desperation of not only me, but of every worthy son of this motherland."

"For God's sake, your grace, how have we sinned against our motherland so?"

"How? By lawlessness, by wantonness, by riotousness and drunkenness. . . . Oh, how lightly our people take such things! But they do not know how this disease is spreading, they do not see what is happening to the walls of this wonderful edifice and how the ceiling is about to collapse over our heads. A war is threatening us; it still is not known whether the pagan will turn his might against us, and you—Christian soldiers—what is the best that you do? Trumpets are calling to battle, and all you think about is wine and wantonness. And with a merry heart you cut down the guardians of laws that establish whatever kind of order remains. Who made these laws? Nobles! And who is trampling them? Nobles! How is this country supposed to present itself on the field of glory, this *antemurale Christianitatis*, when it is inhabited not by soldiers, but by drunkards, not by citizens, but by carousers and brawlers?"

Here Pan Serafin broke off and, pressing his hand to his forehead, once again began to stalk about the room, while they looked at each other with amazement and confusion, for they had not expected to hear anything like this from his lips.

But he sighed, and went on:

"You were summoned against pagan blood, but you spilled Christian; you were summoned to defend this country, but you have revealed yourselves its enemies, for, of course, the greater the disorder in a fortress, the weaker the fortress. . . . Fortunately there are still worthy children of this mother, but that there are such offspring as you, a legion as I said; that there is no freedom, while licence flourishes, no obedience, but impunity, no stern morals, but immorality, no love of country, but self-love; that here the diets are tearing apart; that the treasury is devastated; that disorder is increasing; and that civil wars are trampling the country like unbridled horses; that drunken heads are determining the country's fate; that there is oppression of the peasants, and from top to bottom lawlessness—that is why my heart bleeds and why I fear defeat and God's anger. . . ."

"For God's sake, should we hang ourselves then?" cried out Lukasz.

And Pan Cyprianowicz paced the room a few more times and spoke on, as if to himself now, and not to the Bukojemskis:

"There is one great banquet as long and wide as the Commonwealth, and on the wall an unknown hand is writing: '*Mane — Tekel — Fares!*' Wine is flowing, but blood and tears will also flow. I am not alone in seeing this; I was not alone in predicting this. But it is useless to place a lighted candle before a blindman's eyes or sing songs to a deaf person. . . ."

Silence followed. In increasing confusion, the brothers continued to look now at one another, now at Pan Serafin. Finally Lukasz whispered:

"May I be damned if I understand anything!"

"Me too."

"And I."

"We only drank a couple of times, so. . . ."

"Quiet, don't mention it. . . ."

"Let us go home. . . ."

"Let's go. . . ."

"Farewell, your grace!" said Marek, moving forward and bending down to Pan Serafin's knees.

"And where are you off to?"

"To the forester's lodge. God will help us. . . ."

"And I will help you," replied Pan Cyprianowicz. "Sorrow seized my heart and I had to express my feelings. Go upstairs, gentlemen, and rest; you will learn later what I have decided."

An hour later he had the horses harnessed and he drove to Father Woynowski's.

The priest was likewise scandalized no little bit by the deeds of the Bukojemskis, but at times he could not restrain from laughing, for having served many years in the army, he recalled various adventures that had befallen him and his comrades. But he could not forgive the brothers drinking away the horses.

"A soldier will often get into trouble," he said, "but to lose one's horse is to betray one's service. I will tell the Bukojemskis that I would have been glad if the marshall's court had chopped off their heads—and it is certain that the example would have been of benefit to the rioters—but I will tell you this, sir, that I would have been sorry for them, for all four fellows are first-rate. I know about these things from years of experience and can tell right away what each person is worth. As to the Bukojemskis, it will be unhealthy for those pagans who battle them. What do you intend to do with them?"

"I will not leave them without assistance, but I think that if I sent them off alone, the same type of thing might happen to them a second time...."

"True!" said the priest.

"So it has occurred to me to accompany them and hand them over directly to the cavalry captain. Once they are in a company and under discipline, they will not be able to do anything like this again."

"True! A splendid idea. Accompany them to Cracow, for that is where the regiments will be assembling. Hey! Perhaps I will go along with you, for that way I will be able to see our boys, and then we will return in a more cheerful mood."

At this Pan Cyprianowicz laughed, and said:

"Only you will have to come back alone."

"Why so?"

"For I am also enlisting."

"Do you wish to serve in the army again?" asked Father Woynowski in amazement.

"Yes and no, for it is one thing to join the army and make a career out of service, and another thing to go on a single expedition. I am old, it is true, but older men than I stood in the ranks at the trumpet call of Gradiva. I have sent my only son—that is true—but one can never give too much to the motherland! Thus did my fathers, and for this the motherland showed them the greatest honor she could give. So for her I would give my last cent! My last drop of blood! And if I were to die—think, your grace: a more beautiful death, a greater happiness cannot meet a person. A man must die, and is it not better to die on the field of glory, at the side of one's son, than in a bed—and from a saber or a bullet than from illness, and in addition to this, against pagans for the faith and the country?"

Here Pan Cyprianowicz, moved by his own words, spread out his arms, and exclaimed: "God grant this! God grant this!" And Father Woynowski embraced him, saying:

"God also grant that in this Commonwealth there be many citizens like you, for one will not find many as worthy as you, and certainly none more so. Certainly it is more suitable for a noble to die on the battlefield than in a bed, and in olden days everyone thought the same, but worse times have now come. Our country and our faith is one great altar, and man is a stick of myrrh that is predestined to burn for the glory of that altar.... But, yes! These days are worse times.... I understand that war is nothing new to you?"

Pan Serafin felt about his chest.

"I have a few saber and gun wounds from years gone by."

"It would be more of a pleasure for me to defend the flag than to listen to old women's sins around here! More than one of them tells me any little thing, as if she had come to confession to shake fleas. At least when a man sins he has something to speak of—a soldier even more! Right after I put on this priest's robe, I became a chaplain in the hussar regiment of Pan Modliszewski. It's good to remember those days. In between absolving sins, I had to raise a sword or a gun.... Ha! Many chaplains will be needed now. I would also like to go, but the parish is large, there is a lot of work to do, and the curate is a little indolent—and the worst is that one gunshot I received a long time ago doesn't allow me to stay in a saddle longer than an hour."

"I would be happy to have such a companion," replied Pan Serafin, "but I understand that even if it were not for the wound, you would not be able to leave your parish."

"Well, I shall see. For a couple of days I will sit on a draft horse and test how long I can stay in the saddle. Perhaps something has eased up. But who will look after your estate when you are gone?"

"I have a forester, a simple man, but so honest that he is almost a saint."

"I know. He is the one whom the wild beasts follow. Some say that he is a wizard, but you know better, however. But he is an old man and sick."

"I also wish to engage that fellow, Wilczopolski, who served Pagowski once. Perhaps you remember him? A young noble, missing one leg, but a stout and brave person. Krzepecki dismissed him, for he asserted himself too proudly. He was at my place two days ago to offer his services—and today I will hire him for sure. Pagowski did not like him much either, since the lad did not allow anyone to lead him by the nose, but he praised his loyalty and resourcefulness."

"How are things in Belczaczka?"

"I have not been there in a while. Wilczopolski does not praise the Krzepeckis, of course, but I did not have time to ask him about all the particulars."

"I will look in there tomorrow, though they are not too glad to see me, and then I will go to your place to scold the Bukojemskis. I will command them to go to confession, and for penance their backs will be smarting. Let them give one another fifty lashes; that will serve them."

"Certainly it will serve them, but now I must take farewell of your grace because of this Wilczopolski."

Saying this, Pan Cyprianowicz shortened his sword belt, so that his saber would not be in the way when he got on the britzka, and a moment later he was on his way to his Jedlinka, thinking along the way of the upcoming expedition and smiling at the thought that he would be fighting stirrup-to-stirrup with his only son against the pagans. Passing Belczaczka, he spotted two packhorses and a cart with trunks driven by Wilczopolski.

He told him to sit over in his carriage, and asked:

"That's it with Belczaczka?"

Wilczopolski pointed to the trunks, and wishing to show that though he served others, he was not just a simple fellow, he said:

"See, your grace: *omnia mea mecum porto* [I am taking all my things with me]."

"So there was a great hurry?"

"There was no hurry, but a necessity; that is why I also accept all your grace's conditions with joy and in case you go away, as you have mentioned, I will guard your house and possessions faithfully."

Pan Serafin was pleased with this answer and the lively, plucky face of the lad, so after a moment of thought, he said:

"Of faithfulness I have no doubt, for I know that you are a noble. But I fear inexperience and carelessness. In Jedlinka one must sit like a stone and be on watch day and night, for it is almost in the wilderness, and in great forests there is usually no lack of bandits, who at times attack homes."

"I do not wish an attack upon Jedlinka, but I would like this duty for myself, so that I could prove my vigilance and courage to you."

"Indeed, you look as if you have both," replied Pan Cyprianowicz.

And he became silent, but after a moment spoke again:

"One more important thing which I must warn you of. Pan Pagowski is before God's tribunal and *de mortuis nihil nisi bene* [one should speak only good of the dead]; but it is known that he was hard on his subjects. Father Woynowski rebuked him for this, and from this arose their discord. The sweat of peasants was not spared there, and the punishments were severe and judgment swift. Let us speak the truth: there was oppression, and the officials behaved too cruelly with the people. I will tell you that this does not happen in my place. Discipline must exist, but paternal discipline, as I consider excessive severity to be a sin against God and country. Make note of this well, that the peasants are not curds and one shouldn't press them too much. I do not live on people's tears and I never forget that we are all equal before God."

A moment of silence followed, after which Wilczopolski seized Pan Serafin's hand and raised it to his lips.

And the old man said:

"I see that you understand me."

"I understand, your grace," replied the young man, "and will just say that more than a hundred times I wanted to tell Pan Pagowski to his face to look for another steward, more than a hundred times I wanted to leave his service. But I couldn't!"

"Why? There is no lack of work in the world."

And Wilczopolski became confused and began to stammer:

"No—it did not happen—I couldn't—I held off from day to day. Besides—there was severity and there wasn't. . . ."

"How is that?"

"It is true that the people were driven too hard to work, and no one could prevent that; but as to punishments, as to beatings, I will just say that instead of sticks, straw ropes were used."

"Who was so merciful? You?"

"No. But I chose to obey the will of an angel rather than the will of a devil."

"I understand. But tell me: whose will?"

"Panna Sieninska."

"Ah! So she was like that?"

"Exactly like an angel. She also was in fear of the deceased, who only recently began to pay attention to her every word. But already everyone loved her and would rather have risked the anger of the deceased than refuse what she asked."

"May God bless her for this! So that is how you all conspired against Pagowski?"

"Yes, your grace."

"And it was never discovered?"

"Once, but I did not betray the young lady. The deceased flogged me himself, for I told him if anyone else did this or, because I am a noble, if a carpet wasn't placed below me, then I would set his house on fire and shoot him myself. And that is the way it would have been, even if I would have had to join forest bandits afterward."

"You please me for this," replied Pan Serafin.

Wilczopolski continued:

"It was difficult to stay with Pan Pagowski, but in that house was—well, quite simply—God's cherub, and that is why one wanted to leave, but remained. Later, as the young lady grew up, the deceased started to pay more attention to her, and recently completely so. He knew that she would often give wheat to the poor from the granary, that, as I said, she had straw ropes used instead of sticks, that she had villein service remitted—and he pretended not to notice. In the end he was so ashamed before her that she didn't need to hide anything. She was a real advocate for the peasants, and for that, as your grace said, let God bless and save her."

"Why do you say 'save her'?" asked Pan Cyprianowicz.

"Because it is worse for her now than before."

"Dear God! Why is that?"

"The old ladies are shrews, and young Krzepecki apparently restrains them, but I know why. But he should be careful that someone does not shoot him in the head like a dog."

The night was deep already, but very clear, for in the sky the moon was full, and by its light Pan Cyprianowicz saw that the eyes of the young steward were glittering like a wolf's.

"What do you know of this?" he asked with curiosity.

"I know that he removed me not just because of my pride, but because I watched and listened carefully to what the people in the house said. I left because I had to, but it is not far to Belczaczka, just in case. . . ."

He became silent, and on the road was heard only the sound of pine trees rustling in the night wind.

CHAPTER 22

IT was not only bad for the young lady at Belczaczka, but getting worse. A good deal of time had passed since that moment when old Pagowski, seeing Marcian Krzepecki staring at the still not fully mature girl with too much of a goat's look, had thrown him out of his house. But Marcian had seen her later at church, and occasionally at the houses of neighbors, and always her springlike beauty awakened lust in him once more. Now that he was living under the same roof with her, and saw her daily, he fell in love with her in his own way, that is, with a passionate and animalistic love that only he was capable of. Changes had also occurred in his resolutions. At first he intended, after dishonoring her, to marry her only if a will should be found in her favor. Now he was ready to stand with her before the altar, as long as he could have and possess her forever. Reason, which when subjugated by desire becomes its obedient assistant, told him, besides, that a young lady bearing the name of Sieninska is a great and very advantageous match, even without a dowry. But even if reason had told him the opposite, Marcian would not have listened, for with each day he lost mastery over himself. He burned, went mad, and if he had restrained himself from using force so far, it was only because desire, even the most ardent, wants and craves willing assent, a willing surrender, and likes reciprocation, seeing in it the greatest pleasure, while deceiving itself even when there is no cause. Thus Krzepecki deceived himself, and fell in love with the idea of that wonderful moment in which the young lady herself, passionate and willing, would surrender to his embraces.

He feared, however, to lose by leaving everything to chance, and when he asked himself what might follow in that event, he was seized by fear of himself and the danger that would hang over him, for the laws of the Commonwealth regarding the protection of a woman's honor were merciless, and around him were the sabers of hundreds of nobles, which would flash over his head without fail. But at the same time he felt that the hour might come in which he would not pay attention to anything, that in his wild and audacious spirit resided a desire for battle and a hunger for danger; so the idea of a horde of nobles besieging Belczaczka, the glow of a fire above his head, and a red executioner standing somewhere, as if behind a mist, in some distant city, was not without a certain attraction.

And so lust, fear, and also a longing for battle struggled within him like three strong winds. Meanwhile, wishing to give vent to that storm and at the same time cool the blood that was seething in him like boiling water, he raged, gave free rein to his passions in village inns, rode his horses down, accosted people, and drank his fill in every tavern in Jedlinka, Radom and Przytyk. He gathered about himself a company of loafers, who were not going to war because of bad reputations or privation, and he paid for their expenses and tyrannized over them. He did this with the idea that such company might be useful to him in the future. He did not confide in any of them, however, and never mentioned the name of the girl in their presence, and when once a certain Wysz from some Wyszkow spoke of her in a rude and obscene manner, he smacked him across the face with his saber, drawing blood.

He usually returned home at the first light of day, galloping at breakneck speed, but the mad ride would sober him up completely. He dropped down in his clothes on the horse skin which covered his bed, and slept like a rock. He would sleep for several hours and, after waking, put on his best attire, go to the women and try to be pleasing to the young lady, whom his eyes did not leave for an instant; and crawling all over her, he would arouse his lust. And more than once when he remained alone with her, his lips pushed forward, his abnormally long arms shook, as if they could not resist the desire to seize her in an embrace, his voice became choked, the words muddled, bold and double-meaning, entwined with both flattery and the dull growl of a threat that was difficult to restrain.

And Panna Sieninska feared him as if he were a tame wolf or bear— and with difficulty hid her repugnance, with which the sight of him filled her. For despite the parrotlike colors in which he readily dressed himself, despite the shining jewels about his neck and the expensive flute that he never let go of, he looked worse and uglier with each day. Sleepless nights, licentiousness, drunkenness and flaming desires had made their impression: he grew thin, his shoulders drooped, causing his long arms to appear even longer, so that his hands extended beyond human proportion to reach below his knees. His gigantic torso began to look like a knotty tree trunk, and his short bowlegs were bent even more from his frenzied rides. Furthermore, the skin on his face took on a kind of green pallor, and because of his sunken cheeks, his protruding eyes and lips were completely pushed forward. Particularly in moments when he laughed, he became simply horrible-looking, for from his eyes, lit up with laughter, peered out a kind of inflamed, unrestrained rage and menace.

But her adversity, deep sadness and unhappiness produced in Panna Sieninska a certain kind of dignity, of which she had not a trace before, and which impressed Krzepecki. Once she had been a chattering girl, rattling all day long like a mill; now she learned silence and her eyes took on a certain fixed glance. Though her heart trembled often in fear of Krzepecki, she restrained him with her silence and calm glance, while he drew back, as if fearing to offend such majesty. She seemed still more desirable to him, it is true, but less approachable at the same time.

Sensing, however, that great danger threatened from his side, and later becoming completely certain of this, she endeavored to avoid him, to be with him alone for the shortest period of time, to switch the conversation from things that could make his confession easier, and finally to become bold enough at times to allude to the fact that she was not so abandoned by the world and left to the mercy of fate as might seem.

She avoided mentioning Jacek Taczewski, understanding that after what had passed between them he could not be, and would never be, any defense to her. She felt, besides, that every word concerning him would rouse Marcian's anger and rage. But noticing that the Krzepeckis steered clear of Father Tworkowski and looked upon him with what seemed a hidden fear, she let it be understood frequently that she was under his special protection, arising from a secret agreement which Pan Pagowski had concluded with him just in case. The prelate, who from time to time visited the Krzepeckis, helped her splendidly in this. He played with them for his own amusement, expressed himself mysteriously, quoted phrases in Latin that had double meanings, and let Marcian presume various things that he could interpret as being meant for him personally.

But, above all, the young lady was loved by the servants and the entire village. People considered the Krzepeckis as intruders, and her as the rightful lady of the manor. All feared Marcian, except Wilczopolski. But even after the departure of this young noble, the girl was surrounded by the unseen protection of people, and Marcian understood that the fear he aroused in people had its limits, beyond which there would be real danger for him. He also understood that Wilczopolski, in whose eyes was boldness, would not go far away, and should the lady need protection, he would not stop at anything—so in 'his heart he admitted that she was not really as deserted by everyone as he himself thought at first and as he had once assured his father.

"Who will take her side? No one," he had said to his father when the old man told him to not forget the terrible punishments of the laws of the Commonwealth against dishonoring a woman.

And now he understood that such persons could be found.

This raised one more obstacle, though difficulties and danger were only stimulants to a nature like Marcian's. He still deceived himself that he would be able to obtain her and capture her affections; but there were moments when he saw, as clearly as if it was in the palm of his hand, that he would accomplish nothing—and then he "raged," as said his companions of nightly revels; he went mad, and if it were not for a dull, but strong and irresistible feeling that if he snatched the girl he would lose her forever, he would have set loose the wild animal within him long before.

And precisely in moments such as these, he drank without measure and to forgetfulness.

Meanwhile, relations in Belczaczka became unendurable, seasoned with poison and animosity. The Krzepecki ladies despised the girl not only because she was young and more beautiful than they, but because she was loved by the people and because Marcian stood up for her for any reason and for no reason. Eventually, an implacable hatred flared up within them toward their brother, but seeing that Panna Sieninska never complained, they bothered her even more. Once Agnieszka burned her, as if by accident, with a red-hot poker. Marcian, hearing of this from the servants, went to apologize to the young lady and entreated her to always seek his protection, but at the same time he began to kiss her hand so greedily and disgustingly, and push so near to her, that she fled from him, unable to stifle her abhorrence. Then he fell into a rage and beat his sister so viciously that for two days she pretended to be sick.

Both "old maids," as they were called in Belczaczka, did not spare biting words on the young lady, or open invective and humiliation, taking vengeance in this manner for everything they had to endure from their brother. But out of hatred for Marcian, they warned her of him, and at the same time imputed that she gave in to his lusts, for they saw that nothing wounded and humiliated her as much as this implication. The house became a hell for her, therefore, and every hour she spent in it was torture. Hatred toward these people, who themselves hated one another, began to poison her heart. She began to think of a cloister, but she kept this thought a secret, for she knew that they would not allow her to go, and that by unleashing Marcian's anger, she would expose herself to great danger. Suffering and fear dwelt in her heart and created a desire that never resided in her—a desire for death. Meanwhile, each day added new drops of bitterness to her cup. Once, early one morning, Agnieszka surprised Marcian looking through the keyhole of the orphan's room. He withdrew, gritting his teeth and threatening her with his fist, but the "old maid" called her sister immediately, and both of them, finding the girl undressed, began to persecute her as usual.

"You knew that he was standing there," said the oldest sister, "for the floor squeaks outside the door, and you can hear if someone stops there, but one can see that you were not bothered by this."

"Bah! He was licking his lips at the dainties, and she was not hiding them," interrupted Joanna. "Have you no fear of God, you hussy?"

"Such a person should be put before the church at a pillory."

"And thrown out of the house. Sodom and Gomorrah!"

"Indeed!"

"And when it will be necessary to send for a woman from Radom?"

"And what name will you give it?"

"Indeed! Trollop!"

And they began to spit on her. But her heart raged, for the measure had been passed.

"Leave!" she cried out, pointing to the door.

But her face turned pale as a sheet, darkness fell before her eyes, and for a moment it seemed as if she were flying into some bottomless abyss, after which she lost consciousness, and feeling and memory of what was happening with her.

She woke up covered with water and her chest pained from pinching. The faces of the Krzepecki ladies bending over her showed fear, but seeing after a while that the girl had recovered consciousness, they became calm again.

"Complain, complain!" said Joanna. "Your lover knows how to defend you."

"And you will thank him in your own way. . . ."

But she, setting her teeth, did not respond with a single word.

Marcian, however, guessed at what had happened upstairs without hearing any complaint, for a few hours later screams came from the chancellery, in which he had shut himself up with his sisters, that terrified the entire house.

In the afternoon, when the elder Krzepecki arrived, both ladies fell with a cry to his knees, entreating him to take them away from this "den of licentiousness and torments"; but he, as much as he loved his youngest daughter, hated the older ones, and so not only took no pity on the unfortunate shrews, but began to call for a whip and commanded them to stay.

The only being in that terrible house in whom Joanna and Agnieszka could have found compassion, sympathy, or even protection, had they wanted to be good and friendly toward her, was Panna Sieninska herself. But they preferred to bother and torment her for, with the exception of Tekla, this was a family in which each member did everything in his or her power to poison the life and increase the misery of the other. But Panna Sieninska feared the love of Marcian more than the hatred of his sisters. And he imposed himself on her more and more; with greater brazenness he pushed himself forward, more insistently, and looked upon her with greater greed. One could see that he was losing control over himself completely, that a wild desire was tearing at him as a strong wind tears a tree, and that any moment he would burst.

That moment came soon.

Once, after the arrival of warm weather, Panna Sieninska went at daybreak to bathe in a shady stream. Before she began to undress, she saw Marcian's face on the other bank, peering out from thick bushes. She immediately began to run away, breathless, while he rushed after her. But wanting to jump over the stream, he failed and fell into the water. He was barely able to climb out of it, and returned home wet through and through, and in a rage. Before dinner, he beat a number of servants until he drew blood, and during dinner he did not say a single word. Only at the end of the meal did he turn to his sisters and say:

"Leave me alone with Panna Sieninska, for I have to talk with her on important matters!"

Hearing this, the sisters began to look meaningfully at each other, while the young lady grew pale from emotion, for though he had long tried to seize every moment that he could be alone with her, he had never openly insisted on such a moment.

So when the sisters had left, he rose, looked behind one door and then the other to make sure that no one was eavesdropping; then he approached the girl and said:

"Give me your hand—for reconciliation."

But she instinctively drew back both hands and moved away from him.

Marcian seemed to be trying to constrain himself, but he nevertheless jumped twice on his bowlegs, for he could never stop this habit, and said in a subdued voice:

"You do not want to! But I came very near to drowning myself for your sake today. I beg your pardon for having frightened you, but this did not happen because of some lechery, but because there are mad dogs on the loose between Belczaczka and Wyrabek, so I went with a matchlock to watch over your safety."

Her knees trembled a bit, but she said calmly and with good presence of mind:

"I want no protection that would bring me shame."

"But I want to protect you not only now but always—to death! And without offending God, but with God's blessing. Do you understand?"

A moment of silence followed. Through the open windows came the sound of wood being chopped, with which an old lame man was engaged near the kitchen.

"I do not understand," replied the girl.

"Because you do not want to," answered Marcian. "You have seen for a long time that I cannot live without you. You are as necessary to me as air is for breathing. You are wonderful to me, and dear beyond anything in the world. I cannot live without you! I will burn up without you! I will come to a bad end without you! If I did not restrain myself, I would have seized you a long time ago, as a hawk seizes a dove. Without you my throat becomes dry as if it had no water. All my emotions revolve around you. I cannot sleep nor live. See, even now . . ."

And he broke off, for his teeth began to chatter as if in a fever. He stiffened, grabbed the arms of the chair with his bony hands, as if in fear of falling, and panted loudly for a while.

After this, he began to speak again:

"You lack a fortune—that is nothing! I have enough. I need you, not a fortune. Do you want to be mistress of the house? You were to marry Pagowski—I am not any worse, after all. Just do not tell me No! By the living God, do not tell me No, for I do not know what will happen. You are wonderful! You are my . . ."

Suddenly he knelt down, embraced her knees with his hands and began to press them to his breast. But—beyond even her own expectation—her fear passed without a trace in that terrible moment. Her knightly blood was kindled, a readiness for battle to the last breath was roused within her. She began with her entire strength to push back his sweat-covered forehead with her hands, which was snuggling up against her knees.

"No! No! I would rather die a thousand times. No!"

He rose, pale, hair bristling, full of cold rage. For some time his mustache quivered; long, decayed teeth glittered underneath. But he still maintained control over himself; presence of mind had still not left him completely. But when the lady drew back suddenly toward the door, he jumped to block her way.

"So that is it?" he asked in a hoarse voice. "You do not want me? Tell me once again to my face! You do not want me?"

"I do not want you! And do not threaten me, sir, for I am not afraid."

"I am not threatening you, I just want to take you for my wife. Bah! I ask once more: consider well! For the love of God! Consider well!"

"What should I consider well? My will is my own, for I am a noble— and I tell you to your face: Never!"

And he came so close to her that his face was up to hers, and he said:

"Then perhaps instead of being mistress here, you would rather carry firewood to the kitchen? You do not want this either? So how will it be, noblewoman? To which of your estates will you go now? And if you stay, whose bread will you eat here? On whose kindness will you live? In whose power will you be? In whose bed, in whose room will you sleep? What will happen if I have the door latches removed? And you ask, what do you have to consider? This: which to choose! Marriage, or no marriage!"

"You are contemptible!" cried Panna Sieninska.

At that moment something unheard of happened. Seized with sudden fury, Krzepecki roared with an inhuman sound and, grabbing the girl by her hair, began to beat her mercilessly and mindlessly with a type of wild, animalistic joy. The longer he had restrained himself before, the worse was his terrible and blind madness now. And he would have killed her for sure, if her cry had not brought in the servants. First the caretaker who was chopping wood by the kitchen, climbed into the room through the window with his axe; after him rushed in the kitchen staff, both the Krzepecki ladies, the butler and two of Pan Pagowski's longtime servants.

The butler, who was a noble from a distant settlement in Mazovia and, moreover, a man of uncommon strength, though old, seized Marcian's arms from behind, drew them in so much that his elbows almost touched each other behind this back, and said:

"This is not allowed, your grace! Shame!"

"Let me go!" roared Krzepecki.

But the iron hands held him as if in a vice, and a stern, low voice was heard near his ear:

"Your grace, control yourself, or else I will break your bones!"

Meanwhile the Krzepecki sisters grabbed, or rather carried, the girl from the dinning room. The butler continued:

"Allow me to accompany your grace to the chancellery—to take a rest! I seriously advise this."

And he began to push Marcian before him as if he were a child, while Marcian snapped his teeth, wriggled on his short legs, cried for a rope and a hangman, but he could not resist, for a moment later he weakened suddenly after his outburst to such an extent that he was unable to stand up on his own strength.

So when, in the chancellery, the butler threw him on the horse skin, which covered the bed, he did not even attempt to rise, and lay motionless like a stump of wood, panting with heaving sides like an overstrained horse.

"A drink!" he shouted.

The butler opened the door, called a servant and, whispering a few words, handed him keys; the servant returned presently, carrying a demijohn of aqua vitae and a pint glass.

The noble filled it to the brim, sniffed it, and coming up to Marcian, said:

"Drink, your grace."

Krzepecki seized the glass with both hands, but they shook so much that the liquid began to spill onto his chest, so the butler raised him on the bed, put the glass to his lips and tilted it.

Marcian drank and drank, holding onto the glass greedily when the noble tried to remove it from his lips.

Finally he drank it to the bottom and fell backward.

"Perhaps it is too much," said the butler, "but your grace was terribly weak."

Marcian wished to answer, but he merely sucked in air, like a person who has burned his lips with a hot liquid.

Meanwhile, the noble continued:

"Hey! You owe me a good bit, for I have rendered your grace no mean service. God forbid had you gone further. It's the axe and the executioner for such an act, not to mention that bad things could happen now. The people love the lady very much. And it will be difficult to hide what has happened from Father Tworkowski, though I will enjoin the servants to be quiet. How do you feel, your grace?"

And Marcian looked at him with whitened eyes, gasping continually with open lips. Once, then twice, he tried to say something, after which he was seized by the hiccoughs; his eyes looked with a fixed stare. Suddenly he shut his eyes and began to wheeze like a dying man.

The butler looked at him for a moment, then muttered:

"Sleep or die, you filthy dog."

And he went from the room out to the farm, but after half an hour had passed he returned to the manor, knocked on Panna Sieninska's door, and finding both of Marcian's sisters there, he said to them:

"Your gracious ladies should look in on the young lord in the chancellery, for he has grown very weak. But if he is sleeping, it is better not to wake him."

Then, when he was alone with Panna Sieninska, he bowed to her knees and said:

"Lady, we have to flee from this house. Everything is ready."

And she, though beaten and barely able to stand on her legs, sprang up in an instant.

"Fine. I am ready. Save me!"

"There is a harnessed britzka waiting beyond the stream. I will lead you. I will bring your clothing tonight, for Pan Krzepecki is dead drunk and will be lying like a board until tomorrow. Just take a tunic and let's go. No one will stop us, have no fear."

"God reward you! God reward you!" she repeated feverishly.

And they went out, going through the garden to the gate by which Taczewski usually entered from Wyrabek. Along the way, the butler said:

"Wilczopolski arranged this some time ago. He made an agreement with the people that if there were any attempt on you, they would set fire to the barn. Pan Krzepecki would then have to rush to the fire, and you would have time to escape through the garden to the stream, where a man was to wait with a carriage. But it is better that this will happen without anything getting burned, for that is always a crime. I tell you that Krzepecki will be sleeping like a rock until tomorrow, so do not be afraid of any kind of pursuit."

"Where am I to go?"

"To Pan Cyprianowicz's, for defense is easy at that place. Wilczopolski is there, as are the Bukojemskis and the foresters. Krzepecki will surely try to take you back, but he will not succeed. As to where Pan Cyprianowicz will take you afterward, whether to Radom or farther, this can be discussed with the priests. . . . Well, here is the carriage. Do not be afraid of pursuit! It is not far to Jedlinka—and God has made the evening wonderful. I will bring you clothing tonight, and if they try to guard it, I will not pay attention. May the Most Holy Mother, guardian and protector of orphans, be with you!"

Saying this, he took her by the hand like a child and, seating her in the carriage, called out to the servant:

"Move on!"

It had already grown dark in the world and the evening glow was expiring, coloring the stars in the clear sky a rosy hue. The calm evening was filled with the odors of the earth, the leaves and blossoming elders, while, like the warm rain of spring, nightingales filled the garden, the alder forest and the entire region with their song.

CHAPTER 23

THAT evening Pan Cyprianowicz was sitting in front of his house entertaining Father Woynowski, who had come to see him after vespers, and the four Bukojemskis, who were still staying at Jedlinka. Before them, on crossed legs, stood a table, and on it glasses and a jar of mead, while they, listening to the quiet murmur of the wilderness, drank at leisure, raising their eyes to the heavens in which the crescent moon was shining brightly, and talked about war.

"Thanks to God and your grace we shall soon be ready for the road," said Mateusz Bukojemski. "What has happened, has happened. Even saints have sinned, so how could it be with imperfect man who can do nothing without the grace of God. But when I look upon that moon, which is the Turkish sign, my fist itches me straightaway, as if mosquitoes had bitten it. Well, may God grant it happen as soon as possible, so that relief can be found."

The youngest Bukojemski thought for a moment, and said:

"Why is it, reverend father, that the Turks have some kind of reverence for the moon and bear it on their standards?"

"Do not dogs have a reverence for the moon?" asked the priest.

"For certain, but why the Turks?"

"Precisely because they are sons of bitches."

"Ah, as God is dear to me, that is right!" replied the young man, glancing at the priest in amazement.

"But the moon is not to blame," noted the host, "and it is pleasant to see, when in the calm of night, it spreads its light over the trees, as if someone had sprinkled them with silver. On such a night, I dearly love to sit and gaze at the sky and marvel at the almightiness of God."

"It is certain that at such times the human soul flies as if on wings to its creator," replied the priest. "The merciful God created the moon as well as the sun—and this is a great blessing. As to the sun, well, in the day everything is quite visible, but if there were no moon people would then break their necks riding at night, not to mention that devilish licence would be greater in complete darkness."

For a while they were silent, passing their eyes over the clear sky; after which the priest took a pinch of snuff, and added:

"Do not forget, gentlemen, that kind Providence thinks not only of the needs of the people, but of their comfort."

Further conversation was interrupted by the rattle of wheels, which, in the night quiet, reached their ears clearly. Pan Cyprianowicz rose, and said:

"God is bringing some guest, for the entire household is at home. I wonder who this could be?"

"Perhaps it is someone with news of our boys!" replied the priest.

And all of them rose, while a carriage drawn by two horses entered through the open wicket.

"There is some woman on the seat!" called Lukasz Bukojemski.

"True!"

Passing halfway around the courtyard, the britzka stopped before the porch. Pan Serafin looked at the face of the unknown woman, recognized her in the moonlight, and cried out:

"Panna Sieninska!"

He almost lifted her in his arms from the carriage, but she bent down immediately to his knees and burst out sobbing.

"An orphan who asks for rescue and refuge!" she exclaimed.

Saying this, she nestled up to his knees, embracing them with greater strength and weeping more sorrowfully. Everyone was seized with such great astonishment that for a moment no one could say a word. Finally Pan Cyprianowicz raised her up, pressed her to his heart, and called out:

"As long as there is breath in me, I will be a father to you, orphan. But what happened? Were you driven out of Belczaczka, or what?"

"Krzepecki beat me, and threatened me with disgrace," she replied in a barely audible voice.

But Father Woynowski, who stood right next to Pan Serafin, heard the reply, seized his white hair and cried out:

"Jesus of Nazareth, King of the Jews!"

And the four Bukojemski looked on with open mouths and wide eyes, understanding nothing. It is true that their hearts were moved at once by the weeping of the orphan, but, on the other hand, they remembered that Panna Sieninska had done a great wrong to their friend, Taczewski, they remembered also the teaching of Father Woynowski that a *mulier* is the cause of all evil in the world; so they began to look at one another with questioning glances, as if in hope that some clear thought would come to the mind of one or the other.

Finally Marek said:

"Oh, well, those Krzepeckis . . . in any case we should take care of Marcian . . . no?"

He grabbed at his left side, and following his example, the remaining three brothers began to feel for the hilts of their sabers also.

Meanwhile, Pan Cyprianowicz led the young lady inside and put her in the hands of the housekeeper, Pani Dzwonkowska, a woman with a sensitive heart and irrepressible eloquence, to take care of her as a most honored guest. He commanded the housekeeper to give up her own bedroom to the young lady, light the house, put on a fire in the kitchen, find medicines for calming convulsive sobbing and ointments for bruises, heat some caudle and prepare various delicacies, while he advised the girl herself to lie down in bed until everything could be served her and to rest, putting off discussion of details until the morrow.

But she wanted to unburden her heart immediately to the people with whom she sought rescue. She wanted to cast out from her soul immediately all the suffering that had been accumulating for a long time, as well as the distress and shame and humiliation and torment in which she had been living in Belczaczka. So, shutting herself up with Father Woynowski and Pan Serafin, she spoke as if to a confessor and a father. She confessed everything: her grief over Jacek, and the fact that she wanted to marry her guardian simply because she thought Jacek held her in contempt and because she had heard from the Bukojemskis that he was to marry Panna Zbierzchowska; finally she explained what her life, or rather her torment, had been in Belczaczka; in other words, the troublesome hatred of the Krzepecki ladies and the horrible courtship of Marcian, and what had happened that day that had been the decisive cause of her flight.

And they seized their heads as they listened. Father Woynowski, an old soldier, reached involuntarily to his left side, in the manner of the Bukojemskis, though he had not carried a saber for a long time, and the worthy Pan Serafin placed his hands, quivering with emotion, on the girl's temples, and repeated:

"Just let them try to take you back. I had one son, but now God has given me a daughter."

But Father Woynowski was struck most by what the girl said concerning Jacek. Remembering everything that had occurred, he found all this quite confusing.

So he thought and thought, smoothing down his milky hair with his open hand; finally, he asked:

"Did you know of the letter that the late Pagowski wrote to Jacek?"

"I asked him to write it."

"Then I understand nothing. Why did you do this?"

"Because I wanted him to return."

"How was he to return?" cried out the priest with a certain anger. "It was precisely because of what was in the letter that Jacek left with a broken heart into the wide world to forget and cast out that love which you, lady, trampled on."

She began to blink her eyes from amazement and put her hands together as if in prayer.

"My guardian told me that he had written a fatherly letter. Most Holy Mother! What was in the letter?"

"Scorn, insults and an attack on a man's poverty and honor. Do you understand?"

A cry of such real pain was rent from the girl's lips that the priest's honest heart quivered. He approached the girl, parted the hands with which she had covered her face, and cried out:

"Then you didn't know?"

"I didn't, I didn't!"

"And you wanted Jacek to return?"

"Yes!"

"In God's name! Why?"

Then quick and abundant tears, as large as pearls, began to drop from under her closed lashes; her face turned red from girlish shame; she began to gasp for air with open lips; her heart beat within her as if in a captured bird, and finally she whispered with effort:

"Because . . . I love him!"

"Dear God, child!" the priest cried out.

But his voice broke in his breast, for tears were choking him also.

At the same time he was seized with joy, and a boundless compassion for the girl, and amazement that a *mulier* was not in this case the cause of all evil, but an innocent lamb on which such suffering had fallen, God knows why.

So he seized her in his arms, pressed her to his heart, and began to repeat, over and over:

"My child! My child!"

Meanwhile, the Bukojemskis moved over to the dining room, with glasses and a jug; there they thoroughly emptied the mead to the bottom while waiting for the priest and Pan Serafin, in the hope that once the two would show up supper would be served.

They finally returned, their faces showing emotion and their eyes moist. Cyprianowicz sighed once, then twice, and said:

"Pani Dzwonkowska is putting the poor thing to bed now. One truly cannot believe one's own ears. We are to blame, also, but the Krzepeckis—that is quite simply dishonorable and a disgrace! And one cannot allow it to go unpunished."

"For sure," replied Marek. "We will talk with that 'Stump.' Yes, yes!"

After which he turned to Father Woynowski:

"We are sincerely sorry for the girl, but I think, after all, that God punished her for Jacek. Is that not so?"

And the priest replied:

"You are a fool, sir!"

"How so? Well?"

So the old man, whose heart was filled with remorse, began to speak rapidly and passionately of the innocence and torment of the girl, as if wanting in this manner to make amends for the injustice which he had permitted concerning her; but after a certain time his narrative was interrupted by the arrival of Pani Dzwonkowska, who burst into the room like a bomb into a fortress.

Pani Dzwonkowska's face was covered with tears, as if she had submerged it into a full bucket, and immediately at the threshold she began to cry out with her arms stretched out before her:

"People, whosoever believes in God! Vengeance, justice! Dear God, her back is covered in bruises, her back that was as white as a sheet; her hair is torn out by the handful, her golden hair. My dearest dove, my precious flower, my innocent lamb. . . ."

Upon hearing this, Mateusz Bukojemski, already moved by the narrative of the priest, roared, then was joined by Marek, Lukasz and Jan, until the servants rushed to the room, and the dogs began to bark in the hall. But Wilczopolski, who a moment later returned from his nightly rounds inspecting the haystacks, saw the brothers in another mood. Their hair was standing on end, their eyes were pale with rage, their right hands were grasping at the hilts of their sabers.

"Blood!" shouted Lukasz.

"Give him to me, that son of a bitch!"

"Strike!"

"With the sword!"

And they moved toward the door as one man, but Pan Cyprianowicz sprang between them and the door.

"Stop!" he cried out. "He deserves the executioner, not the sword."

Pan Serafin had to spend a long time soothing the furious brothers. He explained to them that if they were to cut down Marcian Krzepecki at once, it would not be the act of nobles, but of assassins. "First," he said, "we have to make the rounds of our neighbors, come to an understanding with Father Tworkowski, have the judgment of the nobles and the clergy behind us, obtain the testimony of the servants at Belczaczka, then take the matter to the tribunal, and only when the sentence is passed, support it with force. If," he continued, "you cut up Marcian straightaway, his father would not fail to proclaim that you had done so in collusion with Panna Sieninska, so her reputation might suffer, and the old man would summon you, and instead of going to war, you would have to drag about tribunals, for not being under the command of the hetman as yet, you could not evade the terms. And that is how it is."

"How so?" asked Jan with sorrow. "Are we then to overlook the wrong done to this dove?"

"Do you think," noted the priest, "that life will be pleasant for Marcian Krzepecki when *infamia* or an executioner's axe is hanging over him and, in addition, when general contempt surrounds him? That is a worse torment than a quick death, and I would not like to be in his skin now for all the silver in Olkusz."

"And if he wriggles out of it?" asked Marek. "His father is a sly old fox who has won more than one lawsuit."

"If he wriggles out of it, then Jacek will whisper a little word to him when he returns. . . . You still do not know Jacek! He has girlish eyes, but it is safer to take cubs from a she-bear than to sting him to the quick."

Wilczopolski, who had been silent so far, now spoke up in a gloomy voice:

"Pan Krzepecki has delivered his own sentence, and who knows whether he will live to see the return of Taczewski. But I will say something else: For certain he will attempt to take the lady back by force of arms, and then—"

"Then we shall see!" interrupted Pan Cyprianowicz. "Let him just try! That is something else!"

And he shook his saber threateningly, while the Bukojemskis began to gnash their teeth and repeat:

"Let him just try! Let him just try!"

But Wilczopolski said:

"But you gentlemen are leaving for the war. . . ."

"We will find a remedy!" replied Father Woynowski.

Further conversation was interrupted by the arrival of the butler. He brought trunks containing the lady's items, which, as he said, he had accomplished with some difficulty. The Krzepecki ladies tried to stop him and even wanted to wake their brother, so that he could stop him also. But they could not awaken him, and the butler convinced them that they had to let him take the things for their own good, as well as their brother's, or they would be accused of stealing another's property and taken to court. As women who did not know the law, they became frightened and yielded. The butler likewise thought that Marcian would want to get back the young lady for certain, but he did not think that he would resort immediately to force.

"He will be restrained from this," he said, "by old Krzepecki, who understands all about *raptus puellae*! He does not know anything yet of what happened, but I will go to him directly from here and explain the entire affair, and I will do so for two reasons: first, so that he will restrain Marcian, and second, because I do not want to be in Belczaczka tomorrow when Marcian awakens and learns that I assisted the lady in escaping. He would attack me for sure, and then *casus paskudeus* might happen to one of us."

Pan Serafin and Father Woynowski praised the butler's discernment and, seeing that he was a kindhearted person, and experienced besides, one who had eaten bread from more than one oven, and to whom even the law was familiar, asked him to join them in solving the problem. Two councils were formed then, for in the annex the Bukojemskis had set up their own.

Pan Cyprianowicz, knowing how to restrain their murderous intentions in the best possible manner and detain them at home, sent a large demijohn of splendid young wine to the annex, which they attacked immediately, drinking to one another. Their hearts were moved, and they could not help to think about that night in which Panna Sieninska first crossed the threshold of the house in Jedlinka. They remembered how they had immediately fallen in love with her and how, because of her, they had quarreled, and later *unanimitate* given her to Stanislaw Cyprianowicz, making a great sacrifice of their passion for friendship.

Finally, Mateusz took a drink, rested his head in his hand, sighed, and said:

"Jacek was sitting that night in a tree like a squirrel. Who would have thought at that time that the Lord God had destined her for him?"

"And He had us continue in our orphanhood," added Marek.

"Do you remember," asked Lukasz, "how all the rooms were brightened by her presence? It would not have been brighter had one hundred candles been glowing. She would get up, sit down, laugh. . . . And when she looked at you, you became as warm inside as if you had drunk heated wine. . . . Let us drink now for our terrible sadness."

They drank again, after which Mateusz hit the table with his fist and cried out:

"Eh, if she had not loved that Jacek so!"

"Then what?" snarled Jan. "Do you think she would immediately fall in love with you? Look at what a refined gentleman we have here!"

"It's good that you are such a handsome lad!" replied Mateusz.

And they began to look at one another with ill will. But Lukasz, though usually greatly susceptible to fighting, began to calm them.

"She is not for you, nor for you, nor for anyone of us," he said. "Another will get her and lead her to the altar."

"For us there are only sorrow and tears," said Marek.

"Then let us at least love one another. No one in the world loves us! No one. . . ."

"No one! No one!" they repeated, one after the other, mixing their wine with tears.

"And she is sleeping there," said Jan suddenly.

"Sleep, poor thing!" repeated Lukasz. "She is lying like the flower cut by a scythe, like the lamb torn apart by a wicked wolf. My brothers by blood, is there no man who will even pull that wolf by its long hair?"

"That cannot be!" cried out Mateusz, Marek and Jan.

And they began to rage once again, and the more they drank, the more frequently did one and the other clench his teeth, or hit the table with his fist.

"I have an idea!" cried out the youngest suddenly.

"Speak! Have God in your heart!"

"Here, listen! We promised Pan Cyprianowicz that we would not cut 'Stump' down, correct?"

"True, but speak, don't ask questions!"

"We have to take revenge for our young lady, however. As they said, old Krzepecki will be coming here trying to get Pan Cyprianowicz to freely give back the young lady. But we know that he will not give her back! Eh?"

"He will not give her back! He will not give her back!"

"So what do you think? Don't you think that Marcian will hasten to meet with his father on the way back to see and ask what he has accomplished?"

"As God is in heaven, he will do just that."

"Well, halfway between Belczaczka and Jedlinka there is a wood distillery by the road. What if we waited for Marcian in that place?"

"Good! But what for?"

"Hush! Quiet!"

"Hush! . . ."

And they began to look around the room—though they knew that besides themselves there was not a living soul present—and then fell to whispering. They whispered for a long time, now louder, now softer; finally their faces lit up, they finished their drinks in one gulp, embraced each other in turn, and silently, like geese, went out of the room one after the other.

In the greatest quiet, they saddled horses and led them by the bridle from the courtyard. Passing the wicket, they mounted the horses and rode stirrup by stirrup until they reached the highway. Once there, Marek, who though the youngest, took command over his brothers this time, said:

"Jan and I will go to the distillery at once, while you go and bring that barrel before dawn."

CHAPTER 24

AS the butler had foreseen, the elder Krzepecki arrived at Jedlinka the very next day in the afternoon, but beyond all expectation he arrived with such a merry and kindly face that Pan Cyprianowicz, who having the habit of taking a nap after dinner, was a bit drowsy, and became wide awake from amazement at the sight. The old fox also began to talk of neighborly friendship almost as soon as he crossed the threshold and of how delightful it would be for his old age to have more frequent mutual visits; he gave thanks for the hospitable reception, and only after the preliminary courtesies were over did he get to the real issue.

"My dear neighbor," he said, "I have come with due greetings, but at the same time—as you must have guessed—with a request that, in view of my age, I trust you will graciously listen to."

"I will gladly fulfill every proper demand you may make, sir," replied Pan Serafin.

The old man began to rub his hands:

"I knew it! I knew it from the start!" he exclaimed. "How wonderful it is to deal with a man of sound wisdom! One can come to an agreement immediately. I told my son: 'Leave this to me! If the matter is with Pan Cyprianowicz,' I said, 'then everything will go well, for there is not another man in this entire region who is so wise and such an honorable citizen."

"You flatter me too much."

"No, no! I do not say enough! . . . But let us come to the point."

"Let us."

The elder Krzepecki was silent for a moment, as if looking for the appropriate words, and merely moved his jaws, so that his chin met his nose. Finally he laughed joyfully, placed his hand on Pan Serafin's knee, and said:

"Dear Sir . . . you know that our goldfinch has escaped from her cage."

"I know. Because the cat frightened it."

"Is it not pleasurable to talk to such people?" cried the old man, rubbing his hands. "What wit! Father Tworkowski would burst from envy, as God is dear to me!"

"I am listening, sir. . . ."

"Well, *ad rem* and without mincing things: we would want to take this goldfinch back."

"And why not?"

Pan Krzepecki moved his chin toward his nose once, then twice, for he was made uneasy by the fact that the affair was progressing too well. But he clapped his hands and cried out with feigned joy:

"Well, then it is settled! If only there were more people like you!"

"The matter is settled, as far as I'm concerned," replied Pan Serafin. "One just has to ask this little bird if she wants to go back, but it is not possible today, since your son has so crushed her that she is barely breathing."

"Is she sick?"

"She is sick, and lying in bed."

"Perhaps she is just pretending to be sick?"

Pan Serafin's face clouded over all of a sudden, and he said:

"My dear sir, let us speak seriously. Your son Marcian has acted toward Panna Sieninska shamefully, inhumanely, ignobly—quite simply, in a disgraceful manner. Before God and man you have committed a grave offense to give the orphan into hands such as these and entrust her to such a shameless brute."

"There is not a bit of truth in what she says!" cried out the old man.

"How is that? You do not know, after all, what she has said, and already you deny it. It is not she who speaks, but the black and blue marks that my housekeeper saw on her young body. And as to Marcian—all of the servants at Belczaczka saw his wooing and then his cruelty, and are ready to testify if need be. Wilczopolski is here; today he will go to Radom to relate to Father Tworkowski what has happened."

"But you promised, sir, to give the girl back."

"No! I only said that I would not detain her. If she wants to return—fine! If she wishes to stay here—that is fine also! Please do not demand of me that I refuse a roof and a piece of bread to an orphan who has been grievously offended."

Old Krzepecki's jaws began to move. For a moment he was silent, and then said:

"You are right—and you are not right. To refuse a roof and a piece of bread to an orphan would not be proper, but, as a wise man, consider that it is one thing not to refuse hospitality and another thing to support rebellion against a father's authority. I love my youngest daughter, Tekla, sincerely, but it happens at times that I give her a clout. So how would it be? If, after being punished by me, she fled to you—would you not allow me to take her or would you let her decide? What kind of order would there be in the world if women could follow their own will? Why, a married woman, even if she is old, has to yield to her husband and follow his orders. What about an immature girl who is commanded by a father or a guardian?"

"Panna Sieninska is not your daughter, sir, nor even your relative."

"But we have inherited her guardianship from Pan Pagowski. If Pan Pagowski had punished the girl, you would not have said a word for sure; and it is the same situation in regard to me, and to my son, to whom I have entrusted the care of Belczaczka. It is too bad! Someone must rule, someone must have the right to punish! I do not deny that Marcian, as a young and impulsive man, may have gone too far, particularly as she repaid him with ingratitude. But that is my affair! I will examine, judge and punish—but I will take the girl back, and I think, with your pardon, that even His Majesty the King would not have the right to create any difficulties in this matter."

"You speak as in a tribunal," replied Pan Cyprianowicz, "and I do not deny that you have appearances on your side. But appearances are one thing, and truth another. I do not wish to hinder you in anything, but I will tell you truthfully what people think, and you should reckon with that. You are not concerned about Panna Sieninska or the guardianship over her, but you suspect that Father Tworkowski may have a will with a provision for the girl, and so you are afraid that Belczaczka, as well as she, may slip away from you. It wasn't that long ago that I heard one of the neighbors say: 'If it were not for this uncertainty, they would have run this orphan out of the house, for these people do not have God in their hearts.' It is quite disagreeable for me to tell you such things in my own house, but I must, so that you may know."

Flames of anger sparkled in the eyes of old Krzepecki, but he kept control of himself, and spoke in a calm, though somewhat broken, voice:

"The malice of people! A base malice, nothing more, and in addition one that is without reason. How is that? We would run out of the house a girl that Marcian wants to marry? Think about this, sir, for the love of God! The two things do not agree with each other."

"This is what they say: if it is shown that Belczaczka is hers, then Marcian will marry her, if it is shown otherwise, then he will simply dishonor her. I am not any man's conscience, so I simply repeat what people say, with this personal addition, however, that your son threatened the girl with shame. I know this for sure, and you, sir, who knows Marcian and his lecherous desires, know it also."

"I know this and that, but I do not know what you are getting at."

"What am I getting at? Only what I have already told you. If Panna Sieninska agrees to go back to you, then I have no right to oppose you or her will; but if she does not agree, then I will not drive her out of this house, for I already have promised not to do so."

"It is not a question of driving her out of your house, but that you would permit me to take her, just as you would permit me if she were one of my daughters. I only ask that you not stand in our way."

"Then I will tell you clearly: I will not permit any use of force! I am master in my house, and you, sir, who have just mentioned the king, should understand that even the king himself could not deny me."

Hearing this, Pan Krzepecki clenched his fists so strongly that his fingernails pierced his palms, and he said:

"Force? This is precisely what I fear. If ever I have had to act against people (and who has not had to deal with people's animosity), I have acted against them using the law, not violence. And what the proverb says is untrue, that the apple does not fall far from the tree. Sometimes it falls far away. . . . For your welfare and safety, I want to settle this affair peacefully. You are defenseless here in the forest, while Marcian— it is difficult for a father to speak this way of his son—has not quite taken after me. I am ashamed to admit it, but I am not able to answer for him. The entire district fears his impetuosity—and rightfully so, for he is reckless and has fifty swords at his disposal. While you, sir, you are, *repeto*, defenseless here in the forest. . . . I urge you to consider this. I am frightened myself of what can happen. . . ."

Pan Cyprianowicz rose at this, and getting close to Krzepecki, he looked him right in the white of his eyes.

"Do you wish to frighten me, sir?" he asked.

"I am frightened myself," repeated the old Krzepecki.

But further conversation was interrupted by sudden shouts issuing from the courtyard in the direction of the granary and kitchen, so both men sprang to the open window and froze with amazement in the first instant. There, between the fences, ran with terrible impetus in the direction of the gate and courtyard an unusual monster unlike any creature on earth, and behind him, on raging horses, dashed the four

Bukojemskis, shouting and waving riding crops in the air. The monster sped into the courtyard, and after him descended the brothers, looking like bats out of hell, and they began to chase him about the garth.

"Dear Jesus!" cried out Pan Cyprianowicz.

He rushed to the porch, and old Krzepecki followed in similar quick step.

Only then could they see better what was happening. The monster had the shape of a giant bird, but at the same time a rider on a horse, for it ran with some figure on its back and on four legs. But the rider and the horse were so covered with down that their heads looked like two feathered billows. There was no possibility, though, of distinguishing anything clearly, for the Tartar horse rushed like a whirlwind in a circle about the courtyard, while the Bukojemskis followed closely, not sparing blows, from which the feathers were torn away to fall to the ground or wander about the air like snowflakes.

Meanwhile the monster roared like a wounded bear, the brothers also roared, and in the general uproar were lost the voices of Pan Cyprianowicz and old Krzepecki, who were shouting at the top of their lungs:

"Stop! For the love of God, stop!"

But the others pressed on, as if madness had overtaken them, and circled the courtyard five times. From the kitchen, from the annexes, from the stables, from the direction of the barns rushed a considerable number of servants who, having heard the outcry of "stop!" repeated with apparent desperation by Pan Serafin, jumped at the horses of the Bukojemskis and began to check them, grabbing bridles and bits. Finally, the Bukojemkis' steeds were reined in, but the most difficult work was with the feathered horse. Without a bridle, cut by whips, beaten and terrified, the beast reared at the sight of the people or with a lightning move sprang to the side, so that it was only stopped when preparing to spring over the fence. One of the servants seized the horse by the forelock, another by the nostrils, several by its mane. With such a burden, the horse could not jump and fell on its forelegs. In truth, the horse sprang back up immediately, but did not attempt to escape any more; only its entire body began to tremble.

At that point, the rider was removed from the horse, and it became apparent that he had not been thrown from the horse because his legs were restrained firmly under the beast's belly. The feathers were brushed from his face. But under the down appeared a face so covered with thick tar that no one could recognize the features. Besides, the rider gave only faint signs of life, and not until he was taken to the porch did old Krzepecki recognize him, as did Pan Serafin, and both cried out in horror:

"Marcian!"

"Here is that scoundrel!" said Mateusz Bukojemski, panting. "We have punished him a little and have driven him here so that Panna Sieninska can know that there are still loving souls in the world."

Pan Cyprianowicz put his hands to his head:

"The devil take you and your loving souls! You are just bandits!"

Then he turned to Pani Dzwonkowska, who, having run up with the others, was repeatedly crossing herself, and he cried out:

"Pour some vodka into his mouth, let him regain consciousness—and then straight to bed!"

There was movement and disorder. Some rushed to prepare the bed, others for hot water, still others for vodka, while several began to pull the feathers off Marcian, a process in which they were helped by old Krzepecki, who was gritting his teeth and repeating:

"Is he alive? Is he dead? He's alive! Vengeance! Vengeance. . . ."

Then he suddenly rose, sprang over to Pan Serafin and, bending his fingers in the shape of talons right in front of Pan Serafin's face, began to shout:

"You were in on this! You have killed my son, you Armenian assassin!"

Cyprianowicz grew very pale and seized his saber, but at the same moment he remembered that he was the host and Krzepecki a guest, so he let go of the hilt, and instead raised two fingers in the air, and said:

"By the God who is above us, I swear that I knew nothing about this—and I am ready to swear on the cross as well—amen!"

"We are witnesses!" called out Marek Bukojemski.

And Cyprianowicz added:

"God has punished you, for you threatened me, a defenseless old man, with the rage of your son. Here is his rage!"

"A crime!" roared the old man. "The executioner awaits you all, and your heads will be under the sword! Vengeance! Justice!"

"See what you have done!" said Pan Serafin, turning to the Bukojemskis.

"I said it was better to cut him up straightaway," replied Lukasz.

Meantime, Pani Dzwonkowska rushed in with Gdansk vodka and began to pour it straight from the bottle into Marcian's open mouth, who choked and immediately opened his eyes.

His father fell to his knees by his side.

"Are you alive! Are you alive?" he cried out in an outburst of wild joy.

But Marcian could not yet give a reply and lay like a great eagle owl, that shot by a matchlock, falls on its back and pants on outstretched wings. But his consciousness was returning, and with it, memory. His glance traveled to his father's face, then to Pan Serafin's, and stopped at the Bukojemskis. At that point his visage became so terrible that if there had been even the smallest place in the brothers' hearts for fear, they would have trembled from head to toe.

But they merely made a step toward him, like four bulls ready to gore someone, and Mateusz inquired:

"What? That wasn't enough for you?"

CHAPTER 25

A few hours later, old Krzepecki took Marcian to Belczaczka, though the young man was unable to stand on his legs and did not know exactly what was happening to him. Previous to this, the servants had bathed him, washing him with great trouble, and had dressed him in fresh linen, but after all of these things had been done such a great weakness had overcome Marcian that he fainted several times, and was only brought back to consciousness thanks to the angelica and pimpernel bitters which Pani Dzwonkowska gave him. Pan Serafin advised to place him in bed and put off the departure till recovery was complete, but Pan Krzepecki, whose old heart was raging, did not wish to owe gratitude to a man against whom he was planning a lawsuit for harboring Panna Sieninska. Therefore, he had hay put in a wagon, and, placing a rug under Marcian as a bed, he moved toward Belczaczka, while threatening the Bukojemskis and also the host himself. But it was a funny situation in that he was continually threatening vengeance, even as he was forced to accept Cyprianowicz's assistance, and borrow from him hay, clothing and linen; but, blinded by anger, he did not sense this at all, while Pan Serafin had no mind whatever for laughter, since the action of the four brothers disturbed and concerned him much more.

Meantime, Father Woynowski arrived, having been summoned by letter. The Bukojemskis, now greatly confused, were sitting in the annex, not showing their faces, so Pan Cyprianowicz himself had to tell all that had happened, and the priest listened and listened, at times hitting the skirt of his soutane, but he did not become as shocked as Pan Serafin had expected.

Finally he said:

"If Marcian dies, then woe to the Bukojemskis; but if, as I think, he squirms out of it, I suppose that he will take private vengeance rather than raise a lawsuit."

"Why?" asked Pan Serafin.

"Because it is no small thing to open oneself up to the laughter of the entire Commonwealth. Besides which, his conduct toward Panna Sieninska would be revealed, and this also would not give him a good reputation. He has led an ignoble life, therefore it would be better for him if witnesses did not tell *publico* what they know of him."

"Perhaps so," said Cyprianowicz, "but it is difficult nevertheless to forgive the Bukojemskis such antics."

The priest waved his hand.

"The Bukojemskis are the Bukojemskis."

"What?" asked Pan Serafin in amazement. "I thought that your grace would be more outraged."

"My honorable sir," replied the old man, "you served in the army, but not as long as I. I have seen so many soldiers' antics during my time that not just any case can surprise me. It is bad that such things happen, and I will censure the Bukojemskis, but I have seen worse things, particularly when the orphan was in question. Bah! I will state openly that I would have been more outraged had Marcian's actions gone unpunished. Think of it, sir. We are old, but if we were young our blood would have boiled also. That is why I cannot blame the Bukojemskis completely."

"True, true, but Marcian may not live to see tomorrow."

"That is in God's hands; but you said that he is not wounded?"

"He is not, but he looks like one big black-and-blue mark, and was fainting continually."

"Then he will pull through, for he fainted from pain. But I must go to the Bukojemskis and make inquiries of them about what happened."

And he went. The brothers received him with joy, for they hoped that he would take their side with Pan Cyprianowicz. They began to quarrel immediately as to who should tell the tale—and stopped only when the priest gave Mateusz priority.

So he took the floor and spoke thus:

"Father benefactor, God saw our innocence! Because when we learned from Pani Dzwonkowska that the orphan had black-and-blue marks all over her little body, we came into this room in such grief that if it had not been for the jug of wine which our host sent us, our hearts would most probably have burst. I will tell you this, your grace, that we drank and we wept, we drank and we wept! And we had this in mind also, that she was no common girl, but a lady descended from senators. It is known, for example, that the higher the blood a horse has, the thinner his skin is. Slash a common nag with a whip, he will barely feel it, but strike a noble steed, and a welt rises straightaway. Think, Father benefactor, what kind of skin such a little lady must have on her shoulders, and elsewhere. Just like a wafer—don't you agree?"

"What concern is her skin to me?" replied Father Woynowski gruffly. "Tell me better, how you caught Marcian."

"We promised Pan Cyprianowicz that we would not cut him up, but we knew that old Krzepecki would come here, and at the same time it occurred to us that Marcian would rush to meet him. So, as we had agreed, two of us dragged a great salt-barrel filled with torn feathers that we got from a forester's wife over to the wood distillery before daylight, while the other two picked out a cask of the thickest tar in the place, and we waited by the house there. We looked—old Krzepecki came riding along—that's nothing! Let him ride! We waited and waited, until we become tired of waiting and thought about going to Belczaczka, but at that moment a boy from the distillery told us that Marcian was coming up the road. We rode out and stopped in front of him: 'Greetings!' 'Greetings!' 'Where are you off to?' 'Straight ahead,' he said, 'through the woods.' 'But to whose harm?' 'Whether to harm or profit,' he says, 'get out of my way!' And he reached for his saber. And we seized him by the scruff of his neck. Oh, it cannot be! In a twinkling we pulled him down from his horse, which Jan grabbed, and dragged him. He began to cry out, kick, bite, gnash his teeth, and in a lightning flash we took him to the barrels that stood one next to the other, and said: 'Oh, you son of a bitch, so you will harm orphans, threaten young ladies with disgrace, disregard high blood, whip the backs of girls, and think that no one will stand up for them? Know that there are caring souls.' And we plunged him head down into the tar. 'Know that there is chivalry!' And a second time he went into the tar! 'Know the Bukojemskis!' And then he went into the feathers! We wanted to do it a third time, but the wood distiller began to cry out that he would be smothered, and indeed he was well coated, so that neither his nose nor his eyes could be seen. Then we sat him on the saddle and tied his feet firmly under the horse's belly, so that he would not fall off. We painted the horse with a mop, and also covered him with feathers, and then we flogged this rather wild-natured Tartar horse with whips and, taking off his bridle, chased him ahead of us."

"And you drove him here?"

"As an odd beast, for we wanted to cheer up the young lady even a little and show her our brotherly affection."

"You certainly cheered her up! She almost died of fright when she saw him through the window."

"Well, when she recovers she will think of us gratefully for sure. An orphan always likes to feel that there is protection over her."

"You have done her more harm than good. Who knows if the Krzepeckis will not take her away again?"

"How's that? Dear God! Will we let them?!"

"But who will defend the girl when you are locked away in prison?"

Hearing this, the brothers became greatly concerned and began to look at one another with anxious eyes.

Finally, Lukasz struck his forehead, and said:

"They will not lock us up in a prison for, first, we will go join the military expedition; and if it happens, then help will be found if the safety of Panna Sieninska is at issue."

"For sure! For sure!" cried out Marek.

"What kind of help?" asked the priest.

"We will send a challenge to Marcian as soon as he recovers. He will not get out of our hands alive!"

"But if he dies now?"

"Then God will find a way."

"And you will pay with your necks!"

"Before that we will cut up the Turks, for which the Lord Jesus will reward us. Only let your grace take our side with Pan Cyprianowicz, for if Stanislaw had been here, he would have also been giving Marcian a bath with us."

"And Jacek would not?" asked Mateusz.

"Jacek will give him a better bath!" cried out the priest despite himself.

"And so you see, your grace."

Further conversation was interrupted by the arrival of Pan Cyprianowicz, who apparently came with an important, ready-made decision, for he spoke with great gravity:

"I have been thinking about what we should do—and does your grace know what I have decided? I have decided that we should all go to Cracow with Panna Sieninska. I do not know if we will see our boys there, for no one knows where the regiments will be and under what order they will go to the field; but we have to place the girl under the protection of the king or the queen, or if that is not possible, to secure her in some cloister for the time being. I have determined, as your grace knows, to join the expedition in my old age, so that I can serve with my son, and die with him, if that is God's will. During our absence the girl would not be safe even under the protection of Father Tworkowski in Radom. These gentlemen,"—here he pointed to the Bukojemskis—

"need to be under the office of the hetman as soon as possible. No one knows what will happen here. I have acquaintances at court—Pan Matczynski, Pan Gninski, Pan Grothus—and I think that I can get their protection for the orphan. When that happens, I will inquire about Zbierzchowski's regiment and go straight to my son, where I shall also see your Jacek. Well?"

"By God!" cried out Father Woynowski. "This is a splendid idea. And I will go with you! I will go with you! To Jacek! And as to Panna Sieninska—of course! The Sobieskis owe the Sieninskis a great debt! She will be safe in Cracow—and nearer. For I am certain that Jacek has not forgotten her. And when the war ends—what God wills, will happen. . . . They will give me a substitute here in the parish from Radom—and I will go with you!"

"All together!" boomed the Bukojemskis with joy. "To Cracow!"

"And to the field of glory!" added the priest.

CHAPTER 26

CONSULTATIONS now followed concerning the expedition, for there were no voices against it, and even Father Woynowski began to make attempts to get a substitute pastor from Radom. This decision was by now an old one, however, modified only by the intention of taking Panna Sieninska to Cracow and securing protection for her from the king or the cloister against the pursuit of the Krzepeckis. Pan Cyprianowicz foresaw that the king, taken up with the war, would have no time to talk about private matters, but there remained the queen, to whom access would be made easy through the dignitaries he was acquainted with and who were related, for the greater part, with the houses of the Sieninskis and the Taczewskis.

There were also concerns that the Krzepeckis might attack Jedlinka after the master of the house and the Bukojemskis had left, and rob the great wealth in furniture and silver that were to be found in the mansion. But Wilczopolski guaranteed that he would defend the place with the servants and the foresters, and would not let the Krzepeckis touch anything. Despite this, Pan Serafin transported the silver to Radom and left it in a Bernardine cloister, where he had already placed large sums of money, not wanting to keep it at home in the midst of the expansive Kozienicki Wilderness.

Meanwhile, Pan Serafin kept an attentive ear open for news from Belczaczka, for much depended on what happened there. If Marcian were to die, a serious liability would fall on the Bukojemskis; in the opposite case, there would be hope that even a lawsuit would not occur, for it was difficult to imagine that the Krzepeckis would want to expose themselves willingly to ridicule. A more likely possibility, according to Pan Cyprianowicz, was that he would not leave him at peace concerning Panna Sieninska; but he thought that if the orphan were to be under the king's care, then the essence of any lawsuit would be lost.

They learned, through the butler, that the older Krzepecki had been going to Radom and Lublin, but only for brief amounts of time.

As to Marcian, he was seriously ill for the first week after the incident, and there was fear that the tar which he had swallowed in abundance might choke him or completely stop up his intestines. But in the second week he became better. He did not, it is true, leave his bed, for he could not stand on his legs, his bones pained him mercilessly, and he felt *in summo grado fatigatus*, but he began to hurl insults at the Bukojemskis and take pleasure in thoughts of vengeance. After the passage of two weeks, even his "Radom Company" began to visit him: a variety of scoundrels with sabers hanging from hempen cords, holes in their boots and sunken stomachs, continually hungry and thirsty. And he counseled with them and plotted something not only against the Bukojemskis and Pan Cyprianowicz, but also Panna Sieninska, of whom he could not think without gnashing his teeth; and he invented such scandals against her, that his father had to warn him that they bordered on the criminal.

The echo of these plots and threats reached Jedlinka and produced various impressions on different people. Pan Serafin, a courageous but cautious man, was somewhat alarmed by them, particularly when it came to him that this hostility on the part of evil and dangerous people would fall on his son also. Father Woynowski, who had hotter blood in his veins, was greatly indignant and predicted that the Krzepeckis would end in a bad way, and though he was entirely won over to the young lady, he turned from time to time to Pan Cyprianowicz or the Bukojemskis, and said:

"Who caused the Trojan War? A *mulier*! Who causes fights and quarrels? A *mulier*! And so it is now! Innocent or not, a *mulier*!"

But the Bukojemskis took lightly the danger which threatened everyone from Marcian, and even promised themselves various amusements because of it. They were seriously warned, however, from many sides. The Sulgostowskis, the Silnickis, the Kochanowskis, and others, all greatly indignant at Marcian, came one after the other to Jedlinka with news that he was gathering a party, including even bandits from the wilderness. They offered assistance, but the brothers did not want help, and Lukasz, who spoke for most, replied thus to Rafal Silnicki, when the later beseeched them to be on the alert:

"My, my! There is no harm in thinking of our craft, and straightening out and fixing our touch, which has grown somewhat rusty from disuse. Belczaczka is no fortress, so let Marcian think of his own safety, for who knows what may meet him yet; and if he wishes to give us a dish of ingratitude, then by all means, let him try!"

Pan Silnicki glanced at the brothers with a certain astonishment, and said:

"A dish of ingratitude? Well, he certainly doesn't owe you gratitude."

But Lukasz became sincerely indignant at this:

"He doesn't owe us gratitude? We could have cut him up to pieces. Who gave him life? Once, Pani Krzepecka, and the second time our discretion. But if he is always going to count on it, then tell him, sir, that he is mistaken."

"And also tell him that he will see Panna Sieninska as much as his own ears," added Marek.

And Jan finished:

"Why should he not see her then? It is not difficult for a man to see his own ears if they are cut off."

And so the conversation ended. The brothers repeated it to Panna Sieninska in order to calm her, which was not necessary, however, for the young lady was not timid by nature, and besides, in the same measure as she feared the Krzepeckis, and in particular Marcian, at Belczaczka, she was now convinced that no danger threatened her in Jedlinka. When, on the day following her arrival at Jedlinka, she saw Marcian covered in feathers through the window, resembling some loathsome beast chased by the whips of the Bukojemskis, after her first moments of frightful horror mixed with amazement and even pity, she took on such confidence in the power and strength of the brothers that she could not even imagine how anyone could not fail to fear them. Marcian, after all, was considered a dangerous person and a bully, and see what they did with him. It is true that Jacek had cut them all up at one time, but Jacek in her eyes had outgrown ordinary people, and in general he appeared to her before the last separation in such a mysterious manner that she did not know how to measure him at all. The remarks made about him by the Bukojemskis themselves and Pan Cyprianowicz, together with the words of the priest, who spoke of him the most, confirmed in her only amazement for that friend from her childhood, who had been once so close to her, but now was so far away and different. They confirmed in her not only a longing for him, but an even sweeter feeling, which once confessed to the priest in a moment of excitement, she closed off again in the depth of her heart, as a pearl is closed off in a mussel shell.

Besides this, she had a particular unswerving certainty in her soul that she must meet him, and even that she would meet him soon. She had torn herself from the house of the Krzepeckis; she felt over her the formidable protection of warmhearted people; therefore that certainty became the cheer and joy of her existence. Her health returned, her gaiety returned—and she blossomed again like a flower in spring. Her presence brightened the entire Jedlinka mansion, which had been so serious up till then. She had completely won over Pani Dzwonkowska, Pan Cyprianowicz, and the Bukojemskis. The whole house was filled with her presence, and wherever she showed her upturned nose and wherever her young, happy eyes glowed, delight and smiles turned up on all faces. She only feared Father Woynowski a little, for it seemed to her that he held in his hands her fate, as well as Jacek's. She also looked upon him with a certain submissiveness but he, having a compassionate heart for all of God's creatures that in general was like soft wax, became truly fond of her, and what's more, when he got to know her better, he valued her pure soul more and more, though at times he called her a jay-bird and a squirrel, for as he said: "She's here, then she's there."

After that first confession, they did not speak anymore of Jacek, as if by mutual agreement. Both felt that it was too much of a "delicate matter." Pan Serafin did not speak of him with her in front of people, but in private he did not feel so constrained, and when she asked once if he would meet his son in Cracow as soon as he got there, he replied with a question himself:

"And would you not wish to meet someone there also?"

And he thought that she would wriggle out of it with a joke, but a shadow of sadness appeared on her face, and she replied seriously:

"I would be glad to apologize as soon as possible to anyone whom I have wronged."

So he looked at her with some emotion, but after a moment one could see that another thought had entered his mind, for he stroked her rosy cheek and said:

"Oh, you have the means to reward so that the king himself could not reward better!"

Hearing this, she lowered her eyes, and stood before him beautiful and ruddy like the morning dawn.

CHAPTER 27

PREPARATIONS for the expedition went forward at a brisk pace. Attendants were chosen with care—strong, healthy and sober men. Arms, horses, wagon and carts were ready. According to the customs of the day, even dogs were not forgotten, which during a march walked under the wagons, and at places of rest were used to hunt foxes and rabbits. The amount of preparations and supplies surprised Panna Sieninska, who did not expect that a war expedition would require so much effort. Thinking that perhaps this trouble was taken for her safety, she began to inquire of Pan Serafin on these matters.

And he, as a wise and experienced man, answered her questions thus:

"Certainly we have you in our consideration, for I think we will not pass by Marcian without encountering some violence from him. You have heard that he is gathering bullies with whom he is conspiring and drinking. We would be disgraced if we were to allow anyone to snatch you away from us. What will be, will be; but even if we were to fall one after the other, we must get you to Cracow unharmed."

Hearing this, the young lady kissed him on the hand, saying that she was not worthy of putting their lives in danger, but he simply waved this away:

"We would not dare show ourselves to people if we did not do this," he said. "Besides, matters have arranged themselves so that one coincides with the other, for it is not enough just to go to war, one must prepare for it carefully. You are surprised that each of us needs three to four horses, as well as attendants, but know that in war a horse is fundamental. Many of them die along the way, crossing rivers and bogs, or from various camp accidents. And then what? If you buy another horse in haste, one which has various *vitia* and faults, this horse will fail you at the most critical moment. That is why, though my son and Jacek Taczewski took sizeable retinues, and excellent horses also, we thought that each should get a new steed just in case; and Father Woynowski, who is more knowledgeable about horses than anyone else, bought for a good price from old Pan Podlodowski such a Turkish horse for Jacek that even the hetman himself would not be ashamed to appear on him."

"Which one is for your son?" asked the young lady.

Pan Cyprianowicz looked at her, shook his head, smiled and said:

"I see Father Woynowski is right in what he says about women. 'Though the devil were to be most friendly, he will be just as crafty.' You ask which horse is for my son? I will answer thus: Jacek's horse is that sorrel with the arrow sign on his forehead and a white left fetlock."

"You're teasing me, sir!" cried the young lady.

And snorting at him like a cat, she spun around and vanished. But that very day bread crumbs from rolls and salt from saltshakers disappeared, and the following day Pan Lukasz Bukojemski saw something very interesting: at the well in the courtyard the sorrel horse had his nose in the white hands of Panna Sieninska, and when he was led afterward to the stable, he looked around at her time after time, expressing his yearning with short neighs. Pan Lukasz could not ask her at that time about the cause of this confidence, for he was much occupied with loading a wagon, so it was only in the afternoon that he approached the girl, his eyes full of admiration, and said:

"Have you noticed one thing?"

"What?" asked the young lady.

"That even a beast recognizes what is a real delicacy."

And she, forgetting that he had seen her in the morning, and seeing the admiration in his eyes, raised her wonderful brows in surprise, and asked:

"Whom are you thinking of?"

"Whom?" repeated Bukojemski. "Jacek's horse."

"Ah, his horse!"

Saying this, she burst into laughter and ran from the porch to her room, while he stood there astonished and a little confused, not understanding why she had run away or what had caused her sudden gaiety.

One more week passed, and the preparations were nearing completion, but somehow Pan Cyprianowicz was in no rush to leave. He put off the departure from day to day, improved various odds and ends, complained of the heat, and finally became completely anxious. The young lady yearned to start the journey. The Bukojemskis were becoming completely restless, and at last Father Woynowski acknowledged that further delay would simply be a worthless waste of time.

But Pan Serafin answered their urgency thus:

"I have news that His Majesty the King is still not in Cracow and will not be there soon; meanwhile, the troops are to assemble there, but not all, and it is unknown when. I told Stanislaw to send me a man every month with a letter detailing exactly where the regiments are quartered, where they are to go and under whose command. Seven weeks have passed already without any information. I am expecting a letter any day now, and that is why I am delaying. I will tell you that I am a bit worried. Do not think that it is certain that we will find them at Cracow. Bah! It may even happen that they will not be there at all!"

"How is that?" asked Panna Sieninska with concern.

"Well, the regiments do not need to march through Cracow. Wherever a regiment stands, it can move from there as straight as an arrow, but where Pan Zbierzchowski may be at the moment I do not know. What if he has been sent to the Silesian border, or to the army of the grand hetman who is coming from Russia? It frequently happens that before a war regiments are moved about from one place to the next, if just to train them in marching. In the course of seven weeks various orders might have been issued, of which Stanislaw should have informed me. But because he has not done so, I am worried, for it is well known that there are frequent arguments and duels in camps. What if something has happened? But even if nothing has happened, we need to know, after all, where his regiment is and from where it will move."

Everyone was saddened by these words, but Father Woynowski said:

"A regiment is not a needle, though, nor is it a button that is found with difficulty when it is torn from a cloak and falls into the grass. Do not worry yourself over this, sir! We will learn of the regiment quicker in Cracow than here in Jedlinka."

"But we may miss the letter on the road."

"Then tell Wilczopolski to send the letter on after us. That is what should be done! Meanwhile we will find in Cracow the safest shelter for Panna Sieninska, and when the time comes for us to move on, our minds will be at rest."

"True! True!"

"Then this is my advice: If we get nothing by tomorrow, then we should start in the cool of the evening for Radom, and then farther, to Kielce, Jedrzejow and Miechow."

"Perhaps we should leave for Radom the day after at dawn, so as not to pass through the forests at night and leave ourselves vulnerable to an ambush from the Krzepeckis."

"That shouldn't stop us!" exclaimed Mateusz Bukojemski. "Better to go when it is cool. If they are going to attack, they will do so in the day as well as at night, and now things are visible in the night."

Saying this, he began to rub his hands in glee, and his three other brothers followed suit.

But Father Woynowski was of a different mind. He doubted much that the Krzepeckis would be so bold as to attack them out in the open.

"Marcian might do it, but old Krzepecki is too smart for doing something like this, and knows well, moreover, how such an affair smells and how more than one man who has forced himself on a woman has paid for *raptus puellae*. Marcian also could not count on a victory against our strength, but if he could succeed, he can count on vengeance from Jacek and Stanislaw."

The words of the priest threw cold water on the joy of the Bukojemskis, but their spirits were raised by Wilczopolski, who took the opposite view, shaking his head, striking the floor with his wooden leg, and saying:

"Even if you meet no adventure as far as Radom, bah, even as far as Kielce or Miechow, I advise you not to neglect any precaution, for along the road there are woods everywhere, and I, as someone who knows the young Krzepecki the best, am convinced that this devil will plan something."

CHAPTER 28

FINALLY the day of departure arrived. The procession moved out of Jedlinka at the break of day, in beautiful weather, and with a grand number of people and horses. Besides the sheet-iron and leather-covered coach intended for Panna Sieninska and Pani Dzwonkowska, and also for the priest in case his old gun wound should annoy him on horseback too greatly, there were three well-laden wagons, each drawn by four horses. At each wagon were three men, including the driver. Behind Pan Serafin Cyrprianowicz six mounted attendants, in turquoise-colored livery, led reserve horses. The priest had two attendants, each Bukojemski also had two, and there was a forester who guarded the trunk-laden wagons. Altogether the party consisted of thirty-four persons well armed with muskets and sabers. It is true that in case of attack some could not aid in defense, since they would have to guard wagons and horses, but even in that case the Bukojemskis felt sure that they could go through the world with those attendants, and that it would not be healthy for a party three or four times their number to attack them. Their hearts were swelling with a joy so enormous that they could hardly stay put in their saddles. They had fought manfully in their time against Tartars and Cossacks, but those were common, small wars, and later on, when they settled in the wilderness, their youth had been entirely spent in inspecting enclosures, in a ceaseless watch over foresters, in killing bears when it was their duty to preserve them, and in drunken frolics at Kozienice and Radom and Przytyk. But now, for the first time, when each put his stirrup near the stirrup of his brother, when they were going to a war against the immense might of Turkey, they felt that this was their true destination, that their past life had been vain and wretched, and that now had begun in reality the deeds and achievements for which God the Father had created Polish nobles, God the Son redeemed them, and the Holy Ghost made them sacred. They could not think this out clearly, or express it in words, for in those things they had never been adept, but so strong was their feeling that they wanted to shout for joy. Their advance seemed too slow to them. Ah, if they could only rush like a whirlwind on their horses and fly toward that great destination, to that great battle of the Poles with the pagans, to that triumph through Polish hands of the cross above the crescent, to a splendid death, and to glory for the ages! They felt loftier in some way, purer, more honorable, and in their nobility still more ennobled. They had scarcely a thought then for Marcian and his rioting company, or for barriers and engagements on the roadway. All that seemed to them now something trivial, vain, and unworthy of attention. And if whole legions had stood in their way, they would have shot over them like a tempest, they would have ridden right across them, they would have put them under the bellies of their horses, and rushed farther on. Their inborn lionlike impulses were roused, and warlike, knightly blood had begun to run through them with such vigor that if a command had been given to those four men to charge the whole body-guard of the Sultan, they would not have hesitated for one instant.

Similar feelings, and furthermore founded on old recollections, filled the hearts of Pan Serafin and Father Woynowski. The priest had passed the flower of his life on the field with a lance in his hand or a saber. He remembered a whole series of defeats and victories, he remembered the dreadful rebellion of Chmielnicki, Zolte Wody, Korsun, Pilawce, Zbaraz the Renowned, and the great battle of Beresteczko. He remembered the Swedish war with its never-ending battles, and the attack of Rakoczego. He had been in Denmark, for the victorious Polish nation, not content with crushing and driving out Sweden, had sent Czarniecki's invincible regiments to the borders of a distant ocean in pursuit of the enemy; he had helped rout Chowanski and Dolgoruk; he had known the noblest knights and greatest men of the period; he had been a pupil of the immortal Wolodyjowski; he had loved battle, slaughter, assaults and bloodshed. But all that had lasted only until personal misfortune had broken his spirit, and he took holy orders. From that day he changed altogether, and when, turning to people in front of the altar, he said to them: "Peace be with you," he believed himself uttering Christ's own commandment, and that every war, being opposed to that commandment, is "disgusting" to Heaven, a sin against mercy and a stain on Christian nations. He made one exception, however: a war against Turks. "God," he said, "put the Polish people on horseback, and turned their breasts eastward; by that same act He showed them His will and their calling. He knew why He chose us for that position, and put others behind us; hence, if we wish to fulfill His command and our mission with worthiness, we must face that vile sea, and break its waves against our bosoms."

Father Woynowski also thought that God had purposely placed on the throne a sovereign who when still a hetman had shed pagan blood in great quantity, so that his hands might give the last blow to the enemy, and avert ruin from the Christian world once and for all. It seemed to him that just now had the great day of destiny arrived, the day to accomplish God's purpose; therefore, he considered that war a sacred way of the cross, and was delighted at the thought that age, toil and wounds had not pressed him to the earth so utterly that he might not take part in it.

Once again, he would be able to drive away standards; once again, he, an old soldier of Christ, would spur on his horse, and charge with a cross in his hand into the thickest of the battle, with the certainty in his heart that behind him and that cross a thousand lances would enter pagan bodies and a thousand sabers would descend on their skulls. Finally thoughts flew into his head which were personal and more in accord with his earlier disposition. He could, after all, hold the cross in his left hand and a saber in his right. As a priest he could not raise a sword against Christians, but against Turks it was just! Just, indeed! Then, he would show young men how pagan lights should be extinguished, how pagan champions must be mowed down and cut to pieces; he would show what kind of warriors were the soldiers of olden days. Ha! Men had marveled at his prowess on more than just one field; perhaps now the king himself will be astounded! And this thought filled him with so much happiness that he began to make mistakes in saying his rosary: "Hail Mary — attack! slay! — The Lord — at them! — is with Thee — cut them down!" Until finally he collected himself: "Wait! To hell with this! Glory is illusory. Have I gone mad? *Non nobis! Non nobis, sed nomini tuo. . . .*" And he began to pass the beads through his fingers more attentively.

Pan Serafin was repeating also his litany of the morning, but from time to time he looked now at the priest, now at the young lady, now at the Bukojemskis, who were riding at the side of the coach, now at the trees and the dew-covered glades. At last, when he had finished the final "Ave," he turned to the old man and, sighing deeply, said:

"Your grace seems to be in rather good spirits."

"And also your grace," replied the priest.

"For sure. Until a man starts, he is bustling, rushing about and worried; only when the wind blows around him in the field does it become light in his heart. I remember when, ten years ago, we were marching to Chocim, there was a strange willingness in every warrior, so that even though the action took place in the harsh weather of November, more than one person threw his coat off because of the warmth coming from his heart. Well, God, who gave such a victory that time, will undoubtedly give it now, for the leader is the same, and the vigor and valor of the men not inferior. I know the glory of the Swedish army, the French, and even the Germans, but there is no one better against Turks than our soldiers."

"I have heard how his grace the king said the same," replied the priest. "'The Germans,' he said, 'stand under fire patiently, though they blink when attacking, but,' he said, 'if I can bring my men up nose to nose I am satisfied, for they will sweep everything before them as can no other cavalry in existence.' And this is true. The Lord Jesus has gifted us richly with this power, not only the nobles, but the peasants as well. For instance, our field infantry, when they spit on their palms and advance with their muskets, the best of the Janissaries cannot match them in any way. Both of us have seen this and not just once."

"If God has kept Stas and Jacek in good health, I am glad that their first campaign will be against the Turks. But what does your grace think, against whom will the Turks turn their main forces?"

"According to my opinion, they will move against the Emperor, for they are warring against him, and helping rebellion in Hungary. But the Turks have two or three armies, so it is unknown where we shall meet them exactly."

"That is why, no doubt, our side has not organized a main camp, and regiments move from one place to another, as reports arrive. The regiments under Pan Jablonowski are now at Trebowla; others are moving toward Cracow; and even others as events happen. I do not know where the voivod of Wolyn is quartered at present, nor where Zbierzchowski's command is. Sometimes I think that my son has not written for a long time because his regiment may be moving toward those parts."

"If he is ordered to Cracow, it is certain that he must march near us. That, however, depends upon where he was earlier and from where he is starting at present. We may get news at Radom. Is not our first night's halt at Radom?"

"It is. I would also like it if the prelate Tworkowski saw the girl and gave her definite advice. He will furnish us with letters to help her in Cracow."

The conversation stopped for a time; then Pan Cyprianowicz raised his eyes again to Father Woynowski, and asked:

"But what do you think will happen should she meet Jacek in Cracow?"

"I do not know: they will meet or not meet. That will happen which God wishes. Jacek could, with time, restore his family fortune through a marriage, while she is as poor as a church mouse. Wealth alone is nothing but *furda*; the issue is the splendor of the family line."

"But she is of high lineage. And I do not even have to mention that this girl is like gold; besides it is well known that they love each other to death."

"Oh, to the death, for sure!"

It did not seem that the priest wished to speak much on this subject, for he turned the conversation to another issue.

"Well," he said, "let us not forget that a robber is after that gold. Do you remember what Wilczopolski said?"

Pan Serafin glanced around the forest, and said:

"The Krzepeckis would not dare; they would not dare! Our party is fairly large, and as you see, there is quiet all around. I wanted the girl to sit in the coach for safety, but she declined. She fears nothing."

"Well, that is because she has good blood," muttered the priest. "But I note that she has won you over thoroughly."

"Eh, and you too, somewhat," responded Cyprianowicz. "But as for me, I admit it openly. When she asks for something, she knows how to move her eyes in such fashion that you must yield where you stand. Women have various methods, but have you noticed that she has that way of blinking, and that she folds her hands at the same time? Near Belczaczka, I will tell her to enter the coach, but meanwhile she wanted desperately to ride on horseback, because, she says, it is healthier."

"And in such weather it is surely healthier."

"Look, reverend father, at how rosy she is already—just like a euphorbia laurel."

"What is her rosiness to me?" said the priest. "But as to the day, you are right; it is lovely."

In fact the weather was really wonderful, and the morning fresh and dewy. Single drops on pine needles glittered with the rainbow colors of diamonds. The interior of the forest was bright from the hazel woods strewn with the rays of the morning sun. Farther on, orioles were twittering with joy. All about was the odor of pine, and the whole earth seemed to be glad of the sun and the cloudless blue sky.

Thus pushing forward, they finally reached the same tar pit at which Marcian Krzepecki had been seized by the Bukojemskis not too long ago. But the fear that some ambush might be lurking there proved groundless. Near the well were two tar-laden wagons, and to these were attached two wretched little horses, whose heads were sunk in bags of oats. The drivers stood by the horses, and were eating cheese and bread, but at sight of the grand party they put away these provisions as quickly as possible and, removing their caps, looked on in curiosity at the travelers. When asked if they had seen armed men, they answered that since morning a rider had been waiting, but that a moment ago, on seeing this party from a distance, he had rushed away with all the speed of his horse in the opposite direction. The news alarmed Pan Serafin, for it seemed to him that this horseman had been sent as a scout by the Krzepeckis. Therefore, as the leader, he doubled their watchfulness. He commanded two attendants to ride at both sides and examine the forest; he sent two others ahead with an order that if they spotted an armed group, they should fire their muskets and return with all haste to the wagons. An hour passed, however, without any kind of alarm. The party pushed forward slowly, carefully watching its front, its rear and its sides, but it was quiet in the forest. Only orioles twittered, while here and there was heard the hammering of those little smiths of the forest, the woodpeckers. At last they reached a wide field, but before going out on it, Pan Cyprianowicz and the priest insisted that the young lady get off the mount and sit inside the coach, as they were to pass not far from Belczaczka, the trees of which, and even the mansion peering between them, were visible to the naked eye. Panna Sieninska looked on the house with emotion, for in it she had passed many of the best, as well as the worst, days of her life. She had wished to look, above all, at Wyrabek, but the lindens of Belczaczka so covered it that the dwelling was not to be seen from the coach. It occurred to her that she might never again see those places, so she sighed quietly and became sorrowful.

The Bukojemskis looked sharply and challengingly at the mansion, the village and the neighborhood—but everywhere there was great quiet. Along broad fallow lands, which were flooded in sunlight, were grazing cows and sheep, guarded by dogs and groups of children. Here and there flocks of geese seemed like white spots, and had it not been for the summer heat, one might have thought from afar that they were tracts of snow lying on the hill slopes; aside from this, the region actually seemed empty. Pan Cyprianowicz, who did not lack the dash of a cavalier, wished to show the Krzepeckis how little he cared for them, and purposefully ordered the first halt right there to give the horses "a breath." So the party stopped in the midst of fields of wheat waving under the wind and rustling gently, and in the midst of the silence of the plain broken only by the snorting of horses.

"To your health! To your health!" answered the attendants to them.

But that calm was not to the taste of the youngest Bukojemski, Marek, who turned toward the mansion and began to shout to the absent Krzepeckis, as he waved his hand:

"Come out here, you sons of bitches! Show your dog snout, Stump, and we will soon put a cross on it with our sabers!"

Then he bent toward the carriage:

"Your ladyship," he said, "you see that Marcian and his company are not in a hurry to attack us, nor are the bandits in the wilderness."

"Do bandits attack?" asked the young lady.

"Oh, they do, but not us! There are quite a few of them in the Kozienicki Wilderness and in the forests toward Cracow. If his grace the king would grant pardon, enough would be found of those bandits right here in this neighborhood to make two good regiments."

"I should rather meet bandits than Pan Marcian's company, of which people tell in Belczaczka such terrible stories. I have not heard of bandits attacking a mansion."

"They do not, for a bandit has the same kind of sense that a wolf has. Consider, young lady, that a wolf never kills sheep or horned cattle in the neighborhood where his lair is."

"Yes, he speaks well!" called out the other brothers.

Marek, glad of this praise, explained further.

"The bandit also does not attack any village or mansion in this wilderness, in which he lives, for the reason that if the neighboring people should pursue, then they, knowing the forests and all the hiding places in them, would hunt him out all the more easily. That is why bandits make their attacks in farther regions, or fall on travelers, regardless of whether they are in great or small parties."

"Have they no fear?"

"They have no fear of God, so why should they fear men?"

But Panna Sieninska was already thinking of something else, so that when Pan Serafin approached the coach, she began to blink in her distinctive way, and asked:

"Why should I stay in the coach when no attack threatens? I can go on horseback, can't I?"

"Why?" replied Pan Serafin. "The sun is high, and it would burn your face. What if someone would be displeased at that?"

Hearing that, the young lady withdrew with a sudden movement to the interior of the coach, and Pan Cyprianowicz turned to the brothers:

"Is that not true?"

But not being quick-witted, they did not know what was being talked about, and started to ask:

"Who? Who?"

So Pan Cyprianowicz shrugged his shoulders, and said:

"The prince bishop of Cracow, the German emperor, and the king of France."

After which, he gave the sign, and the cavalcade moved on.

They passed Belczaczka, and once again rode though tilled fields, fallow land, meadows, and broad airy regions which were bordered on the horizon by the blue rim of a forest. At Jedlinka they stopped for a second rest, during which the brewers, the citizens and the peasants took farewell of Father Woynowski—-and before evening they stopped for their first night's lodging at Radom.

Marcian Krzepecki had not given the least sign of life. They learned that he had passed the previous day in Radom, and had drunk with his company, but had gone home for the night; so the priest and Pan Cyprianowicz breathed with more freedom, judging that no danger now threatened them on the journey.

CHAPTER 29

THE prelate Tworkowski furnished them with letters to Father Hacki, to the vice-chancellor Gninski, who, as they knew, was enrolling a whole regiment for the coming war at his own cost, and to Pan Matczynski. He was quite overjoyed to see Panna Sieninska and Father Woynowski, for whom he felt a great friendship, and Pan Cyprianowicz, whom he prized as a skilled Latinist who understood every quotation and maxim. He, too, had heard of Marcian Krzepeck's threats, but had lent no great weight to them, judging that if an attack had been planned it would have been made in the Kozienicki Wilderness, a place more favorable for that kind of deed than the forests between Radom and Kielce. "The young man will not attack you," he said to Pan Cyprianowicz, "and his father will not bring an action, for then he would have to deal with me, and he knows that I have other weapons against him besides church censure." The prelate then entertained them all day, and let them start only toward evening. Since danger seemed like it had been most decidedly set aside, Pan Cyprianowicz agreed to night travel, all the more since the weather was becoming hot.

The first few miles, however, they still traveled in daylight. Along the Oronka river, which here and there formed marshes, began again, in those days, extensive pine forests, which took in Oronsk, Sucha, Krogulcza, and extended as far as Szydlowiec, and beyond—up to Mroczkow and Bzin, and even to Kielce. They moved slowly, for in some places the old road lay among sandy hillocks and holes, while in others it sank very notably and became a muddy, stick-covered ridgeway. This ridge lay in a quagmire through which a man could pass neither with wagon nor horse, nor go on foot at any season, except during very dry summers. These places enjoyed no good repute, but the travelers, confident of their strength, had little concern about this and were glad to move in cool air, when heat did not trouble men, or flies annoy horses.

Night descended soon, but it was pleasant and clear. Above the woods rose a large, red full moon, which decreased and grew pale as it made its way upward, after which, paling completely, it sailed like a silver swan through the navy blue night sky. The wind ceased. The motionless forest was buried in a stillness broken only by the voices of gnats flying in from distant pools, and by the playing of landrails in the grass of the neighboring meadows.

Father Woynowski intoned: "Hail, Oh Wise Lady, the residences dear to God," to which the four bass voices of the Bukojemskis and the voice of Pan Cyprianowicz answered immediately: "Adorned by the golden table and seven columns." Panna Sieninska joined the chorus, after her the attendants, and soon the pious hymn was resounding through the forest. But when they had finished all the canonical hours and repeated all the "Aves," silence set in again. The priest, the brothers and Pan Serafin conversed for some time yet in lowered voices; then they began to doze, and at last they fell asleep for good.

They heard neither the "hup! hup!" of the drivers, nor the snorting of horses, nor the sucking sounds made when hoofs were drawn out of mud on that long ridgeway which lay in the sticky and reed-covered quagmire, and which they came to shortly before midnight. The shouts of attendants, who were advancing in front, first roused the sleepers.

"Stop! Stop!"

Everyone opened their eyes. The Bukojemskis straightened in their saddles and galloped ahead lively.

"What is it?"

"The road is blocked. There is a ditch across it, and beyond the ditch an abatis."

The sabers of the brothers screeched in their scabbards and then gleamed in the moonlight.

"To arms! An ambush!"

Pan Cyprianowicz found himself at the obstacle in one moment, and understood. There was no mistaking it: a broad ditch had been dug across the ridgeway, and beyond the ditch lay whole pine trees which, with their branches sticking up, formed a great obstruction. The men who stopped the road in that fashion had evidently intended to let the party enter the ridge, from which there was no escape on either side, and then attack in the rear.

"To your guns! To your muskets!" thundered the voice of Father Woynowski. "They are coming!"

In fact about a hundred yards behind them dark figures—strange, squarish, quite unlike men—appeared on the ridge, and came running toward the wagons very quickly.

"Fire!" commanded the priest.

A report was heard, and brilliant flashes pierced the night gloom. Only one figure rolled to the earth, but the other men ran the more swiftly toward the wagons, and after them denser groups appeared.

Experienced in many years of war, Father Woynowski realized straightway that the men were carrying bundles of straw, reeds or willows, and that was why the first discharge had such little effect.

"Fire! In order! Four at a time! And at their knees!" he shouted.

Two attendants had blunderbusses loaded with buckshot. When these men took their places alongside others and fired at the knees of the attackers, cries of pain were heard, and this time the whole front rank of bundles tumbled down to the mud on the ridgeway. But the next rank of men sprang over those who were prostrate, and came still closer to the wagons.

"Fire!" came the command for the third time.

And again came a salvo, this time with more effect, for the onrush was stopped momentarily, and disorder arose among the attackers.

The priest acquired courage, for he knew that the attackers had outwitted themselves in their choice of position. In truth, if they had gotten the upper hand, not a living soul would have been able to escape, and the attackers had this particularly in mind; but, not having men to hem in the party on all sides, they were forced to attack only over the ridgeway, and therefore in a thin body, which made defense much easier. In this manner, five or six brave and strong men could defend the passage all night, if necessary.

The attackers began to fire also, but because their weapons were apparently of poor quality, they caused no great damage. Their first fire struck only a horse and one attendant in the thigh. By that time, the Bukojemskis were begging to charge the enemy, and promising to sweep right and left into the quagmire any men whom they might not crush in the mud of the roadway. But the priest, who kept their strength for the last, would not send them; he commanded the brothers, however, as excellent marksmen, to shower bullets at the attackers from a distance and guard Pan Cyprianowicz from the direction of the ditch and the obstruction.

"If they attack us from that side," he said, "they may accomplish something, but they will not get us cheaply."

Then he hastened for a moment to the coach, in which Panna Sieninska was sitting with Pani Dzwonkowska. Both were reciting prayers, though without any great fear.

"It is nothing!" he said. "Have no fear!"

"I am not frightened," answered the girl. "But I would like to get off and . . ."

Her further words were drowned out by shots. The attackers, confused for a moment, pressed along the ridge now, with strange and singular blind daring, since it was clear that they would not effect much on that side.

"Hm!" thought the priest. "Were it not for the women, we might charge them."

And he had begun to think of sending the Bukojemski brothers with four good attendants, when he looked at both flanks and trembled.

On the two sides of the quagmire appeared crowds of men, who, springing from hillock to hillock, or along sheaves of reeds, which had been thrown in soft places on purpose, were running toward the wagons.

As quickly as possible, the priest turned on them two ranks of attendants, but he understood at the same time the enormous danger of the situation. His party was now surrounded on three sides. The attendants were, it is true, chosen men, who had been involved in a variety of entanglements, but they were insufficient in number, especially as some had to guard the extra horses. Therefore it was evident that after the first volley, inadequate because of so many attackers, and before guns could be loaded again, there would be a hand-to-hand struggle in which the weaker would fall.

Only one plan remained, to retreat by the ridgeway, that is, leave the wagons, command the Bukojemskis to sweep all before them, and push on behind the four brothers, keeping the women among the horses in the center. So when they had fired at both sides again, the priest ordered the women to mount, and arranged all for the onrush. In the first rank were the four brothers, behind them six attendants, then Panna Sieninska and Pani Dzwonkowska, at the side the priest and Pan Serafin, behind them eight attendants, four in a rank. After the charge and retreat from the ridgeway he intended to reach the first village, collect all the peasants, return with them and rescue the wagons.

Still he stopped for a moment, and only when the attackers were little more than a dozen or so yards distant and when wild sounds were heard suddenly beyond the obstruction, did he shout out:

"Strike!"

"Strike!" roared the Bukojemskis, and they flew forward like a hurricane destroying all things before it. When they had ridden up to the enemy, the horses rose on their haunches and plunged into the densest crowd of robbers, trampling some, pushing others into the quagmire, overthrowing whole lines of people. The brothers cut with sabers unsparingly, and without pause. There was great shouting and splashing of bodies as men fell into the water near the ridgeway, but the four dreadful horsemen pushed forward; their arms moving like those of a windmill to which a gale gives dreadful impetus. Some attackers sprang willingly into the water to save themselves; others put up pitchforks and billhooks against the onrushing brothers. Clubs and spears were raised also; but again the horses reared and, breaking everything before them, swept on like a whirlwind in a young forest.

If the road had not been so narrow, and if those who were slashed had a means of flight and those behind not pushed on those in front, the Bukojemskis would have cleared the whole ridgeway. But since more than one of the bandits preferred battle to drowning, resistance continued and even became more stubborn. The hearts of the robbers became inflamed. They began to fight then not merely for plunder or kidnaping, but from rage. At moments when shouts ceased, the gritting of teeth and curses became audible. The rush of the Bukojemskis was finally arrested. It came to their minds at that moment that death might meet them.

And when, suddenly, they heard the tramping of horses to their front, and loud shouts were raised in all parts of the thicket surrounding the quagmire, they felt sure that the moment of death was approaching. So they fought ferociously; they would not sell their lives cheaply in any case.

But now something marvelous happened. Behind the splashing, many voices were heard shouting: "Strike!" Sabers gleamed in the moonlight. Certain horsemen fell to cutting and hewing in the rear of the robbers, who, because of this sudden attack, were seized in a single instant with terror. Escape in the rear was now closed to them; nothing remained but escape at either side of the roadway. Only some, therefore, offered a desperate resistance. The greater number of them sprang like ducks to the turfy quagmire on both sides, but the quagmire broke under them. Then grasping grass, clumps and reeds, they clung to hillocks, or lay on their bellies not to sink right away.

Only a small company, armed with scythes fixed to poles, madly defended themselves for some time yet, and because of this many horsemen were wounded. But at last even this handful, seeing that for them there was no rescue whatever, threw down their weapons, fell on their knees, and begged mercy. They were taken alive to be witnesses.

Meanwhile horsemen from both sides stood facing one another, and raised their voices:

"Halt! halt! Who are you?"

"And who are you?"

"Cyprianowicz of Jedlinka."

"Dear God! Our own people!"

And two riders pushed from the ranks quickly. One bowed down to Pan Cyprianowicz's saddle and grabbing his hand, began to cover it with kisses; the other threw himself into the arms of the priest.

"Stanislaw!" exclaimed Pan Serafin.

"Jacek!" cried out the priest.

The greetings and embraces lasted for a while, after which Pan Cyprianowicz regained speech first:

"For God's sake, how did you come to be here?"

"Our regiment is marching to Cracow. Jacek and I had permission to visit you at Jedlinka, but meanwhile we learned at Radom, while halting for food there, that you, father, and the priest, and the Bukojemskis had set out an hour earlier by the high road toward Kielce."

"Did Father Tworkowski tell you this?"

"No! The Jews at Radom. We did not see the priest. After they told us this, we did not go to Jedlinka, together with our regiment, in fear that we might miss you. And then, after midnight, we heard firing. . . . So we all rushed to give assistance, thinking that bandits had fallen upon travelers. It did not occur to us that you were the people. God be thanked, God be thanked, that we arrived in time!"

"Bandits and not bandits, but the Krzepeckis. It is because of Panna Anulka, who is here."

"Dear God!" exclaimed Stanislaw. "Then I think that his heart will leave Jacek."

"I wrote to you about her, but I see that my letter did not reach you."

"No, for we have been marching for three weeks. I have not written of late because I was to come here myself."

Shouts of triumph from the Bukojemskis, the attendants and the soldiers interrupted further conversation. At that moment also attendants ran up with lighted torches, a supply of which had been taken by Pan Cyprianowicz so that the dark nights could be lit up. It became as clear on the road as in daylight—and in those bright gleams Taczewski saw the gray horse on which Panna Sieninska was sitting.

He became dumbfounded at the sight of her, and seeing his amazement, Father Woynowski said:

"Yes. She is with us."

Then Jacek urged his horse forward and halted before her, after which he uncovered his head and stood thus before her—staring speechless, almost without breath, and with a face as white as chalk.

After a moment the cap slipped from his hand and fell to the ground; his eyes closed, and his head dropped onto the mane of his horse.

"He is wounded!" cried out Lukasz Bukojemski.

CHAPTER 30

INDEED, Jacek was wounded. One of the assailants who had defended themselves to the last, had cut him with an upright scythe, and since the soldiers marched without wearing armor and brassards, the very end of the iron had cut into his arm rather deeply from the shoulder to the elbow. The wound was not too grievous, but it bled profusely, and so the young man had fainted. The experienced Father Woynowski ordered him placed in the wagon and, after dressing the wound, left him in the care of the women. Almost immediately after that, Jacek opened his eyes and began to look once again, as at a rainbow, into the face of Panna Sieninska, who was leaning over him.

Meanwhile the attendants filled the ditches and took apart the abatis in no time. The transport and company passed to the dry road beyond the dam, where they halted for a rest and to introduce order into the camp and question the prisoners. From Taczewski the priest went to the Bukojemskis to see if they had sustained any injury. But they had not! Their horses were scratched up, and even pricked by pitchforks, but not seriously, while they themselves were not only in good shape, but in splendid humor, for they were admired by everyone for a valor that had "pommeled more people before the war than could many a soldier during years of campaigning."

"You should join the regiment under Pan Zbierzchowski," said this one and that one from the company. "It has been known for a long time, and God willing will be shown again, that our regiment is the finest, even among the hussars. Pan Zbierzchowski admits not just anyone, and it is not easy to enter it, but he will accept such worthy cavaliers gladly, and we will be happy to have you with us."

The Bukojemski brothers knew that this could not be, for they did not have the means of obtaining either suitable retinues or the equipment necessary in such a superior regiment. They listened to these words with joy, however, and when the flasks went around from hand to hand, they did not let anyone surpass them.

While this was happening, the soldiers were taking out the captured attackers from the mud by their heads, and they led them before Pan Zbierzchowski, Pan Cyprianowicz and the priest. Not even a single assailant had escaped, for in that sizeable regiment counting more than three hundred men and nine hundred posts, there were enough men to surround the entire bog and both ends of the dam. The sight of the prisoners surprised Pan Serafin greatly, however. As he had told his son, he expected to find Marcian Krzepecki among them, as well as his company of Radom nobles, but instead he found before him a ragged assembly of ruffians, smeared with mud and reeking of turf, and made up—as all such groups—of deserters from the recruited infantry, of outcasts from society, runaway personal servants, serfs—in a word, of all kinds of wild and evil scoundrels engaged in robbery in the wilderness and in the woods. Many such groups prowled about, especially in the wooded region of Sandomierz, and since they attracted men who were ready for anything and who were threatened with terrible punishment if captured, their attacks were uncommonly bold, and battles with them were particularly savage.

The search through the bog lasted for some time yet, and afterward Pan Cyprianowicz turned to Zbierzchowski, and said:

"Gracious colonel, we thought that these people were someone else, but these are common bandits and this was an ordinary act of robbery. We thank you with grateful hearts no less, however, and your entire company for the effective help, for without it we might not have seen the sun rise this morning."

And Pan Zbierzchowski smiled, and replied:

"God grant these marches in the night! The heat is not a problem, and one can render service to others. Do you wish to interrogate these captives straightaway?"

"Since I have looked at them close up, it is not necessary. The court in the city will interrogate them, and the executioner will devote himself to them."

At this, a tall, bony fellow with a sullen face and light shaggy hair stepped forward from the row of captives and, bending to Pan Cyprianowicz's stirrups, said:

"Great lord, spare our lives and we will tell the truth. We are common bandits, but the attack was not common."

Hearing this, the priest and Pan Serafin looked at each other with interest.

"Who are you?" asked the priest.

"The superior. There were two of us, for the band was formed in two groups, but the other man is dead. Spare us, your graces, and I will tell everything."

The priest thought for a moment, and then said:

"We cannot save you from justice, but it is better for you if you tell us the truth of your own free will rather than be forced to declare it under torture. Perhaps, in such a case, man's judgment, as well as God's, will be less severe."

The fellow began to look at his companions, uncertain whether he should speak or remain silent, and meanwhile the priest added:

"And if you tell us the honest truth, then we can do one more thing for you, namely intercede for you with the king and commend you to his mercy, and since he needs affable soldiers, he frequently recommends mercy to judges now."

"In that case, I will tell everything," answered the man. "My name is Obuch, and the superior of the other group was Kos, and the both of us were hired by one noble to fall upon you."

"Do you know the name of this noble?"

"I did not know him, for I am from distant places, but Kos knew him and said his name was Wysz."

The priest and Cyprianiowicz looked at each other again in astonishment.

"Wysz, did you say?"

"Yes."

"And no one was with him?"

"There was someone else—a lean, thin young man."

Pan Serafin turned to the priest and whispered:

"It is not them."

"But they could be from Marcian's company."

After which he said aloud to the fellow:

"What did they tell you to do?"

"This is what they said: 'What you do with the people is your business; the wagons and plunder are yours. But in the train there is a young lady whom you are to take and bring through the wilderness between Radom and Zwolenie toward Policzna. Beyond Policzna our company will fall upon you and seize the young lady. You will pretend to defend her, but in such a way as to do no harm to our men. You will get a thaler apiece, aside from what you find in the wagons.'"

"As if in the palm of your hand!" said the priest.

And after a moment he continued his questioning:

"Then only these two talked with you?"

"Later a third person came in the night with them, and he gave us as an advance payment of a zloty apiece, but though it was as dark as in a cellar, one of my men recognized him, for he had been a serf of his, and he said that it was Pan Krzepecki."

"Ha! It is he!" exclaimed Pan Cyprianowicz.

"Is that man of yours here or has he also fallen?" asked the priest.

"I am here!" responded a voice nearby.

"Come closer. Did you recognize Pan Krzepecki? How could you do so when it was so dark that a person couldn't see his own hand in front of him?"

"Because I know him from childhood. I recognized him by his bowlegs, and by his head, which sits as if in a pit between his shoulders, and by his voice."

"So he spoke to you?"

"He spoke to us, and then I listened as he talked to those who came with him."

"What did he tell them?"

"He said this: 'If I could have trusted you with money, I would not have come, even if the night were even darker.'"

"And you will testify to this before the mayor or the starost in the city?"

"I will testify."

Hearing this, Pan Zbierzchowski turned to his attendants:

"Guard this man with special care for me."

CHAPTER 31

AFTERWARD, they began to take counsel. The opinion of the Bukojemskis was to disguise the first reasonably good-looking peasant woman
they came across in the dress of the young lady, put her on horseback,
surround her with attendants and soldiers dressed up as bandits and go
to the place designated by Marcian, and when he made the attack as
agreed upon, surround him, and either wreak vengeance right then and
there, or take him to Cracow and hand him over to the court. With
great willingness, they volunteered to lead the expedition and swore that
they would throw a bound Marcian at the feet of Panna Sieninska. Their
proposal pleased everyone greatly at first, but when it was examined
with more care, its execution seemed difficult and even unnecessary. Pan
Zbierzchowski could, and had the right, to rescue people from danger
whom he met on his march, but he did not have the right, and he did
not want the right, to send out soldiers on private expeditions. On the
other hand, since a man had been found among the bandits who knew
and was ready to indicate to the courts the chief author of the ambush,
it was possible to bring that same author to account at any moment and
have a sentence of infamy issued against him. Because of this, both Pan
Serafin and Father Woynowski came to the conclusion that there would
be enough time for this after the war, for there was no fear that the
Krzepeckis, who owned large estates, would abandon them and flee.
This did not please the Bukojemskis, however, for they had an intense
desire to have the matter settled at once. They even declared that if such
was the decision, they would go themselves with their own attendants
after Marcian, but Pan Cyprianowicz forbade them to do so, and they
were stopped finally by Jacek, who implored them by all that was
sacred to leave Krzepecki to him and him alone.

"I will not use the law against him," he said, "but after what I have
heard from you here, if I do not perish in the war, then as God is in

heaven, I will find the man, and it will be shown whether a *kondemnata* would not have been better and more merciful than that which I have in store for him."

And his "girlish" eyes glittered so terribly at that moment that a shiver went through the Bukojemskis, though they were cavaliers who did not frighten easily. They knew, however, in what a strange fashion gentility and passion were intertwined in Jacek's spirit, together with a portentous memory for wrongs experienced.

He still repeated several times: "Woe to him! Woe to him!" And once again he paled from loss of blood. Before this, the day broke completely. The dawn painted the world in rosy and green colors, and sparkled in the dewdrops hanging on the reeds, rushes and tree leaves, and also on the needles of dwarf pine trees growing here and there along the edge of the bog. Pan Zbierzchowski commanded the prisoners to bury the dead, which went quickly, for the turf gave way easily to the spades, and when no trace of battle remained on the dam, the march proceeded toward Szydlowiec.

Pan Cyprianowicz advised Panna Sieninska to move over to the coach, in which she could get sound sleep before the next halting place, but she declared so decisively that she would not leave Jacek's side that even Father Woynowski did not try to dissuade her from this resolution. So they rode together, just the two of them aside from the driver, as Pani Dzwonkowska was so tortured by lack of sleep that after a brief while she transferred herself over to the coach.

Jacek was lying on his back on bundles of hay arranged lengthwise on one side of the wagon, while she sat on the other side, leaning over every minute to his wounded arm and checking to see that blood was not coming through the bandages. At times she placed a wine-bag to the lips of the wounded man, which apparently had a good effect, for after a while he became tired of lying down and had the driver remove the bundles of straw under his legs.

"I prefer to ride sitting up," he said, "for I feel I have all my strength now."

"And your wound? Will it not hurt you in that position?"

Jacek turned his eyes to her rosy face, and he began to speak in a low and sad voice:

"I will give the same answer as a certain knight gave so, so long ago when King Lokietek saw him on the battlefield pierced with the spears of the Teutonic Knights, and asked if he was in great pain. The knight showed his wounds, and said: 'This pains me less.'"

Panna Sieninska lowered her eyes.

"And what pains you more?" she whispered.

"A yearning heart and separation pain me more, and the memory of inflicted wrongs."

For a while there was silence, but both their hearts began to beat with greater strength, for they understood that the time had come in which they could and should confess everything each had against the other.

"It is true," said the young lady, "that I did you an injustice when, after the duel, I received you with an angry face and inhumanly. . . . But that was just one time, and though only God knows how much I regretted this later, I say to you, nevertheless, that it was my fault! And I ask your forgiveness from my entire soul."

Jacek put his sound hand to his forehead.

"That was not my anguish," he replied; "that was not my greatest pain!"

"I know. It wasn't that, but Pan Pagowski's letter. . . . How could you suspect that I knew of it, or that I contributed to it?"

And she began to tell in a broken voice what had happened: how she had implored Pan Pagowski to make a step toward reconciliation, how he had promised to write a fatherly and heartfelt letter, but wrote something entirely the opposite, and how she had found this out only later from Father Woynowski and learned from the letter that Pan Pagowski, having other plans, wished to separate them forever.

At the same time, since her words were a confession to a certain extent, and also a renewal of sad and painful memories, deep blushes came to her cheeks from duress and shame, and her eyes became dim with tears.

"Did Father Woynowski," she asked finally, "not write to you that I knew nothing about the content of this letter and that I could not even understand why I received such repayment for my sincere heart?"

"Father Woynowski," replied Jacek, "only wrote me that you were going to marry Pan Pagowski."

"But he did not write that I agreed to this only from pain, from orphanhood and abandonment—and also out of gratitude to Pan Pagowski. . . . For at that time I did not yet know how Pan Pagowski had treated you, and only knew that I was scorned and forgotten."

Hearing this, Jacek closed his eyes and began to speak with great sadness:

"You were forgotten? Dear God! I was in Warsaw, I was in the king's court, I rode through the country with my regiment, and whatever happened to me and wherever I was, not for one moment did you go from my mind and heart. You followed me as a shadow follows a man. And frequently when I was in distress and pain, I called out to you in simple exhaustion during sleepless nights: 'Have pity! Be lenient! Let me forget about you!' But you did not leave me at any time, not in the day, not at night, not on the field, not under a roof. . . . Until I finally understood that I could only tear you from my heart if I tore that very heart from my breast."

Here he stopped, for his voice was choked from emotion, but after a moment he continued:

"So after that I would often say in my prayers: 'God, grant me death, for You see Yourself that I cannot be with her and I cannot live without her.' And this was before I had expected that favor of seeing you once again in life—you, the only one in the world, my love!"

Saying this, he leaned toward her and placed his temple against her arm.

"You," he whispered, "are like that blood which gives life, you are like that sun in the heavens. . . . The mercy of God is upon me that I see you once more, my love, my love! . . ."

And it seemed to her that Jacek was singing some beautiful song. Her eyes were filled with a wave of tears, and her heart with a wave of happiness. Silence rose between them once again, but the girl wept long with such a sweet weeping as she had never wept before in her life.

"Jacek," she said finally, "why have we worried ourselves so much?"

And he replied:

"God has rewarded us a hundredfold."

And for the third time silence rose between them; only the squeaking of the wagon could be heard as it moved slowly over the sand of the wide roadway. Beyond the forest they came out into expansive sun-bathed fields that rustled with wheat and that were dotted richly with red poppies and blue cornflowers. There was great calm. Over the already reaped plots of ground here and there, skylarks could be seen, motionless, lost in song; in the distance, along the edges of the fields, sickles glittered; from distant green pastures came the cries and songs of herdsmen. And it seemed to both that the wheat was rustling because of them, that the poppies and cornflowers were twinkling because of them; that because of them the larks were ringing, the herdsmen calling out, and that the entire peace of those fields and all those voices were simply echoing their happiness and rapture.

They were roused from this enrapture by Father Woynowski, who had moved up to the wagon unnoticed, and said:

"How are you feeling, Jacek?"

Jacek gave a start and looked at him with shiny eyes, as if he had been just awakened from sleep.

"What, reverend father?"

"How are you feeling?"

"It will not be better in paradise!"

The priest looked carefully first at him, then at the young lady.

"Is that true?" he asked.

And he galloped back to the company.

But they were once again swept away by joyful reality: they began to gaze at each other and sink into each others eyes.

"I cannot stop looking at you!" exclaimed Jacek.

She lowered her eyes and smiled at the corners of her mouth, till dimples appeared in her rosy cheeks.

"Is not Panna Zbierzchowska more beautiful?" she asked quietly.

Jacek looked at her with astonishment.

"What Panna Zbierzchowska?"

She did not reply, but merely began to laugh into her hand with a laugh as resonant as a silver bell.

Meanwhile, when the priest had galloped off to the company, his companions, who loved Jacek, began to ask questions about him.

"Well, how goes it? Is he wounded badly?"

"He is no longer in this world!" replied the priest.

"Dear God! What happened? How is he not here anymore?"

"Because he says that he is already in paradise. *Mulier!!!*"

The Bukojemskis, as persons who by nature understood things said to them in their simplest form, did not cease to look at the priest with horror, and removing their caps, they were just about ready to say a prayer of eternal rest, when suddenly a general outburst of laughter interrupted their pious thoughts and intentions. But in this laughter there was sincere goodwill and sincere sympathy for Jacek. Some of the men had learned from Stanislaw Cyprianowicz how "sensitive" the cavalier was, and all guessed how much he must have been troubled, so the worlds of the priest delighted everyone greatly. Voices were heard at once:

"By God, we knew, after all, how he struggled with his feelings, how he did not answer questions to the point, how he did not fasten his buckles, how he forgot himself when eating or even drinking, and how he gazed at the moon during the night. These were the sure *signa* of unfortunate love!"

While others said:

"It is certain that he is now as if in paradise, for if there are any worse wounds than those which Amor gives, then you have no sweeter medicine than reciprocity."

These and similar remarks were made by Jacek's companions. Some of them, when they learned of hardships which the young lady had gone through, and how shamefully Krzepecki had treated her, began to shake their sabers and cry out: "Give him to us!" Some took pity on the girl; some, finding out the fate that Marcian had suffered at the hands of the Bukojemskis, praised their inborn wit and valor to the skies.

But after a while everyone's attention became centered again on the lovers.

"Well," cries were heard, "let us shout to their health and good fortune *et felices rerum successus!*" And immediately a crowd of horses moved noisily toward the wagon.

In a flash almost the whole regiment surrounded Jacek and Panna Sieninska. Loud voices thundered: "*Vivant! Floreant!*" And other cried before it was time: "*Crescite et multiplicamini!*"

Whether Panna Sieninska was really frightened by these cries, or whether, as a *mulier insidiosa*, she merely pretended to be frightened, even Father Woynowski would not have been able to guess; it was enough that she nestled her head against Jacek's healthy shoulder and began to ask, confused and embarrassed:

"What is that, Jacek? What is happening?"

And he embraced her with his sound arm, and replied:

"They are giving you to me, and I will take you, my dearest flower."

"After the war?"

"Before the war."

"Dear God, why so quickly?"

But apparently Jacek did not hear the question, for instead of replying to it, he said:

"Let us bow to our dear companions and thank them for their goodwill."

So they began to bow on both sides, which roused still greater enthusiasm among the knights. Seeing the blushing face of the girl, which was as beautiful as the morning dawn, the soldiers could not refrain from striking their thighs in admiration.

"By God!" they called out. "A simply enchanting vision!"

"An angel would fall in love; what about a sinful man?"

"It is wonder that he was wasting away from grief!"

And again hundreds of voices thundered more powerfully:

"*Vivant! Crescant! Floreant!*"

Amid these cries and in clouds of golden dust, they entered Szydlowiec. At the first moment the inhabitants became frightened, and deserting the workshops standing in front of their houses, where they had been cutting out whetstones from sandrock, they escaped into their rooms. But shortly, realizing that these were shouts of a betrothal and not of anger, they rushed in a crowd to the street and joined up with the army. A throng of people and horses resulted. The sound of hussars' kettledrums, trumpets and crooked horns were heard. A general cheerfulness prevailed. Even the Jews, who through fear had stayed longer in their houses, shouted hurrahs, though many did not know well what the question was about.

And Taczewski said to Panna Sieninska:

"Before the war! Before the war, even if death should come an hour later!"

CHAPTER 32

"HOW is that?" asked Father Woynowski at the dinner in honor of Jacek. "In five or six days we are heading off, you may die in the war. Does it make sense to get married before the campaign, instead of waiting for its happy end and only then marrying at your leisure?"

But Jacek's companions, hearing these prudent words, burst into laughter; some of them even held their sides, others cried in a chorus:

"Oh! It is worthwhile, reverend father, and just for the reason that he may die is it worthwhile all the more!"

The priest was a little angry, but when the three hundred best men of the regiment, not excluding Pan Cyprianowicz, insisted, and Jacek would not hear of delay, it had to be as he wished. Renewed contact with the court, and the favor of the king and queen, facilitated the matter greatly. The queen declared that the future Pani Taczewska would be under her protection until the war ended, and the king himself promised to be at the marriage and to think of a fitting dowry when his mind became less occupied. He remembered that many lands of the Sieninskis had passed to the Sobieskis, and how his ancestors had grown strong from them; therefore he felt obligated to the orphan. Besides, she had attracted him by her beauty, and roused his compassion by her harsh fate and the evils which she had suffered.

Pan Matczynski, a friend of old to Father Woynowski, and also a friend of the king, promised to remind him frequently of the young lady, but after the war; for at this time, when on the shoulders of Jan III the fate of all Europe was resting, and of all Christianity, it was not permitted to trouble him with private interests. Father Woynowski was glad at this promise as much as if Jacek had already received a "considerable crown estate," for all knew that one could rely on every word of Pan Matczynski as if it had been given by the legendary knight, Zawisza. Truthfully speaking, he was the author of all the good that had met Panna Sieninska in Cracow; he had mentioned Father Woynowski to the king and queen; he had eventually won over for the young lady the queen who, though capricious in her likings and fickle, began from the first moment to show her special favor and friendship, which seemed even almost too sudden.

A dispensation from banns was granted through protection of the court and the favor of the bishop of Cracow. Even earlier, Pan Serafin had obtained for the young couple handsome lodgings from a Cracow merchant, whose ancestors and those of Pan Serafin had done business together when they were living in Lwow and importing brocades from the Orient. It was a beautiful lodging and, because of the multitude of civil and military dignitaries in the city, such a good one could not be obtained by many a voivod. Stanislaw Cyprianowicz had determined that his friend Jacek should pass those few days before the campaign, as it were, in a genuine heaven, and he ornamented those lodgings exceptionally with fresh flowers and tapestries, while other comrades helped him zealously, each lending the best of what he had—rugs, tapestries, carpets, and similar costly articles, which in wealthy hussar regiments were taken even on campaigns.

In a word, all showed the young couple the greatest goodwill, and helped them as each one was able and with what he commanded, except the four Bukojemskis. They, in the first days after coming to Cracow, went sometimes twice in a day to visit the Cyprianowiczes and Jacek, and to merchants at the inns with whom officers from the regiment of Prince Alexander drank not infrequently, but afterward the four brothers vanished as if they had fallen into water. Father Woynowski thought that they were drinking in the suburbs, where servants had seen them one evening, and where mead and wine were cheaper than in the city, but immediately after that all news of them ceased. This angered the priest as well as the Cyprianowiczes, for the brothers were bound to Pan Serafin in gratitude, and this they should not have forgotten.

"They may become good soldiers," said the priest, "but they are frivolous persons on whose stability we cannot count. It is certain that they have found some wild company in which they pass time more pleasantly than with us."

This judgment proved unjust, however, for on the eve of Jacek's marriage, when his quarters were filled with acquaintances who had come with good wishes and presents, the four brothers appeared in their very best garments, and their faces were calm, but full of mysteriousness.

"What has been happening with you?" asked Pan Serafin.

"We have been tracking a wild beast!" replied Lukasz.

But Mateusz gave him a jab in the side, and said:

"Quiet! Do not say anything before it is time."

Then he looked at the priest, at both the Cyprianowiczes, and turning finally to Jacek, began to clear his throat, like a man who intends to speak at some length.

"Well, begin right away!" urged his brothers.

But he looked at them with dejected eyes, and inquired:

"How was it?"

"How? Have you forgotten?"

"I'm stuck."

"Wait . . . I know!" exclaimed Jan. "It began: 'Our most honorable . . .' Go on!"

"Our most honorable Pilate—" began Mateusz.

"Why Pilate?" interrupted the priest. "Perhaps it was Pylades?"

"You've hit the nail on the head, reverend father!" cried out Jan. "It was Pylades, as I live!"

"Our honorable Pylades!" began Mateusz again in good cheer. "Though not the iron Boristhenes, but the gold-bearing Tagus itself were to flow through our lands, we, being exiled through barbarian attacks, should have nothing but our hearts glowing with friendship to offer you, neither could we honor this day by any gift of thanks as it merits. . . ."

"You speak as if cracking nuts!" exclaimed Lukasz with passion.

But Mateusz repeated several more times: "As it merits . . . as it merits . . . as it merits . . ." He stopped, looked at his brothers, pleading with his eyes for help, but they had forgotten completely what was to come later.

Jacek's companions began to laugh, while the Bukojemskis began to frown. Seeing this, Pan Serafin decided to come to their aid.

"Who composed this speech for you?" he asked.

"Pan Gromyka of Pan Szumlanski's regiment," replied Mateusz.

"There it is. A strange horse is more likely to balk and rear than your own beast; so now embrace Jacek and tell him in your own way what you have to say."

"For sure, that is best."

And they began to embrace Jacek in turn, after which Mateusz said:

"Jacek, we know that you are not Pilate, and you know that after losing Kijowszczyzna we are just poor soldiers; in a word: naked. Here it is! We give you what we can, and receive it with a thankful heart."

Saying this, he handed him some object wound up in a piece of red satin, and at that moment the three younger brothers repeated with feeling:

"Accept it, Jacek! Accept it! Accept it!"

"I accept it, and may God repay you!" replied Jacek.

He put the object on the table, and began to unroll the satin. All at once he started back, and cried:

"Dear God! It is the ear of a man!"

"But do you know whose ear? Marcian Krzepecki's!" thundered the brothers.

"Ah!"

All present were so shocked that a momentary silence followed.

"Ugh!" cried out Father Woynowski finally.

And measuring the brothers, one after the other, with a stern glance, he took them all in:

"Are you Turks to bring in the ears of beaten enemies? You are a shame to this Christian army and all nobles. If Krzepecki deserved death a hundred times, if he were even a heretic, or an out-and-out pagan, it would still be an inexpressible shame to commit such an act. Oh, you have so delighted Jacek, that he has to spit out the bad taste in his mouth! But I tell you that for such a deed you are to expect not gratitude but contempt, and shame also; for there is no regiment in all the cavalry, or even a regiment in the infantry, which would accept such barbarians as comrades!"

At this, Mateusz stepped out in front of his brothers and, flaming with rage, began to speak:

"Here is gratitude for you, here is reward, here is the justice of people, and a judgment. If any layman were to utter this judgment I should cut one ear from him, and also the other to go with it, but since a clerical person speaks this way, let the Lord Jesus judge him, and take the side of the innocent! Your Grace asks: 'Are you Turks?' But I ask: Do you think that we cut off the ear of a dead man? My born brothers, innocent orphans, to what have you come, that they make Turks of you, enemies of the faith! Well?"

Here his voice quivered, for his grief had exceeded his anger. The three brothers, roused by the unjust judgment, began to cry out with equal sorrow:

"They make Turks of us!"

"Enemies of the faith!"

"Vile pagans!"

"Then, confound it, tell us what happened!" said the priest.

"Lukasz cut off Marcian's ear in a duel."

"How did Krzepecki get here?"

The brothers answered:

"He rode here."

"He has been here for five days."

"He rode in behind us."

"Let one man speak." The priest turned to the youngest, Marek: "Speak, but to the point."

"An acquaintance of ours from the regiment of the Bishop of Sandomir," began Marek, "told us by chance, three days ago, that he had seen a remarkable sight in a wineshop in Kazimierz: 'A noble,' he said, 'as thick as a tree stump, with a great head so thrust into his body that his shoulders came up to his ears, on short crooked legs,' he said, 'and he drank like a dragon. A viler monkey I have not seen in my life,' he said. And we, since the Lord Jesus has given us this gift from birth, take everything in quickly; we looked at one another straightaway: Well, is it not Krzepecki? Then we said to the man, 'Lead us to that wineshop.' 'I will take you.' And he led us there. It was dark, but we looked till we saw something black in one corner behind a table. Lukasz advanced, and made sparks fly before the very eyes of the person who was hiding there. 'Krzepecki!' he cried out—and grabbed him by the scuff of his neck. We went to our sabers. Krzepecki sprang away, but saw that there was no escape, for we were between him and the doorway. Did he not jump then? He jumped up time after time like a rooster! 'What,' he said, 'do you think that I am afraid?! Just come at me one by one, not in a crowd! Unless you are murderers and not nobles?'"

"The scoundrel!" interrupted the priest. "Did he want to do act differently with us?"

"This is what Lukasz asked him. 'Oh, you son of a bitch,' he said, 'who was it who sent a whole band of cutthroats against us? It would be well,' he said, 'to hand you over to the executioner, but this is the quicker way!' Then he pressed on, and they fell to slashing at each other. After the third or fourth blow, Krzepecki's head leaned to one side! I looked—and there is an ear on the floor. Mateusz picked it immediately, and cried out: 'Do not cut the other one, leave it to us. This,' he said, 'will be for Jacek, and the other for Panna Sieninska.' But Marcian dropped his saber, for his blood had begun to flow terribly—and he fainted. We poured water on his head, and wine into his mouth, thinking that he would revive and meet the next one of us; but that could not be. He recovered consciousness, it is true, and said: 'Since you have sought justice yourselves, you are not free to seek any other,' and he fainted again. We went away then, sorry not to have the other ear. Lukasz said that he could have killed the man, but he spared him for us, and especially for Jacek. And I do not know if anyone could act more politely, for it is no sin to crush such vermin as Marcian, but it is clear that politeness does not pay these days, since we have to suffer for it and listen as we are called pagans."

"True! He speaks justly!" exclaimed the other brothers.

"Well," said the priest, "if that's the way it was, then it is another matter, but the *donum* is still tasteless."

The brothers looked at one another with amazement.

"Why tasteless?" asked Marek. "We did not bring the ear for Jacek to eat."

"I thank you from the bottom of my heart for your good wishes," said Taczewski. "I do not think that you brought it here for it to be stored away."

"It's true that is has grown a little green; perhaps it should be smoke dried!"

"Let a man bury it at once," said the priest with severity, "for it is the ear of a Christian in any case."

"We have seen better things in Kiovia," muttered Mateusz.

"For sure Krzepecki came here to make a new attack on Anulka," said Jacek.

"He will not take her away from the king's palace," said the prudent Pan Serafin, "but I do not think that he came for that purpose. His attack failed, so I suppose he only wanted to learn whether we knew that he arranged it, and if we had made a complaint against him. Perhaps old Krzepecki did not know of his son's undertaking; perhaps he did know; if he did, then both must be greatly alarmed, and I am not at all surprised that Marcian came here to investigate."

Stanislaw Cyprianowicz began to laugh.

"Well," he said, "he has no luck with the Bukojemskis, that's for sure!"

"God be with him!" exclaimed Taczewski. "For I am ready to forgive everything today!"

The Bukojemskis and Stanislaw Cyprianowicz, who knew the stubbornness of the young cavalier, looked at him with astonishment, and he, as if answering them, added:

"For Anulka will shortly be mine, and tomorrow I shall be a Christian knight and defender of the faith, a man whose heart should be free of all hate and vain private matters."

"God will bless you for this!" exclaimed the priest.

CHAPTER 33

FINALLY the long anticipated day of happiness arrived for Jacek Taczewski. In Cracow a report had gone out among the citizens, and was repeated with wonder, that in the army was a knight who would marry on one day and mount his horse on the next. When the report also went out that the king and queen would attend the marriage, crowds began to assemble in the church and outside it from early morning. At length the crowd was so great that the king's men had to bring order to the square so that the wedding guests might have free passage. Taczewski's comrades assembled to a man; this they did out of goodwill and friendship, and also because it was dear to each one of them to be seen in company where the king himself would be present, and to belong, as it were, to his private circle. Many dignitaries also appeared, even men who had never heard of Jacek Taczewski, for it was known that the queen favored the marriage, and at the court much depended on her inclination and favor.

To some of the lords it was no less wonderful than to the citizens that the king should find time to be at the marriage of a simple officer, while on that king's shoulders the fate of the whole world was then resting, and day after day couriers from foreign lands were flying in on foaming horses; therefore, some considered that this arose from the kindness of the monarch and his wish to endear himself to the army, while others made suppositions that there existed something close to a bond of kinship, difficult to acknowledge; others ridiculed these suppositions, stating justly that in such a case the queen, who had so little forgiveness that the king had been forced more than once to make explanations even for the sins he committed when a bachelor, would not have been so anxious that the lovers be united.

People remembered little of the Sieninskis, and to avoid every calumny and gossip the king intentionally reminded people that the

Sobieskis owed much to that family. People of society then became preoccupied with Panna Sieninska and, as is usual at courts, at one time they pitied her, at another time they were moved by her sufferings, and then lauded her virtue and comeliness. Reports of her beauty spread widely even among the citizenry, and when they finally saw her no one was disappointed.

She came to the church with the queen, so all glances went first to that lofty lady whose charms were still brilliant, like the bright sun before evening; but when they were turned to the bride, all men among dignitaries, the military, nobles and citizens whispered, and even loud voices were heard.

"Beautiful, beautiful! That man owes much to his eyes, who has seen once in life such a woman."

And this was true. In those days, a maiden would not always be dressed in white for her marriage, but the young ladies and assistants arrayed the girl in white, for such was her wish, and that was also the color of her finest robe. So in white, with a green wreath on her golden hair, and with a face a trifle confused and pale, with downcast eyes, she, silent and slender, looked like a snowy swan, or even like a white lily.

Even Jacek himself, to whom she seemed in some way different than usual, was astonished at the sight of her.

"Dear God!" he said to himself. "How can I approach her? She is a genuine queen, or a veritable angel with whom it is sinful to speak unless kneeling."

He almost became alarmed. But when at last he and she knelt side by side before the altar, and heard the voice of Father Woynowski full of emotion, as he began with the words: "I knew you both as little children," when the priest joined their hands with his stole, and Jacek heard his own low voice: "I take you as wife," and the hymn "*Veni, Creator*" burst forth a moment later, it seemed to him that happiness would burst his chest, all the more easily since he was not wearing his armor. He had loved this woman from childhood, and he knew that he loved her, but now, for the first time, he understood how he loved her without measure or limit. And again he began to say to himself::

"I surely must die in battle, for if a man were to be so happy in his life, what more could there be for him in heaven?"

But he thought that before he died he must repay God for this happiness, and suddenly before his eyes he saw legions of Turkish warriors, beards, turbans, sashes, crooked sabers, horsetail standards. So from his heart was rent the shout to God:

"I shall repay! I shall repay!"

And he felt that for those enemies of the cross and the faith, he would become a ravaging lion. That vision lasted only one twinkle, then his breast was filled with a boundless wave of love and rapture.

Meanwhile the ceremony ended, and the retinue moved to the dwelling prepared for the young couple by the Cyprianowiczes and ornamented by his comrades in the regiment. For only one moment could Jacek press the young Pani Taczewska to his heart, for straightaway both ran to meet the king and queen who had come from the church. Two high armchairs had been set for the royal pair at the table, and after the blessing, during which the young people knelt before their majesties, Jacek begged the gracious lord and lady to attend the wedding feast, but the king had to decline.

"Dear comrade," he said, "I should be glad to talk with you, and still more to talk with you as a relative," here he turned to Pani Taczewska, "and discuss the coming dowry, but I cannot. I will stay a moment and drink to your health, but I cannot sit down, for I have much on my head and every hour is precious."

"True, true!" exclaimed several voices.

Taczewski seized the feet of the king, who took a filled goblet from the table.

"Gracious gentlemen!" the king exclaimed, "to the health of the young couple!"

A cry was heard: *"Vivant! Crescant! Floreant!"* Then the king took the floor again:

"Enjoy your happiness while you can," he said to Taczewski, "for it is worth it, and will not be here long. You will remain here a few days; then your must follow us quickly, for we will not wait for you."

"It will be easier for her to hold out without you than Vienna without us," said Pan Marek Matczynski, smiling.

"But cavalier Lubomirski is already cutting up the Turks there," remarked on of the hussars.

"I have good news of our men," said the king, "which I have commanded Matczynski to bring with him so that he can read it to you to cheer up the hearts of our soldiers. Here is what the Duke of Lorraine, the caesar's *generalissimus*, writes about the battle at Presburg."

And he began to read, somewhat slowly, for he read to the nobles in Polish, and the letter was in the French language:

"The emperor's cavalry advanced with effect and enthusiasm, but the action was ended by the Poles who left no work for the Germans. I cannot find words sufficient to praise the strength, valor and bearing of the officers and soldiers led by Pan Lubomirski."

"That is what the Duke of Lorraine writes. The battle was a great one, and our glory not small."

"We will show that we are not worse!" called out the soldiers.

"I believe and am confident, but we must make haste, for subsequent letters portend evil. Vienna is barely able to breathe, and all Christianity has its eyes on us: will we make it in time, or not?"

"Few regiments have remained here," said Father Woynowksi, "and the main forces, as I have heard, are waiting at Tarnowice under the hetmans. But though our hands are needed at Vienna, they are not needed so much as the presence of a leader like your Royal Grace."

The king smiled at this, and said:

"That, word for word, is what the Duke Carolus writes. So, gentlemen, keep the bridles in hand, for at any hour I may order the sounding of trumpets!"

"When, gracious lord?" asked several voices.

The king grew serious all of a sudden.

"Tomorrow I will move those regiments that have remained with me."

After which, he looked keenly at Taczewski, as if testing him, and said:

"Since her grace the queen will accompany us up to Tarnowice, where there will be a review, you may remain here, as long as you quickly catch up to us, unless you ask of us an entirely new posting."

And Jacek put his arm around his wife, made a step forward with her, and said:

"Gracious lord! If the German empire or even the kingdom of France were offered me in exchange for this lady, God, who sees my whole heart, knows that I would not accept either crown, and that I would not give her for any treasure in the world. But God forbid that I should abandon my service, or lose an opportunity, or neglect a war for my faith, or desert my own leader for the sake of private happiness. If I did, I would despise myself, and she, for I know her, would also despise me. Oh, gracious lord, if ill luck or misfortune were to bar the road and I could not join you, I should burn up from shame and from anguish."

Tears dimmed his eyes, blushes came to his cheeks, and, in a voice trembling from emotion, he added:

"Today I blasphemed before the altar, for I said: 'O God, I will repay you!' But what with, if not with my life, with my blood, with my labor could I return thanks for the happiness that has met me. For this very reason I shall ask no new posting, and when you move, gracious leader and king, I will not delay even one day behind you. I will go at the same hour, though I were to perish the following day."

And he knelt at the feet of Sobieski, who, bending forward, embraced his head and said:

"Give me more of such men, and the renown of Poland will thunder throughout the world!"

Father Woynowski had tears in his eyes, and the Bukojemskis were crying their eyes out. Emotion and enthusiasm seized all present.

"On to the pagans! For the faith!" roared many voices.

And then sabers began to rattle.

But when it had grown somewhat quiet again, Pani Taczewska bent to the ear of her husband and, with pale lips, whispered into it:

"Do not wonder at my tears, Jacek, for if you go, I may never see you again—but go."

CHAPTER 34

THEY remained two days together, however. The court, it is true, set out the following day, but the queen, with all her court ladies, and a multitude of lay and church dignitaries, accompanied the king to the camp at Tarnowice where a great review had been announced; but since the retinue was numerous, it moved slowly and was easy to overtake. The advance of the forces that was to come, with the king at the head, from the border to Vienna astonished the world by its swiftness, especially since the king hastened ahead and arrived before the main army, but the queen, with her retinue, dragged on toward Tarnowice for six days. So the Taczewskis caught up with the escort on the second day, after which the new bride took her seat in a court carriage, while Jacek hurried on to the camp to join his regiment for the night. The time of separation was approaching. On August 22 the king took solemn farewell of his beloved "Marysienka, " and in the early morning he mounted a horse to marshall the army before her eyes, and then move at its head to Gliwice.

It was noted that although he always took farewell of the queen with great sorrow, since he loved her as the apple of his eye and was pained by even a short absence, his face this time was radiant. So the church and lay dignitaries took courage, knowing how terrible war was with the enemy, who, besides, had never advanced with such might. "The Turks have moved three parts of the world, it is true," they said to themselves, "but if our lord, their greatest crusher and destroyer, goes with such delight to this struggle, we have nothing to fear." And hope filled their bosoms; the sight of the warriors increased it still more and changed it to complete confidence in victory. The army, with all the camp followers, seemed very considerable. As far as the eye could see the sun sparkled off of helmets, armor, sabers, musket barrels and cannon. The glitter was so bright that eyes were dazzled by its excess. Above the army, rainbow-hued ensigns and banners waved in the blue air. The rolling of drums throughout the foot regiments was mingled with responses from trumpets, kettledrums, crooked horns, with the hellish noise of a Janissary orchestra and the neighing of horses.

Immediately at the start of the review, the supply column moved to one side, so as not to hinder the movements of the army, and only then did the parade actually begin. The royal carriage halted on a plain not too high, a little to the right of the road by which the regiments were to pass. In the first carriage sat the queen wearing plumes, laces and velvets glittering with jewels; beautiful and imposing she was, with the full majesty in her face of a woman who possesses all in life that she could imagine, for she had a crown and the inexpressible love of the most glorious of contemporary monarchs. As was the case with the king's closest dignitaries, she felt most certain that when the king—her husband—mounted his horse for action, he would be followed, as he had been followed at all times, by triumph and the crushing defeat of the enemy. And she felt that at the moment the eyes of all the world, from Constantinople to Rome, Madrid and Paris, were turned on him, that all of Christianity was stretching out its hands to him, and that only in him and his iron soldiers did people see rescue, so her heart rose with a woman's pride. "Our might will grow, and glory will raise us above all other kings," said she in her soul; therefore, though her husband was leading barely twenty thousand or so men against countless Turkish hosts, her breast was filled with delight and no cloud of fear or worry darkened her white forehead. "Look at the victor, look at your father, the king," said she to her children, who filled the carriage as little birds fill a nest. "When he returns, the world will kneel to him in thanks."

In other carriages were visible the charming features of youthful court ladies, the mitres of bishops, and the dignified, stern faces of senators, who remained at home to manage the government while His Majesty was away. The king himself was with the army, but all could see him very clearly on the height at some distance, among hetmans and generals, where he made the impression of a giant on horseback. The army was to pass a little lower, as if at his feet.

First there moved forward, with a deep, rolling sound and the grating of chainlinks, Pan Marcin Kacki's artillery. After it went foot regiments, a musket on the shoulder of each man, under officers with sabers on straps and carrying long canes with which they kept all ranks in order. Those regiments marched four abreast and seemed moving fortresses; their step kept time and thundered. When passing the carriage of Her Majesty each regiment gave a loud shout to salute her and lowered its ensign in homage. Among them were some with a costlier outfit than others, and showing a form beyond common in dignity, but the most showy regiment of all was made up of Kashubians in blue coats and yellow ammunition belts. These Kashubians, large and strong fellows, were so carefully chosen that each seemed a brother to the next man; the heavy muskets moved in the mighty hands of those warriors as would walking sticks. At the sound of the fife they halted before the king as one person, and presented arms with such accuracy that he smiled with delight, and the dignitaries said to one another: "Eh! It would not be healthy for even the Sultan's own bodyguards to meet them. These are real lions, not people!"

But immediately after them moved squadrons of lighthorse. One might have thought them real centaurs, to such a degree had each man and horse become one single entity. These were worthy sons of those horsemen who in their day had trampled all Germany, cleaving apart with their sabers and with horse hoofs whole regiments, nay, entire armies of Luther's followers. The heaviest foreign cavalry, if only equal in number, could not oppose them, and the lightest could not escape them by fleeing. The king himself had said of those men when at Chocim: "If they are led to the enemy, they will cut down all in front of them, as a mower cuts down grass." And though at this moment they advanced past the carriages slowly, each person, even one quite ignorant of warfare, divined very quickly that at the right moment nothing save a hurricane could surpass them in swiftness, mobility and striking force. Crooked trumpets and drums went on thundering in front of them, while they marched forward, squadron after squadron, with drawn sabers which seemed like flaming swords in the shimmering light of the sun. When they had passed the court carriages they advanced like a wave starting suddenly, going first at a trot which turned soon to a gallop, and when they had outlined a great giant circle, they passed again, and this time they rushed like a tempest near the queen's carriage, with an awesome cry of "Attack! Kill!"—and their sabers pointed forward in their extended right hands, as if in attack, on horses whose nostrils were distended to the utmost, with waving manes, as if wild from the impetus of their onrush. And they passed thus a second time, and then at the third turn, without breaking ranks, they stopped almost abruptly. They did this so evenly, concurrently and precisely, that foreigners, of whom there were many at that court, and especially those who saw the Polish cavalry in action for the first time, looked at one another with amazement, as if each man were questioning his own eyesight.

After this, the entire field glittered and bloomed like a flower with dragoons. Some of these regiments had appeared under Pan Jablonowski from Trebowla, some had been assembled by magnates—and one regiment by the king himself, from his own private fortune, which was commanded by Count Maligni, Her Majesty's brother. In the dragoons served common folk for the greater part, but men trained to riding from childhood, experienced in fighting of various sorts, stubborn under fire, less terrible at close quarters than nobles, but disciplined and most enduring of military labor.

But the greatest delight for the eyes and the spirit began only when the hussars advanced. They moved on in calmness as was proper for regiments of such quality; their lances pointed upward seemed like a forest, and at the points, moved by the light breeze, was a rainbow cloud of streamers. Their horses were heavier than those in other squadrons; their steel armor was inlaid with gold; on their shoulders were wings, in which the feathers, even when moving slowly, made that sound heard in forests by branches. The great dignity and pride that issued forth from them, made so deep an impression that the queen and court ladies, the senators and, particularly, the foreign visitors, rose in their carriages to see them more clearly. There was something tremendous in that march, for it came to the mind of each man unwittingly, that when an avalanche of iron like that should rush forward, it would crush, grind and drive apart all things in front of it, and that there was no human strength which could stop it. And this was true. Not so distant at that time was the day when three thousand such horsemen had rubbed into dust Swedish legions five times their own number; still less remote was that other day when one squadron of the same kind had passed, like a spirit of destruction, through the whole army of Karl Gustav; and quite recent was the day when, at Chocim, those same hussars under that same king had trampled into the earth Turkish guards formed of Janissaries as easily as standing wheat in an open field. Many of the men who had shared in that shattering of the enemy at Chocim were still serving under the banners of that day, and these warriors, proud, calm and confident, were starting now toward the walls of a foreign capital to reap a new harvest.

Terror and strength seemed the soul of that body. An afternoon breeze suddenly rose behind them, whistled in their streamers, blew forward the waving manes of their horses, and made so mighty a sound in the wings at the shoulders of each mounted warrior, that the horses from Spain which drew the court carriages rose on their haunches. The squadrons approached to a line twenty yards from the carriages, turned to one side, and marched past in squadrons.

It was then that Pani Taczewska saw her husband for the last time before the expedition. He rode in the second rank at the edge of the squadron, all in iron, with winged armor at his shoulders and in a helmet whose ear pieces hid his cheeks altogether.

His large golden bay Turkish stallion bore him easily despite the weighty armor, throwing his head upward, rattling his bit and snorting loudly, as if in good omen for the rider.

Jacek turned his iron-covered head toward his wife and moved his lips, as if whispering; though no distinct word reached her ears she understood, after all, that he was giving her the last "Farewell!"—and such an impulse of yearning and love seized her heart that if she could have, at the cost of her life, changed at that moment to a swallow, she would have perched on his shoulder, or on the flag of his lance point, and accompanied him; she would not have hesitated for one moment.

"Take care, Jacek! May God protect you!" she cried, stretching her hands to him.

And her eyes became wet with tears, and he rode past her—gleaming in the sun, solemn, and as if made sacred by the service he was to perform.

Behind Prince Alexander's regiment, other regiments came up and marched by, equally terrible and equally brilliant; and then, following the tracks of the other companies, they described a great circle and halted on the plain almost in the places from which they had started during review, but now in marching order.

* * *

From the carriages on the height, the eye could embrace almost all the regiments. Far away and nearby were seen crimson uniforms, glittering armor, the flashing of swords, the upturned forest of lances, the broad cloud of streamers, and above them great banners like giant blossoms. From the regiments standing nearer, the breeze brought the odor of horse sweat, and the shouts of commanders, the shrill note of fifes, and the deep sound of kettledrums. But in those shouts, in those sounds, in that delight and that eagerness for battle, there was something triumphant. A perfect confidence in the victory of the cross above the crescent flowed through every heart.

* * *

The king remained yet for a moment at the carriage of Her Majesty, but when a blessing had been given him with a cross and relics by the

bishop of Cracow, he rushed at a gallop to the army. The air was pierced
suddenly by the keen sound of trumpets, while masses of foot soldiers
and cavalry stirred, began slowly to lengthen, and finally those masses
moved, all of them, westward. In advance were the banners of the
lighthorse squadrons, behind them hussars; the dragoons brought up
the rear.

*   *   *

The prince bishop of Cracow raised the cross with both hands,
holding the relics as high above his head as was possible:
"Oh, God of Abraham, Isaac, and Jacob, have mercy on Thy people!"

*   *   *

And at that moment, from more than twenty thousand breasts came
the anthem which apparently Pan Kochowski had composed especially
for that expedition:

> *For Thee, Pure Lady,*
> *Mother Immaculate,*
> *We go to defend Christ,*
>   *Our Lord.*

> *For Thee, Dear Motherland,*
> *And for thee, white eagles,*
> *We will crush the enemy,*
>   *On the field of glory.*

EPILOGUE

(TAKEN FROM ACCOUNTS BY COUNTS JOHN SOBIESKI AND A.J. ORCHOWSKI)

VIENNA had become, under ten successive emperors of the House of Austria, the capital of the Roman Empire in the West. Suleiman the Magnificent was the first Turkish emperor who marched against Vienna in 1529, but he failed in his attempt when Charles V marched to the city's relief with an army of eighty thousand men. Over one hundred and fifty years later, the grand vizier and leader of the Turkish army, Kara Mustapha, flattered himself that he should be more fortunate when he began a siege of the city on the seventh of July in 1683. He saw only a handful of the enemy to oppose him, and was still emboldened by an audience he had at Hesaric with the Sultan, Mohammed IV, who told him and his officers: "Now proceed and combat bravely the enemies of the Koran. Thou wilt return with victory, or die in its arms, if thou art sensible to the honors of this world, or if thou aspirest after immortality in paradise. There the prophet's champions receive their reward."

The vizier pitched his camp in the plain on the southern side of the Danube and filled its whole extent, an expanse of nine miles. This camp abounded with everything that was necessary for so vast a multitude: money, ammunition and provisions of every kind. The different quarters were commanded by pashas, who displayed the magnificence of kings. But all this magnificence was eclipsed by the pomp of the vizier, who simply wallowed in luxury. A grand vizier's retinue usually consists of two thousand officers and servants, but Kara Mustapha had double that number. His park, that is to say, the space enclosed by his tents, was as extensive as the city he besieged. The luster of the richest stuffs of gold and jewels seemed to contend with the highly polished glare of arms. It was furnished with baths, gardens, fountains, and even curious animals and exotic birds for his amusement. He shut himself up with his young favorites oftener than with his generals. The imam, or minister of religion, who attended him in this expedition, threatened him with the divine indignation, but the vizier laughed at his menaces and plunged himself deeper in debauchery.

In the meantime the luxury of the general did not in the least diminish the valor of the Janissaries, nor was the Turkish artillery less formidable. Count Starhemberg, a man of abilities and experience, who was now Governor of Vienna, and had formerly been so under the emperor, had set fire to the suburbs, and by a cruel necessity burned the substance of the citizens, whom his object was to preserve. He had a garrison under him which was reckoned at sixteen thousand men, but in fact amounted only to eleven thousand at most.

The Duke of Lorraine, who had taken post on the island of Leopold-stadt and did his utmost to preserve a communication with the city, determined that it was necessary to withdraw from it by the bridges which he had laid across the Danube and now ordered to be broken down. Never was there a general in a more desperate situation. For, after he had thrown part of his infantry into Vienna, Raab and Comora, he had not thirty thousand men left to keep the field.

The Turks did not get possession of the counterscarp till the seventh of August, after repeated engagements for twenty-three days with great loss of blood on both sides. Their mines, their continual attacks, the decrease of the garrison, the waste of provisions, all contributed to give the utmost uneasiness; and to so many real evils more imaginary ones were added. A rumor was spread that traitors were making subterranean passages to admit the enemy, and everyone received orders to keep watch in their cellars. Others whispered that incendiaries were paid by the Turks to set fire to the city. A young man, who was found by chance in a church that had caught fire, was torn to pieces by a mob. But the Turkish artillery was more to be dreaded than all these fictitious enemies. People were unceasingly employed in extinguishing the flames, which the bombs and hot balls kindled in every quarter of the city.

The Duke of Lorraine wrote letter after letter to the King of Poland to hasten his march. Notwithstanding all the diligence he had used, Sobieski's army could not be got together before the end of the month of August, 1683. Sobieski sent away the first units that arrived and, while the main body was getting ready, took up his residence at Cracow, where he did not throw away his time. His fondness for hunting, play and entertainments never showed itself, but when the Commonwealth was at peace. He examined the details that he received of the siege; studied the situation of Vienna on a topographical map; considered the position of the Turks in every view; settled his order of battle and regulated his marches in order to fix the decisive day. Wishing, moreover, to deal somehow with the threat of Tekeli, whom he regarded as a slave of the Turks, a base Hungarian, who, instead of fighting for the liberty of his country, was rendering it as tribute to the followers of Mohammed, the king sent him a message assuring him that if he and his malcontents burnt so much as a straw in the Polish territories or in those of her allies, Sobieski, her king and defender, would enter Hungary and burn him and his wife alive in their own castle.

When he arrived at Tarnowice, Jan Sobieski reviewed his army which amounted to less than twenty-five thousand men and, consequently, far short of the number stipulated in the treaty. Before the review was over, he received a letter from the emperor, Leopold: "We are convinced that, by reason of the vast distance of your army, it is absolutely impossible for it to come in time to contribute to the preservation of the place which is in the most imminent danger. It is not therefore your troops, Sire, that we expect, but your Majesty's own presence; being fully persuaded that if your Royal person will vouchsafe to appear at the head of our forces, though less numerous than those of the enemy, your name alone, which is so justly dreaded by them, will make their defeat certain."

The emperor concluded his letter with a minute account of all the troops that he was assembling, which were to arrive forthwith at the bridge where they were to pass the Danube, assuring Sobieski that the bridge was already finished.

The critical situation of affairs, and the confidence that Leopold reposed in the Polish ruler, determined Sobieski to take a step which exposed his own person to danger.

Leaving his army to the care of the grand-general, Jablonowski, he resolved to go forward himself, according to Leopold's request, and even to engage in battle if the preservation of Vienna required it. In order to get there, he had no route to take but across Silesia, Moravia and that part of Austria which lies to the north of the Danube, three provinces that were infested by hostile Hungarians, Turks and Tartars, whom the Duke of Lorraine, with all his splendid ability and courage, despaired of keeping within bounds any longer.

Sobieski, in his march, had only two thousand cavalrymen. Other kings, even in the midst of an army, have a second army for their guard. His equipage was no greater than that of the brave soldiers who marched with him. He did not claim for himself more than he could provide for them, a fact which endeared him so much to his soldiers. Nothing but a chaise attended him, which even Prince James, his own son, made no use of; they both traveled all the way on horseback. Peasants ran together from every hamlet to see their deliverer, and considered themselves as already delivered. His own troops that he had conducted through so many dangers, stood also in need of being encouraged, and Sobieski saw to it that every opportunity was made use of to strengthen and encourage them. One morning, when he was a few miles from Olmutz, an eagle flew by him on the right, and as the Poles had retained some faith in omens, he told them a story from Roman history about how the flight of an eagle was considered as a token of victory. Another day, upon the weather's clearing up after a thick mist, an inverted rainbow (a phenomenon not common, but which sometimes happens) was seen upon the surface of a meadow. The symbol of the Turkish power was the crescent, and this rainbow formed a crescent, but was upside down. The soldiers fancied it to be miraculous, and Sobieski did all he could to confirm them in this belief.

At length, the King of Poland reached the banks of the Danube and marched to Tuln, a small town on the right side of the river, fifteen miles from Vienna. Leopold had written to Sobieski that the bridge at Tuln was finished, whereas, they were now at work upon it. The same letter told him that he would find the German troops assembled in readiness, but he saw only the Duke of Lorraine's little army and two battalions that guarded the head of the bridge. At this sight he broke out in a passion: "Does the emperor take me for an adventurer? I have left my own army because he assured me that his was ready. Is it for myself, or him, that I come to fight?" The duke, whose prudence was equal to his valor, quieted his indignation.

The Polish army had a great distance to cover; and yet, to the amazement of every one, it arrived before the Germans. The quickness of its march did great honor to Grand-general Jablonowski, who made his appearance on the fifth of September.

The German generals, leaving their troops behind, had come to attend Sobieski and could not help expressing some disquiet at the great day that was approaching: "Consider," said the king, contemptuously, "the general you have to deal with, and not the multitude that he commands. Which of you at the head of two hundred thousand men would have suffered this bridge to be built within fifteen miles of his camp? This man has no ability to command. We shall conquer him easily."

The Polish army was, by this time, passing the bridge. The cavalrymen were universally admired for their horses, their dress and fine appearance. This was probably one of the most remarkable bodies of cavalry that ever appeared upon a field of battle. Every man was a nobleman, that is, each possessed a title of nobility; every one of them was a knight and commanded by their king, the most knightly man of that age or any other age. The infantry, however, was not so well clothed, and did not make so good an appearance. One battalion among the rest being remarkably ill-clad, Prince Lubomirski advised Sobieski, for the honor of the nation, to let it pass in the night. The king was of a different opinion, and when the battalion was crossing the bridge, he exclaimed: "Look at it well; it is an invincible body that has taken an oath never to wear any clothes but what it takes from the enemy. In the last war they were clad in the Turkish costumes." If this encomium did not furnish them with clothes, it certainly armed them with courage.

The Poles, when they had crossed the bridge, extended themselves upon the right and were exposed for twenty-four hours. They could have been cut in pieces had Kara Mustapha known how to make the most of his advantages. At length units of German troops arrived, one after another, and the whole Christian army was assembled by the seventh of September to the amount of seventy-four thousand men.

From the camp at Tuln, they heard the roar of the Turkish batteries. Vienna was reduced to the last extremity, and many officers of the first merit had already lost their lives. The grave remained open without ever closing its mouth. Dysentery, a disorder as destructive as the sword, carried off sixty persons a day. Starhemberg himself was attacked by it. There were not more than three or four officers left to a battalion; most of these were wounded, and nearly all of their chief officers were gone. The soldiers, worn out with fatigue and bad rations, could scarcely walk to the bridge, and those who escaped the fire of the enemy died of weakness. The citizens, who at first partook in all the labors of the siege, had recourse to prayer as their only defense, and ran in crowds to the churches where the bombs and balls carried terror with them.

The Duke of Lorraine had just received a letter from Starhemberg who, in the beginning of the siege, had the firmness and even confidence to write, "I will not surrender the place, but with the last drop of my blood." At present he had scarce a gleam of hope remaining. His letter contained only these words: "No more time to lose, my Lord, no more time to lose."

It is certain that if at this time Kara Mustapha had made a general attack, Vienna would have fallen. But avarice extinguished the thunder that he held in his hand. He entertained a notion that the place of residence of the emperors of Germany must contain immense treasures; and he was afraid that he should lose this imaginary wealth by the city's being pillaged, as it inevitably would be, if taken by storm. He chose therefore to stay until the place surrendered, an event which, he continued to flatter himself, would occur at any hour. This presumption

blinded him as much as his greed. He jested at the weakness of the
Christian army, which he thought weaker than it was, and could not
suppose it would have the boldness to come and attack him. His intelli-
gence was so bad that he was still ignorant of Sobieski's arrival. Of all
the princes in the league, the vizier dreaded him the most.

Sobieski, when he was about to march, gave out the order of battle
with his own hand. They had only a march of fifteen miles to get at the
Turks who were separated from them by nothing but a chain of mountains. Across these there lay two roads, one over the highest part of the
ridge; the other in a place where the slopes were lower and the passage
more easy. The council of war, being assembled, was for taking the
latter; but the king determined upon the former which was much
shorter; nor did any of the princes murmur, because he convinced them
that the fate of Vienna depended upon a single moment, and that there
are cases when speed ought to be preferred to caution.

On the ninth of September the whole army was in motion. The Germans, after several attempts to draw up their cannons, despaired of success and left them in the plain. The Poles were more persevering, for
Kacki, Palatine of Kiovia, commander of the artillery, succeeded in getting over twenty-eight pieces and none but these were used on the day
of battle.

This march, which was encumbered with all sorts of difficulties, continued for three days. At almost every step it was necessary to widen
the path, to cut open roads, and often to construct bridges across
precipices, on which the cannons had to be dragged. Steep mountains
were to be scaled, and ammunition carried up those laddering heights.
Soldiers were obliged to endure hunger and thirst in the midst of the
forest, and the cavalry horses could only be fed with the leaves of oak
and other trees.

The army at length drew near to the last mountain, called Kahlen-
berg. From the top of this height, the Christians were presented, about
an hour before night, with one of the finest and most dreadful prospects
of human power: an immense plain, and all the islands of the Danube,
covered with pavilions whose magnificence seemed rather calculated for
an encampment of pleasure than to endure hardships of war; an innu-
merable multitude of horses, camels, and buffaloes; two hundred thousand men, all in motion; swarms of Tartars dispersed along the foot of
the mountain in their usual confusion; the fire of the besiegers incessant
and terrible, and that of the besieged such as they could possibly make;
and a great city, distinguishable only by the tops of the steeples, and the
smoke and immense volcanoes of flames that covered it.

The besieged were immediately apprised by signals of the approach of the army to their relief. People, scarcely crediting the blissful tidings, gazed through their telescopes from the tower of St. Stephen's church and saw the lances and banners of the Polish cavalry.

To have an idea of the joy that the city felt, a person must have suffered all the extremities of a long siege, and be destined with his wife and children to the sword of a merciless conqueror, or to slavery in a foreign country. But this gleam of joy was soon succeeded by fear. Kara Mustapha, with such a large army, had reason to still expect success. The Janissaries and Spahis were ranged in order of battle. Sobieski, who was examining the disposition of his forces, said to the German generals: "This man is badly encamped; he knows nothing of war; we shall certainly beat him."

The cannons on both sides were the prelude to the important scene of the following day, which was the twelfth of September, a day that was to decide whether Vienna under Mohammed IV would share the fate of Constantinople under Mohammed II, and whether the Empire of the West would be reunited to the Empire of the East; perhaps also whether Europe would continue as a Christian continent.

* * *

Two hours before the break of day the King Jan Sobieski, the Duke of Lorraine and several of the generals asked the protection of the Son of God, while the Turks were invoking their God by repeated cries of Allah! Allah!

After services, Sobieski spoke to his troops:

"Warriors and friends! Yonder in the plain are our enemies, in numbers greater indeed than at Chocim, where we trod them underfoot. We have to fight them on a foreign soil, but we fight for our own country, and under the walls of Vienna we are defending those of Warsaw and Cracow. We have to save today not a single city, but the whole of Christendom, of which that city of Vienna is the bulwark. The war is a holy one. There is a blessing on our arms, and a crown of glory for him who falls. You fight not for your earthly sovereign, but for the King of Kings. His power has led you unopposed up to the difficult access to these heights, and has thus placed half the victory in your hands. The infidels see you now above their heads, and with hopes blasted and courage depressed, are creeping among valleys destined for their graves. I have but one command to give—follow me. The time is come for the young to win their spurs."

Military music and the shouts of thousands greeted these enbolding words, and as the speech closed, five cannon shots gave the signal for the general advance.

The sun rose opposite the descending Christians, showing the movement of their army as a scene in a vast amphitheatre, where the Turks, with surprise, beheld the dauntless array of their enemies. It was then that the khan of the Tartars made the grand vizier take note of the lances of the Polish cavalry, decorated with their national colors, "the sign," he said, "of their king being at their head." These words imparted to Kara Mustapha some uneasiness, for he had always dreaded Jan Sobieski.

But never was a shout of joy more sincere, never transport more intense, than when the garrison and inhabitants of Vienna saw the champions of their safety approaching them. Children and aged men, the sick and the wounded—all gathered on the ramparts, to cheer themselves with this spectacle; and then betook themselves to the churches, to pour out their gratitude to the God of mercy.

*   *   *

The allied armies continued to descend, pressing forward against every attempt at opposition and at every step gaining ground, notwithstanding the continued fire of the Turks.

The princes and generals at the head of their respective divisions, now with the infantry, now with the cavalry, executed with precision the orders of King Jan Sobieski, who seemed the soul of all, and was himself everywhere. During this day, Sobieski was on horseback fourteen hours; while these, his compatriots, the most distinguished captains in Europe, respecting in him a chief worthy of commanding them, participated willingly in his fatigues and seconded him with zeal, for neither jealousy nor ambition disturbed the loyal harmony that prevailed throughout the whole of the allied forces. Owing to this perfect unanimity, and therefore order, neither the incessant firing, nor the impetuous charges of the Turks and Tartars, who swept over the field when the Christian columns were taking their lines for action, could occasion the least confusion amongst them. The right wing was supported by an occupied village; the left extended to the banks of the Danube; and it may be said that a radius of a league and a half was occupied by the battalia of the Christians.

As soon as Kara Mustapha perceived that the Janissaries were repulsed, a red flag was raised—the signal of vengeance without mercy. All sense of humanity between the grand vizier and the adversary who dared to oppose his ambition seemed annihilated; complete extermination was the word; and he instantly issued orders to the Tartars for putting all their prisoners to the sword. Thirty thousand fell. These prisoners had been gathered together, in the march to Vienna, from towns and villages en route. They were from all classes, rich and poor, bond and free, male and female, and of all ages. At the same time the grand vizier set in motion one hundred fifty thousand men, the bulk of his army, towards a general slaughter of the oncoming foe, and he also detached twenty thousand of his best and fiercest troops to make a general assault on Vienna. At sight of these terrible preparations, despair again seized the city.

To break the impetuosity of the Turks, Sobieski thought it expedient to increase its ardor: he therefore ordered a column of cavalry to advance, with a command to fall back on their own infantry, as if in panic, and so draw after them the eager assailants. The dangerous honor of this military feint was entrusted to the young and brave Potocki, son of the constable of Cracow, that senator into whose hands Sobieski, before his departure, had placed the care of his country and the reins of government. Potocki marched at the head of his troops, and to meet the bold charge, a volley of Turkish musketry was poured into the face of the squadron.

The young hero fell, mortally wounded, and the next instant expired. Thus, in one moment, burying in the grave a father's pride and a nation's hope. Seventeen brave companions of similar generous valor, equally in the flower of their age, experienced the same fate, and with the same honor. Modrzewski, the king's treasurer, an officer of approved courage, succeeded young Potocki. Burning to avenge him and his noble colleagues, he took the post, but was struck with a similar fatal blow, and joined their pale corpses on the field of glory. The Polish squadrons, on this destruction of their leaders, became disheartened, and seriously faltered in their approach. But Felix Potocki, Palatine of Cracow, at the head of his own troops, advanced to the others, re-established order and gallantly avenged his beloved nephew by duly executing the commands of the king. He then withdrew upon the allies' columns, formed in order of a battle, which soon opened upon the rushing ranks of the enemy.

It was not a combat, but a furious storm. The Moslems, proud of an imaginary success, forgot all caution, and threw themselves on the Christian lines; but every arm there was prepared with an unreceding weapon; whole thirty pieces of cannon, perfectly well aimed, poured forth destruction. At length the impetuous human torrent dispersed, like lashing waves from a rock.

When the Moslems fell back, fire and sword pursued them. The Turkish infantry, posted on the sides of the hills, in rocky hollows and in vineyards, at first sustained the allied attack, but soon were entirely broken. The combat increased in emulative ardor from the presence of Sobieski, and the Moslems were pursued from hill to hill, until the great standard-bearer of the Poles, Leszczynski, and Count Maligni got possession of that particular height, which had been marked as the end of the day's toil.

But Sobieski, following up fortune, still pushed on some squadrons, and in the instant of this new movement, he perceived an evident confusion in the Turkish center. He ordered the columns of his own center to advance and occupy the field he had quitted; and after having entrusted his son to Count Maligni, he pointed out to the hussars the floating standard and tent of the grand vizier, exclaiming: "There! You must carry terror and your whole vengeance to that point!" Instantly twenty thousand Polish cavalry—that cavalry, which, according to the expression of Bossuet, darted on their foe like eagles—precipitated themselves, as amidst lightning and with the thunderbolt, towards the object of destruction; the roaring of musketry and of the artillery completing the horrors of the moment in which they poured into the camp of the infidels, while the lances of Prince Royal Alexander Sobieski's hussars pierced and bore down all before them, except those who met their deaths by the Polish saber.

The intrepid comrades, led by the great generals of the crown, Jablonowski and Sienianski, pushed on directly to the grand vizier's pavilions, and a power more than mortal seemed to disperse the flying hordes before them. Tartars, Wallachians, Transylvanians, and those same Janissaries who had possessed the audacity to affront the whole of the right of the Christian line, now fled before the conqueror. The vizier attempted to recover the good opinion of his men by showing courage and good behavior, but he had lost his opportunity. He addressed himself next to the Pasha of Buda and the other generals, who answered him only with a silence of despair. "And thou," said he to the Tartar prince, "dost then too refuse to help me?" The khan saw no safety but in flight.

The Spahis still made a feeble effort, but it was their last, for the Polish cavalry, by an impetuous and heavy charge bearing them down, broke their ranks. The vizier turned his back, and his flight made the consternation universal. It was soon communicated from the center to the wings, which were hard pressed by all the divisions of the Christian army at the same time; the left by Jablonowski, the right by the Electors of Saxony, while the Duke of Lorraine fell upon the center and Sobieski animated the whole by his actions and his orders. That immense multitude, which under an able leader ought to have surrounded and overwhelmed its enemies in so extensive a plain, was deprived by terror of all strength and presence of mind. Had night been farther off it would have been a total defeat; as things were, it was only a hasty retreat.

While the grand vizier was overborne by the Poles, and the left wing and center of his army were put to flight, the right wing, commanded by the Pasha of Diarbekr, was hard pressed by the Saxons and Austrians. Field Marshal Flemming had the honor of fixing the Saxon standard in this quarter of the enemy's camp, while Prince Louis of Baden, at the head of the dragoons of Saxony, Wurtemberg, Baden, and of the Polish hussars, reached the counterscarp of Vienna about half-past six o'clock, and at the Schotten Gate gave his hand to the brave Count Starhemberg. What a moment! They hastened to silence the guns on the works, from where the Turkish artillery still did not cease to batter the town. There the Janissaries had rallied and, standing firm, defended themselves with the same gallantry, as though their camp yet existed. This noble effort was unavailing; they were assailed on every side; and with King Jan Sobieski advancing rapidly towards the same quarter, all were taken, and Vienna liberated.

The victorious troops would willingly have entered the enemy's camp, allured by the immense riches that the Turks had left, but the temptation was a dangerous one at this juncture. The enemy, favored by the darkness of the night, might return and cut to pieces an army which would be too much employed in pillage to make any defense. An order was therefore issued to continue all night under arms upon pain of death.

Sobieski himself passed the night at the foot of a tree, and slept upon the ground, his cloak serving him for a pillow.

* * *

About six in the morning the enemy's camp was opened to the soldiers, whose desire for plunder was at first paralyzed, as it were, by a most shocking spectacle. In several parts of the camp, mothers were butchered, some of whom had their children still hanging at their breasts. It seems to have been a practice for the Moslems to take their families with them upon these campaigns. The women were virtuous wives whom their husbands chose rather to kill than leave to the Christians. The children escaped this slaughter, and five or six hundred of them were saved, whom the Bishop of Neustadt took care of and educated in the religion of the conquerors.

Never did an army get possession of more abundant spoil; for the Turks, who are economists in time of peace, display great magnificence in the field. The hero of the day had his share upon the present occasion. He wrote to the queen that the grand vizier had made him his heir, and that he had found in his tent the value of several millions of ducats. "You will have no room," added he, "to say of me what the women of Tartary say, when their husbands return empty-handed: 'You are no men because you come back without plunder.'"

Among the many things which fell into the hands of the soldiers there were two which attracted the notice of all but excited the covetousness of none. One was the large standard of Mohammed, an emblem of Ottoman might. The other sacred implement that made part of the booty was a picture of the Virgin found in the vizier's tent, with this inscription in Latin:

> *Per hanc imaginem victor eris, Johannes. Per hanc imaginem victor ero Johannes.*

The first line, "Jan, by this image thou shalt conquer," comes from the Virgin; to which Jan answers, "By this image, I, Jan, will conquer." It was evidently an imitation of the sign which Constantine claims to have seen in the air when he was marching to give battle to Maxentius.

The image gave occasion for much speculation. Some thought it very remarkable that the vizier should have in his tent a presage of his approaching ruin which ought rather to have been in King Sobieski's possession. Others insisted that no miraculous facts should be admitted without an application of the test of severe criticism. The image, however, was placed in a magnificent chapel, built by the Queen of Poland and the standard of Mohammed was sent to the Pope as an act of homage to the Lord of Hosts.

All the cannon remained to the Emperor and the Empire also. The Turks lost a great many colors and it is well known that colors are never surrendered but with great effusion of blood; and indeed, if we take only a transitory view of two armies disputing at first against each other, foot to foot, for six hours, a spot of ground full of eminences and vineyards, and afterwards coming to a general action, this would be sufficient to show that it could not be done without considerable bloodshed.

The next day after the victory was a day of glory. Starhemberg, the brave commander of the city, who had so resolutely and so gallantly and with so small a force of men, resisted the mighty hosts of the Turks for two whole months, had come to pay his respects to the deliverer of

Vienna, as King Jan Sobieski entered the city over its ruins amidst the declamations of the people, the chanting of "Te Deum," and the celebratory sounds of bombards, muskets, and the bells of the fortress. His horse could scarce get through the multitudes that fell prostrate before him, coming to kiss his feet and calling him their father, their savior, the noblest of all princes, and the king shed tears as he contemplated these generous effusions of gratitude in creatures whose pale and emaciated faces too plainly demonstrated the extreme pinching misery from which he had rescued them.

Sobieski went to two churches to give thanks, and the celebrations continued with dinner at the residence of the governor, Count Starhemberg. Afterward, back in camp, Sobieski wrote a long letter to his "Marysienka," the queen, and concluded it by stating: "Let Christendom rejoice, and give thanks to the Lord, who did not permit the infidels to insult us and to say, 'Where is now your God?'"

*   *   *

Of the Polish army, more than 300 Polish nobles died on that field of glory, many of the finest of the motherland. It is left to the reader's imagination to decide which, if any, of the heroes of our story perished in that fateful battle. As to the survivors, they saw the sun shine again on a liberated Vienna, triumphantly aware that their efforts, and the efforts of their valiant fallen comrades, had secured for Poland and its leader a glorious page in the annals of history.

The Works of Henryk Sienkiewicz

Quo Vadis
Translated by W.S. Kuniczak
Now available in a beautiful hardcover edition!
Written nearly a century ago and translated into over 40 languages, *Quo Vadis* has been a monumental work in the history of literature. W.S. Kuniczak, the foremost Polish American novelist and master translator of Sienkiewicz in this century, presents a modern translation of the world's greatest bestseller since 1905. An epic story of love and devotion in Nero's Rome, *Quo Vadis* remains without equal an all-encompassing saga set during the degenerate days leading to the fall of the Roman empire and the glory and agony of early Christianity.
589 pages • 6 x 9 • 0-7818-0763-8 • W • $29.95hc • (336)
Also available in paperback: 0-7818-0550-3 • $19.95pb • (648)

In Desert and Wilderness
Edited by Miroslaw Lipinski
This powerful coming-of-age tale, set in Africa, has captivated readers young and old for a century.
278 pages • 5½ x 8½ • 0-7818-0235-0 • $19.95hc • (9)

With Fire and Sword
Translated by W.S. Kuniczak
The first volume of the epic trilogy, it is a sweeping saga of love, adventure, war and rebellion set in Eastern Europe during the 17TH century.
1,154 pages • 6 x 9 • 0-87052-974-9 • NA • $35.00hc • (766)

The Deluge
Translated by W.S. Kuniczak
This second part of the trilogy, a superb account of the Swedish War of 1655-69, which came close to overwhelming the Polish-Lithuanian Commonwealth until the Polish people rallied to the defense of Czetochowa is the structural and thematic heart of Henryk Sienkiewicz's magnificent Trilogy.
2 volumes: 1,808 pages • 6 x 9 • 0-87052-004-0 • NA • $60.00hc • (762)

Fire in the Steppe
Translated by W. S. Kuniczak
The final volume in the famous trilogy.
750 pages • 0-7818-0025-0 • $24.95hc • (16)

The Little Trilogy
Translated by Miroslaw Lipinski
Comprised of three novellas, *The Old Servant, Hania,* and *Selim Mirza.*
267 pages • 0-7818-0293-8 • $19.95hc • (235)

Teutonic Knights, Illustrated Edition
Edited by Miroslaw Lipinski
"Swashbuckling action, colorful characters and a touching love story . . ."
—*Publishers Weekly*
800 pages • illustrated • 0-7818-0433-7 • $30.00hc • (533)

Bilingual Polish Literature from Hippocrene

Pan Tadeusz
Adam Mickiewicz
Translated by Kenneth R. MacKenzie
On the 200TH anniversary of Mickiewicz's birth comes a reprint of Poland's greatest epic poem in its finest English translation. For English students of Polish and for Polish students of English, this classic poem in simultaneous translation is a special joy to read.
553 pages • Polish and English text side by side • 0-7818-0033-1
• $19.95pb • (237)

Treasury of Love Poems by Adam Mickiewicz in Polish and English
Edited by Krystyna Olszer
This new volume marks the bicentennial of the birth of a poet who is second to none in Polish literature. As a full blooded Romantic, Mickiewicz left a treasure of unforgettable love poems. With over 50 poems, this beautiful bilingual gift edition contains poems addressed to Maryla (his Beatrice), as well as sonnets and verses of sensual and spiritual love in all shades of Romantic passion—"To—(In the Alps as Splugen)," "Romanticism," "The Nixie," and "The Akkerman Steppes," along with the editor's informative introduction, are all included in this collection.
137 pages • 5 x 7 • 0-7818-0652-6 • $11.95hc • (735)

Treasury of Polish Love Poems, Quotations & Proverbs in Polish and English
Edited by Miroslaw Lipinski
Works by Krasinski, Sienkiewicz and Mickiewicz are included among 100 selections by 44 authors. In the original Polish with side-by-side English translation.
128 pages • 5 x 7 • 0-7818-0297-0 • $11.95hc • (185)
Also available as Audiobook: 0-7818-0361-6 • $12.95 • (576)

Treasury of Classic Polish Love Short Stories in Polish and English
Edited by Miroslaw Lipinski
This charming gift volume delves into Poland's rich literary tradition to bring you classic love stories from five renowned authors. It explores love's many romantic, joyous, as well as melancholic facets, and is destined to inspire love and keep its flame burning bright.
109 pages • 0-7818-0513-9 • $11.95hc • (603)

A Treasury of Polish Aphorisms: A Bilingual Edition
Compiled and translated by Jacek Galazka
This collection comprises 225 aphorisms by eighty Polish writers, many of them well known in their native land. Twenty pen and ink drawings by talented Polish illustrator Barbara Swidzinska complete this remarkable exploration of true Polish wit and wisdom.
140 pages • 5½ x 8½ • 20 illustrations • 0-7818-0549-X • $14.95hc • (647)

Polish Fables
Bilingual Edition
Ignacy Krasicki
Translated by Gerard T. Kapolka
Sixty-five fables by eminent Polish poet, Bishop Ignacy Krasicki, are translated into English by Gerard Kapolka. With great artistry, the author used contemporary events and human relations to show a course to guide human conduct. For over two centuries, Krasicki's fables have entertained and instructed his delighted readers. This bilingual gift edition contains twenty illustrations by Barbara Swidzinska, a well known Polish artist.
250 pages • 6 x 9 • 0-7818-0548-1 • $19.95hc • (646)

Polish Folk Tales

Glass Mountain
Twenty-Eight Ancient Polish Folktales and Fables
Retold by W. S. Kuniczak
Illustrated by Pat Bargielski
"It is an heirloom book to pass onto children and grandchildren. A timeless book, with delightful illustrations, it will make a handsome addition to any library and will be a most treasured gift."
—Polish American Cultural Network
160 pages • 6 x 9 • 8 illustrations • 0-7818-0552-X • $16.95hc • (645)

Old Polish Legends
Retold by F. C. Anstruther
Wood engravings by J. Sekalski
This fine collection of eleven fairy tales, with an introduction by Zygmunt Nowakowski, was first published in Scotland during World War II, when the long night of German occupation was at its darkest.
66 pages • 7¼ x 9 • 11 woodcut engravings • 0-7818-0521-X
• $11.95hc • (653)

Polish History

Poland's Navy, 1918–1945
Michael Alfred Peszke
Created in 1918 when Poland regained its independence lost for 123 years, the Polish Navy fought in World War II alongside of the Royal Navy. The British First Lord of the Admiralty Alexander said in 1944:

"In view of its small size, the number of operations in which the Polish Navy has taken a part is almost incredible, especially bearing in mind that some of them are continuous. Amongst these operations are Narvik, Dunkirk, Lofoten Islands, Tobruk, Dieppe, attacks on shipping in the Channel, Sicily, Italy, Oran and patrols notably in the Mediterranean, and convoy escorting. The recent work of the Polish ships in the Mediterranean has been especially brilliant."

A total of 22 Polish warships fought in World War II; 2 light cruisers, 8 destroyers, 3 destroyer escorts, 8 submarines and 1 minelayer.
222 pages • 6 x 9 • photos/illustrations • 0-7818-0672-0 • W
• $29.95hc • (770)

Bitter Glory: Poland and Its Fate, 1918–1939
Richard M. Watt
"Admirably fair-minded and meticulous about the achievements and the disasters of the Pilsudski years."   —*The New York Times*
"An able political history of the Polish Republic from its reconstruction at the end of the First World War." —*The New Yorker*
"An American popular historian writes objectively and well, and from a solid base in the existing literature, about Pilsudski and Poland's period of independence between the wars."   — *Foreign Affairs*
511 pages • 6¼ x 9½ • 32 pages b & w photos • 0-7818-0673-9 • W
• $16.95pb • (771)

Poland in World War II: An Illustrated Military History
Andrew Hempel

Poland's participation in World War II is generally little known in the West and is often reduced to stereotypes advanced by the media: of German planes attacking the civilian population in 1939 and of Polish cavalry charging German tanks. In actuality, it was not an easy victory for the Germans in 1939, and after the conquest of Poland, the Poles continued to fight in their homeland, on all European fronts, and in North Africa. This illustrated history is a concise presentation of the Polish military war effort in World War II, intermingled with factual human interest stories and 50 illustrations and maps.

150 pages • 5 x 7 • 50 b/w illustrations/maps • 0-7818-0758-1 • W • $11.95hc • (541)

Forgotten Holocaust: The Poles Under German Occupation, 1939–1945, Revised Edition
Richard C. Lukas
Foreword by Norman Davies

This new edition includes the story of Zegota and the list of 700 Poles executed for helping Jews.

"Dr. Richard C. Lukas has rendered a valuable service by showing that no one can properly analyze the fate of one ethnic community in occupied Poland without referring to the fates of others. In this sense, *The Forgotten Holocaust* is a powerful corrective."
—from the foreword by Norman Davies
"Carefully researched—a timely contribution."
—Professor Piotr Wandycz, Yale University
"Contains excellent analyses of the relationship of Poland's Jewish and Gentile communities, the development of the resistance, the exile leadership, and the Warsaw uprisings. A superior work.
—*Library Journal*

300 pages • 6 x 9 • illustrations • 0-7818-0528-7 • $24.95hc • (639)

Did the Children Cry?
Hitler's War Against Jewish and Polish Children
Richard C. Lukas

Winner of the 1996 Janusz Korczak Literary Competition for books about children.

" . . . [Lukas] intersperses the endless numbers, dates, locations and losses with personal accounts of tragedy and triumph . . . A well-researched book . . ." —*Catalyst*

263 pages • 15 b/w photos, index • 0-7818-0242-3 • $24.95hc • (145)

Your Life is Worth Mine

Ewa Kurek

Introduction by Jan Karski

First published in Poland in 1992 as *Gdy Klasztor Znaczyl Zycie*, this is the story of how Polish nuns saved hundreds of Jewish lives while risking their own during World War II. This long awaited American edition includes a section of interviews with nuns and Jewish survivors which did not appear in the Polish edition.

"A welcome addition to Holocaust literature . . . deserves a wide readership." —*Zgoda*

250 pages • 5½ x 8½ • 0-7818-0409-4 • $24.95hc • (240)

Jews in Poland: A Documentary History

Iwo Cyprian Pogonowski

Foreword by Richard Pipes

Originally published in 1993, this classic historical work is now available in paperback! *Jews in Poland* describes the rise of Jews as a nation and the crucial role that the Polish-Jewish community played in this development. The volume includes a new translation of the Charter of Jewish Liberties known as the Statute of Kalisz of 1264; 114 historical maps; as well as 172 illustrations including reproductions of works of outstanding painters, photographs of official posters, newspaper headlines and cartoons.

402 pages • maps, illustrations, index • 8½ x 11½ • 0-7818-0604-6 • $19.95pb • (677)

Other Polish Interest Titles

Song, Dance & Customs of Peasant Poland

Sula Benet

Preface from Margaret Mead

"This charming fable-like book is one long remembrance of rural, peasant Poland which almost does not exist anymore . . . but it is worthwhile to safeguard the memory of what once was . . . because what [Benet] writes is a piece of all of us, now in the past but very much a part of our cultural background." —*Przeglad Polski*

247 pages • illustrations • 0-7818-0447-7 • $24.95hc • (209)

Polish Folk Dances & Songs: A Step-by-Step Guide

Ada Dziewanowska

The most comprehensive and definitive book on Polish dance in the English language, with in-depth descriptions of over 80 of Poland's most

characteristic and interesting dances. The author provides step-by-step instruction on positions, basic steps and patterns for each dance. Includes over 400 illustrations depicting steps and movements and over 90 appropriate musical selections. Ada Dziewanowska is the artistic director and choreographer of the Syrena Polish Folk Dance Ensemble of Milwaukee, Wisconsin.
672 pages • 0-7818-0420-5• $39.50hc • (508)

The Polish Heritage Songbook
Compiled by Marek Sart
Illustrated by Szymon Kobylinski
Annotated by Stanislaw Werner
This unique collection of 80 songs is a treasury of nostalgia, capturing echoes of a long struggle for freedom carried out by generations of Polish men and women. The annotations are in English, the songs are in Polish.
166 pages • 65 illustrations • 80 songs • 6 x 9 • 0-7818-0425-6
• $14.95pb • (496)

Polish Folk Embroidery
Jadwiga Turska
190 stunning full-color illustrations showcase the folk art of Poland's 31 regions, from Cracow to Podhale, from Silesia to Lowicz, from Mazovia, Kashubia, to Kuyavia and Kurpie; a striking display of folk costumes, furnishings, headgear and decorations. A glossary of terms and a bibliography are included.
336 pages • 8½ x 11⅜ • 190 illustrations • 0-7818-0719-0 • NA
• $75.00hc • (780)

All prices subject to change without prior notice.
To purchase Hippocrene Books contact your local bookstore, call (718) 454-2366, or write to: HIPPOCRENE BOOKS, 171 Madison Avenue, New York, NY 10016. Please enclose check or money order, adding $5.00 shipping (UPS) for the first book and $.50 for each additional book.